REFLECTIONS ON VIOLENCE

REFLECTIONS ON VIOLENCE

BY

GEORGES SOREL

AUTHORISED TRANSLATION

BY T. E. HULME

NEW YORK
PETER SMITH
1941
WGE

First published in 1915.
Reprinted, 1941

57831
331.8862 - S713r

PRINTED IN THE
UNITED STATES OF AMERICA

A LA MÉMOIRE

DE LA COMPAGNE DE MA JEUNESSE

JE DÉDIE CE LIVRE

TOUT INSPIRE PAR SON ESPRIT

A NOTE TO THE THIRD FRENCH EDITION

I HAVE often been asked lately if I have not observed any facts since 1906 which invalidated some of the arguments set forth in this book.   On the contrary, I am more than ever convinced of the value of this philosophy of violence. I have even thought it useful to add to this reprint an " Apology for Violence " which I published in the *Matin* of May 18, 1908, on the day when the first edition appeared.

This is one of those books which public opinion will not permit an author to improve ; I have only allowed myself to change a few words here and there in order to make certain phrases clearer.

CONTENTS

CHAPTER V

CHAPTER VI

CHAPTER VII

INTRODUCTION

MY DEAR HALEVY—I should doubtless have left these
studies buried in the bound volumes of a review if some
friends, whose judgment I value, had not. thought that
it would be a good thing to bring them before the notice
of a wider public, as they serve to make better known
one of the most singular social phenomena that history
records. But it seemed to me that it would be necessary
to give this public some additional explanations, since
I cannot often expect to find judges as indulgent as you
have been.

When I published, in the *Mouvement Socialiste*, the
articles which are now collected in this volume, I did not
write with the intention of composing a book : I simply
wrote down my reflections as they came into my mind.
I knew that the subscribers to that review would have
no difficulty in following me, since they were already
familiar with the theories, which for some years my
friends and I had developed in its pages. But I am convinced that the readers of this book, on the contrary,
will be very bewildered if I do not submit a kind of
defence which will enable them to consider things from
my own habitual point of view. In the course of our
conversations, you have sometimes made remarks which
fitted so well into the system of my own ideas that

they often led me to investigate certain questions more thoroughly.   I am sure that the reflections which I here submit to you, and which you have provoked, will be very useful to those who wish to read this book with profit.

There are perhaps few studies in which the defects of my method of writing are more evident ; I have been frequently reproached for not respecting the rules of the art of writing, to which all our contemporaries submit, and for thus inconveniencing my readers by the disorder of my explanations.   I have tried to render the text clearer by numerous corrections of detail, but I have not been able to make the disorder disappear.   I do not wish to defend myself by pleading the example of great writers who have been blamed for not knowing how to compose. Arthur Chuquet, speaking of J. J. Rousseau, said : " His writings lack harmony, order, and that connection of the parts which constitutes a unity." [1] The defects of illustrious men do not justify the faults of the obscure, and I think that it is better to explain frankly the origin of this incorrigible vice in my writings.

It is only recently that the rules of the art of writing have imposed themselves in a really imperative way ; contemporary authors appear to have accepted them readily, because they wished to please a hurried and often very inattentive public, and one which is desirous above all of avoiding any personal investigation.   These rules were first applied by the people who manufacture scholastic books.   Since the aim of education has been to make the pupils absorb an enormous amount of information, it has been necessary to put into their hands manuals suitable to this extra rapid instruction ; everything has had to be presented in a form so clear, so logically arranged, and so calculated to dispel doubt, that in the end the beginner comes to believe that science is much simpler than our fathers supposed.   In this

[1] A. Chuquet, *Jean Jacques Rousseau*, p. 179.

way the mind is very richly furnished in a very little time, but it is not furnished with implements which facilitate individual effort. These methods have been imitated by political publicists and by the people who attempt to popularise knowledge.[1] Seeing these rules of the art of writing so widely adopted, people who reflect little have ended by believing that they were based on the nature of things themselves.

I am neither a professor, a populariser of knowledge, nor a candidate for party leadership. I am a self-taught man exhibiting to other people the notebooks which have served for my own instruction. That is why the rules of the art of writing have never interested me very much.

During twenty years I worked to deliver myself from what I retained of my education ; I read books, not so much to learn as to efface from my memory the ideas which had been thrust upon it. It is only during the last fifteen years that I have really worked for the purpose of learning ; but I have never found any one to teach me what I wanted to know. I have had to be my own master, and in a way to educate myself. I make notes in which I formulate my thoughts as they arise ; I return three or four times to the same question, adding corrections which amplify the original, and sometimes even transform it from top to bottom ; I only stop when I have exhausted the reserve of ideas stirred up by recent reading. This work is very difficult for me ; that is why I like to take as my subject the discussion of a book by a good author : I can then arrange my thoughts more easily than when I am left to my own unaided efforts.

You will remember what Bergson has written about the impersonal, the socialised, the *ready-made*, all of which contains a lesson for students who need knowledge

---

[1] I recall here a phrase of Renan : " Reading, in order to be of any use, must be an exercise involving some effort " (*Feuilles détachées*, p. 231).

for practical life. A student has more confidence in the formulas which he is taught, and consequently retains them more easily, when he believes that they are accepted by the great majority ; in this way all metaphysical pre-occupations are removed from his mind and he is to feel no need for a personal conception of things ; he often comes to look on the absence of any inventive spirit as a superiority.

My own method of work is entirely opposed to this ; for I put before my readers the working of a mental effort which is continually endeavouring to break through the bonds of what has been previously constructed for common use, in order to discover that which is truly personal and individual. The only things I find it worth while entering in my notebooks are those which I have not met elsewhere ; I readily skip the transitions between these things, because they nearly always come under the heading of commonplaces.

The communication of thought is always very difficult for any one who has strong metaphysical preoccupations ; he thinks that speech will spoil the most fundamental parts of his thought, those which are very near to the motive power of the mind, those which appear so natural to him that he never seeks to express them. A reader has great difficulty in grasping the thought of an inventor, because he can only attain it by finding again the path traversed by the latter. Verbal communication is much easier than written communication, because words act on the feelings in a mysterious way and easily establish a current of sympathy between people ; it is for this reason that an orator is able to produce conviction by arguments which do not seem very comprehensible to any one reading the speech later. You know how useful it is to have heard Bergson if one wants to recognise clearly the tendencies of his doctrine and to understand his books rightly. When one has followed his courses

of lectures for some time one becomes familiar with the
order of his ideas and gets one's bearings more easily
amidst the novelties of his philosophy.

The defects of my manner of writing prevent me
getting access to a wide public ; but I think that we
ought to be content with the place that nature and
circumstances have assigned to each of us, without
desiring to force our natural talent.   There is a necessary
division of functions in the world ; it is a good thing
that some are content to work, simply that they may
submit their reflections to a few studious people, whilst
others love to address the great mass of busy humanity.
All things considered, I do not think that mine is the
worst lot, for I am not exposed to the danger of becoming
my own disciple, as has happened to the greatest philosophers when they have endeavoured to give a perfectly
symmetrical form to the intuitions they brought into
the world.   You will certainly not have forgotten the
smiling disdain with which Bergson has spoken of this
infirmity of genius.   So little am I capable of becoming
my own disciple that I am unable to take up an old work
of mine again with the idea of stating it better, or even
of completing it ; it is easy enough for me to add corrections and to annotate it, but I have many times vainly
tried to think the past over again.

Much more, then, am I prevented from ever becoming the founder of a school ; [1] but is that really a great

---

[1] I think it may be interesting to quote here some reflections borrowed
from an admirable book of Newman's : " It will be our wisdom to avail
ourselves of language, as far as it will go, but to aim mainly, by means
of it, to stimulate in those to whom we address ourselves, a mode of
thinking and trains of thought similar to our own, leading them on
by their own independent action, not by any syllogistic compulsion.
Hence it is that an intellectual school will always have something of an
esoteric character ; for it is an assemblage of minds that think, their
bond is unity of thought, and their words become a sort of *tessera*, not
expressing thought but symbolising it " (*Grammar of Assent*, p. 309).
As a matter of fact, the schools have hardly ever resembled this ideal
sketched out by Newman.

misfortune ? Disciples have nearly always exercised a
pernicious influence on the thought of him they called
their master, and who has often believed himself obliged to
follow them. There is no doubt that his transformation
by young enthusiasts into the leader of a party was a
real disaster for Marx; he would have done much
more useful work if he had not been the slave of the
Marxists.

People have often laughed at Hegel's belief—that
humanity, since its origins, had worked to give birth to
the Hegelian philosophy, and that with that philosophy
Spirit had at last completed its development. Similar
illusions are found to a certain extent in all founders of
schools ; disciples expect their master to close the era
of doubt by giving final solutions to all problems. I have
no aptitude for a task of that kind. Every time that I
have approached a question, I have found that my
enquiries ended by giving rise to new problems, and the
farther I pushed my investigations the more disquieting
these new problems became. But philosophy is after
all perhaps only the recognition of the abysses which lie
on each side of the footpath that the vulgar follow with
the serenity of somnambulists.

It is my ambition to be able occasionally to stir up
personal research. There is probably in the mind of
every man, hidden under the ashes, a quickening fire,
and the greater the number of ready-made doctrines
the mind has received blindly the more is this fire
threatened with extinction ; the awakener is the man
who stirs the ashes and thus makes the flames leap up.
I do not think that I am praising myself without cause
when I say that I have sometimes succeeded in liberating
the spirit of invention in my readers ; and it is the spirit
of invention which it is above all necessary to stir up in
the world. It is better to have obtained this result than
to have gained the banal approbation of people who

repeat formulas and enslave their own thought in the disputes of the schools.

I

My *Reflections on Violence* have irritated many people on account of the pessimistic conception on which the whole of the study rests ; but I know that you do not share this impression; you have brilliantly shown in your *Histoire de quatre ans* that you despise the deceptive hopes with which the weak solace themselves. We can then talk pessimism freely to each other, and I am happy to have a correspondent who does not revolt against a doctrine without which nothing very great has been accomplished in this world. I have felt for some time that Greek philosophy did not produce any great moral result, simply because it was, as a rule, very optimistic. Socrates was at times optimistic to an almost unbearable degree.

The aversion of most of our contemporaries from every pessimistic conception is doubtless derived, to a great extent, from our system of education. The Jesuits, who created nearly everything that the University still continues to teach, were optimists because they had to combat the pessimism which dominated Protestant theories, and because they popularised the ideas of the Renaissance ; the Renaissance interpreted antiquity by means of the philosophers, and consequently misunderstood the masterpieces of tragic art so completely that our contemporaries have had considerable difficulty in rediscovering their pessimistic significance.[1]

[1] " The significant melancholy found in the masterpieces of Hellenic art prove that, even at that time, gifted individuals were able to peer through the illusions of life to which the spirit of their own surrendered itself without the slightest critical reflection " (Hartmann, *The Philosophy of the Unconscious*, Eng. trans., vol. iii. p. 78 ; ii. p. 436).

I call attention to this view, which sees in the genius of the great Greeks a historical anticipation ; few doctrines are more important for an understanding of history than that of anticipations, which Newman used in his researches on the history of dogmas.

At the beginning of the nineteenth century, there was such a concert of groaning that pessimism became odious. Poets, who were not, as a matter of fact, much to be pitied, professed to be victims of fate, of human wickedness, and still more of the stupidity of a world which had not been able to distract them ; they eagerly assumed the attitudes of a Prometheus called upon to dethrone jealous gods, and with a pride equal to that of the fierce Nimrod of Victor Hugo (whose arrows, hurled at the sky, fell back stained with blood), they imagined that their verses inflicted deadly wounds on the established powers who dared to refuse to bow down before them. The prophets of the Jews never dreamed of so much destruction to avenge their Jehovah as these literary people dreamed of to satisfy their vanity. When this fashion for imprecations had passed, sensible men began to ask themselves if all this display of pretended pessimism had not been the result of a certain want of mental balance.

The immense successes obtained by industrial civilisation has created the belief that, in the near future, happiness will be produced automatically for everybody. " The present century," writes Hartmann, " has for the last forty years only entered the third period of illusion. In the enthusiasm and enchantment of its hopes, it rushes towards the realisation of the promise of a new age of gold. Providence takes care that the anticipations of the isolated thinker do not disarrange the course of history by prematurely gaining too many adherents." He thinks that for this reason his readers will have some difficulty in accepting his criticism of the illusion of future happiness. The leaders of the contemporary world are pushed towards optimism by economic forces.[1]

So little are we prepared to understand pessimism, that we generally employ the word quite incorrectly :

[1] Hartmann, *loc. cit.* vol. iii. p. 102.

we call pessimists people who are in reality only disillusioned optimists. When we meet a man who, having
been unfortunate in his enterprises, deceived in his most
legitimate ambitions, humiliated in his affections, expresses his griefs in the form of a violent revolt against
the duplicity of his associates, the stupidity of society,
or the blindness of destiny, we are disposed to look upon
him as a pessimist ; whereas we ought nearly always to
regard him as a disheartened optimist who has not had
the courage to start afresh, and who is unable to understand why so many misfortunes have befallen him, contrary to what he supposes to be the general law governing
the production of happiness.

The optimist in politics is an inconstant and even
dangerous man, because he takes no account of the great
difficulties presented by his projects ; these projects
seem to him to possess a force of their own, which tends
to bring about their realisation all the more easily as they
are, in his opinion, destined to produce the happiest results.
He frequently thinks that small reforms in the political
constitution, and, above all, in the personnel of the government, will be sufficient to direct social development in
such a way as to mitigate those evils of the contemporary
world which seem so harsh to the sensitive mind. As
soon as his friends come into power, he declares that it
is necessary to let things alone for a little, not to hurry
too much, and to learn how to be content with whatever
their own benevolent intentions prompt them to do. It is
not always self-interest that suggests these expressions
of satisfaction, as people have often believed ; self-
interest is strongly aided by vanity and by the illusions
of philosophy. The optimist passes with remarkable
facility from revolutionary anger to the most ridiculous
social pacificism.

If he possesses an exalted temperament, and if unhappily
he finds himself armed with great power, permitting him

to realise the ideal he has fashioned, the optimist may lead his country into the worst disasters. He is not long in finding out that social transformations are not brought about with the ease that he had counted on ; he then supposes that this is the fault of his contemporaries, instead of explaining what actually happens by historical necessities ; he is tempted to get rid of people whose obstinacy seems to him to be so dangerous to the happiness of all. During the Terror, the men who spilt most blood were precisely those who had the greatest desire to let their equals enjoy the golden age they had dreamt of, and who had the most sympathy with human wretchedness : optimists, idealists, and sensitive men, the greater desire they had for universal happiness the more inexorable they showed themselves.

Pessimism is quite a different thing from the caricatures of it which are usually presented to us ; it is a philosophy of conduct rather than a theory of the world ; it considers the *march towards deliverance* as narrowly conditioned, on the one hand, by the experimental knowledge that we have acquired from the obstacles which oppose themselves to the satisfaction of our imaginations (or, if we like, by the feeling of social determinism), and, on the other, by a profound conviction of our natural weakness. These two aspects of pessimism should never be separated, although, as a rule, scarcely any attention is paid to their close connection.

1. The conception of pessimism springs from the fact that literary historians have been very much struck with the complaints made by the great poets of antiquity on the subject of the griefs which constantly threaten mankind. There are few people who have not, at one time or another, experienced a piece of good fortune ; but we are surrounded by malevolent forces always ready to spring out on us from some ambuscade and overwhelm us. Hence the very real sufferings which arouse the

sympathy of nearly all men, even of those who have been
more favourably treated by fortune ; so that the literature
of grief has always had a certain success throughout the
whole course of history.[1] But a study of this kind of
literature would give us a very imperfect idea of pessimism. It may be laid down as a general rule, that in order
to understand a doctrine it is not sufficient to study it
in an abstract manner, nor even as it occurs in isolated
people : it is necessary to find out how it has been mani-
fested in historical groups ; it is for this reason that I am
here led to add the two elements that were mentioned
earlier.

2. The pessimist regards social conditions as forming
a system bound together by an iron law which cannot be
evaded, so that the system is given, as it were, in one
block, and cannot disappear except in a catastrophe
which involves the whole. If this theory is admitted, it
then becomes absurd to make certain wicked men responsible for the evils from which society suffers ; the
pessimist is not subject to the sanguinary follies of the
optimist, infatuated by the unexpected obstacles that
his projects meet with ; he does not dream of bringing
about the happiness of future generations by slaughter-
ing existing egoists.

3. The most fundamental element of pessimism is
its method of conceiving the path towards deliverance.
A man would not go very far in the examination either
of the laws of his own wretchedness or of fate, which
so much shock the ingenuousness of our pride, if he were
not borne up by the hope of putting an end to these
tyrannies by an effort, to be attempted with the help of
a whole band of companions. The Christians would not
have discussed original sin so much if they had not felt

[1] The sham cries of despair which were heard at the beginning of
the nineteenth century owed part of their success to the analogies of
form which they presented to the real literature of pessimism.

the necessity of justifying the deliverance (which was
to result from the death of Jesus) by supposing that this
sacrifice had been rendered necessary by a frightful crime,
which could be imputed to humanity. If the people of
the West were much more occupied with original sin than
those of the East, it was not solely, as Taine thought,
owing to the influence of Roman law,[1] but also because
the Latins, having a more elevated conception of the
imperial majesty than the Greeks, regarded the sacrifice
of the Son of God as having realised an extraordinarily
marvellous deliverance ; from this proceeded the necessity
of intensifying human wretchedness and of destiny.

It seems to me that the optimism of the Greek philosophers depended to a great extent on economic reasons ;
it probably arose in the rich and commercial urban
populations who were able to regard the universe as an
immense shop full of excellent things with which they could
satisfy their greed.[2] I imagine that Greek pessimism
sprang from poor warlike tribes living in the mountains,
who were filled with an enormous aristocratic pride, but
whose material conditions were correspondingly poor ;
their poets charmed them by praising their ancestors and
made them look forward to triumphal expeditions conducted by superhuman heroes ; they explained their
present wretchedness to them by relating catastrophes
in which semi-divine former chiefs had succumbed to
fate or the jealousy of the gods ; the courage of the
warriors might for the moment be unable to accomplish
anything, but it would not always be so ; the tribe must
remain faithful to the old customs in order to be ready
for great and victorious expeditions, which might very
well take place in the near future.

[1] Taine, *Le Régime Moderne*, vol. ii. pp. 121-122.
[2] The Athenian comic poets have several times depicted a land of
Cokaigne, where there was no need to work (A. and M. Croiset, *Histoire
de la littérature Grecque*, vol. iii. pp. 472-474).

Oriental asceticism has often been considered the most remarkable manifestation of pessimism ; Hartmann is certainly right when he regards it as having only the value of an anticipation, which was useful since it reminded men how much there is that is illusory in vulgar riches ; he was wrong, however, in saying that asceticism taught men that the " destined end to all their efforts " was the annihilation of will,[1] for in the course of history deliverance has taken quite other forms than this.

In primitive Christianity we find a fully developed and completely armed pessimism : man is condemned to slavery from his birth—Satan is the prince of the world—the Christian, already regenerate by baptism, can render himself capable of obtaining the resurrection of the body by means of the Eucharist ; [2] he awaits the glorious second coming of Christ, who will destroy the rule of Satan and call his comrades in the fight to the heavenly Jerusalem. The Christian life of that time was dominated by the necessity of membership in the holy army which was constantly exposed to the ambuscades set by the accomplices of Satan ; this conception produced many heroic acts, engendered a courageous propaganda, and was the cause of considerable moral progress. The deliverance did not take place, but we know by innumerable testimonies from that time what great things the march towards deliverance can bring about.

Sixteenth-century Calvinism presents a spectacle which is perhaps even more instructive ; but we must be careful not to confuse it, as many authors have done, with contemporary Protestantism ; these two doctrines

---

[1] Hartmann, *loc cit.* p. 130. " Contempt for the world, combined with a transcendent life of the spirit, had, indeed, in India, already found a place in the esoteric doctrine of Buddhism. But this teaching was only within the reach of a narrow circle of celibate adepts ; ·the outside world had only taken the ' letter which kills,' so that the thought only attained realisation in the eccentric phenomena of hermits and penitents" (p. 81).

[2] Battifol, *Études d'histoire et de théologie positive,* 2nd series, p. 162.

are the antipodes of each other. I cannot understand
how Hartmann came to say that Protestantism "is a
halting place in the journey of true Christianity," and
that it "allied itself with the renaissance of ancient
paganism." [1] These judgments only apply to recent
Protestantism, which has abandoned its own principles
in order to adopt those of the Renaissance. Pessimism,
which formed no part of the current of ideas which characterised the Renaissance,[2] has never been so strongly
affirmed as it was by the Reformers. The dogmas of
sin and predestination which correspond to the two first
aspects of pessimism, the wretchedness of the human
species, and social determinism, were pushed to their
most extreme consequences. Deliverance was conceived
under a very different form to that which had been given
it by primitive Christianity ; Protestants organised themselves into a military force wherever possible ; they
made expeditions into Catholic countries, expelled the
priests, introduced the reformed cult, and promulgated
laws of proscription against papists. They no longer
borrowed from the apocalypses the idea of a great final
catastrophe, of which the brothers-in-arms who had for
so long defended themselves against the attacks of Satan
would only be spectators ; the Protestants, nourished
on the reading of the Old Testament, wished to imitate
the exploits of the conquerors of the Holy Land ; they
took the offensive, and wished to establish the kingdom
of God by force. In each locality they conquered the
Calvinists brought about a real catastrophic revolution,
which changed everything from top to bottom.

[1] Hartmann, *The Religion of the Future*, Eng. trans., p. 23.

[2] "At this epoch commenced the struggle between the Pagan love
of life and the Christian hatred of this world and avoidance of it"
(Hartmann, *op. cit.* p. 88). This pagan conception is to be found in
liberal protestantism, and this is why Hartmann rightly considers it
to be irreligious ; but the men of the sixteenth century took a very
different view of the matter.

Calvinism was finally conquered by the Renaissance ; it was full of theological prejudices derived from medieval traditions, and there came a time when it feared to be thought too far behind the times ; it wished to be on the level of modern culture, and it finished by becoming simply a lax Christianity.[1] To-day very few people suspect what the reformers of the sixteenth century meant by " free examination " ; the Protestants of to-day apply the same method to the Bible that philologists apply to any profane text; Calvin's exegesis has been replaced by the criticisms of the humanists.

The annalist who contents himself with recording facts is tempted to regard the conception of deliverance as a dream or an error, but the true historian considers things from a different point of view ; whenever he endeavours to find out what has been the influence of the Calvinist spirit on morals, law, or literature, he is always driven back to a consideration of the way in which former Protestant thought was dominated by the conception of the path to deliverance. The experience of this great epoch shows quite clearly that in this warlike excitement which accompanies this *will-to-deliverance* the courageous man finds a satisfaction which is sufficient to keep up his ardour. I am convinced that in the history of that time you might find excellent illustrations of the idea that you once expressed to me—that the Wandering Jew may be taken as a symbol of the highest aspirations of mankind, condemned as it is to march for ever without knowing rest.

II

My theses have shocked many people who are, to a certain extent, under the influence of the ideas of natural

[1] If Socialism comes to grief it will evidently be in the same way, because it will have been alarmed at its own barbarity.

justice implanted in us by our education ; very few educated men have been able to free themselves from these ideas. While the philosophy of natural justice is in perfect agreement with that of force (understanding this word in the special meaning that I have given it in Chapters IV. and V.), it cannot be reconciled with my· conception of the historical function of violence. The scholastic doctrines of natural right contain nothing but this simple tautology—what is just is good, and what is unjust is bad ; as if in enunciating such a doctrine we did not implicitly admit that the just must adapt itself to the natural order of events. It was for a reason of this kind that the economists for a long time asserted that the conditions created under the capitalist regime of competition are perfectly just, because they result from the *natural course* of things ; and inversely the makers of Utopias have always claimed that the actual state of the world was *not natural enough*; they have wished, consequently, to paint a picture of a society naturally better regulated and therefore juster.

I cannot deny myself the pleasure of quoting some of Pascal's *Pensées* which terribly embarrassed his con-temporaries, and which have only been understood in our day. Pascal had considerable difficulty in freeing himself from the ideas of natural justice which he found in the philosophers ; he abandoned them because he did not think them sufficiently imbued with Christianity. " I have passed a great part of my life believing that there was justice, and in this I was not mistaken, for there is justice *according as God has willed to reveal it to us*. But I did not take it so, and this is where I made a mistake, for I believed that our justice was essentially just, and that I possessed means by which I could know this and judge of it " (fragment 375 of the Braunschvieg edition). " Doubtless there are natural laws ; but this good reason once corrupted, has corrupted all "[1] (fragment 294) ; " *Veri juris.* We have it no longer " (fragment 297).

Moreover, mere observation showed Pascal the absurdity of the theory of natural right ; if this theory was correct, we ought to find laws which are universally admitted ; but actions which we regard as criminal have at other times been regarded as virtuous. " Three degrees of latitude nearer the Pole reverse all jurisprudence, a meridian decides what is truth ; fundamental laws change after a few years of possession, right has its epochs, the entry of Saturn into the constellation of the Lion marks to us the origin of such and such a crime. A strange justice that is bounded by a river ! Truth on this side of the Pyrenees becomes error on the other. . . . We must, it is said, get back to the natural and fundamental laws of the State, which an unjust custom has abolished. This is a game certain to result in the loss of all ; nothing will be just on the balance " (fragment 294 ; cf. fragment 379).

As it is thus impossible for us to reason about justice, we ought to appeal to custom ; and Pascal often falls back on this precept (fragments 294, 297, 299, 309, 312). He goes still further and shows how justice is practically dependent on force : " Justice is subject to dispute ; might is easily recognised and is not disputed. Thus it is not possible to attribute might to justice, because might has often contradicted justice, and said that it itself was just. And thus not being able to make what was just strong, what was strong has been made just " (fragment 298 ; cf. fragments 302, 303, 306, 307, 311).

This criticism of natural right has not the perfect clearness that we could give it at the present day, because we know now that it is in economics we must seek for a

---

[1] It seems to me that Pascal's editors in 1670 must have been alarmed at his Calvinism. I am astonished that Sainte-Beuve should have said nothing more than that there " was in Pascal's Christianity something which they could not understand, that Pascal had a greater need than they had of Christian faith (Port Royal, vol. iii. p. 383).

type of force that has attained absolutely uncontrolled development, and can thus be identified naturally with right, whilst Pascal under the one heading confuses together all the manifestations of force.[1]

Pascal was vividly impressed by the changes that the conception of justice has experienced in the course of time, and these changes still continue to embarrass philosophers exceedingly. A well-organised social system is destroyed by a revolution and is replaced by another system, which in its turn is considered to be perfectly just ; so that what was just before now becomes unjust. Any amount of sophisms have been produced to show that force has been placed at the service of justice during revolutions ; these arguments have been many times shown to be absurd. But the public is so accustomed to believe in natural rights that it cannot make up its mind to abandon them.

There is hardly anything, not excepting even war, that people have not tried to bring inside the scope of natural right : they compare war to a process in which one nation reclaims a right which a malevolent neighbour refuses to recognise. Our fathers readily acknowledged that God decided battles in favour of those who had justice on their side ; the vanquished were to be treated as an unsuccessful litigant : they must pay the costs of the war and give guarantees to the victor in order that the latter might enjoy their restored rights in peace. At the present time there are plenty of people who propose that international conflicts should be submitted to arbitration ; this would only be a secularisation of the ancient mythology.[2]

[1] Cf. what I say about force in Chapter V.

[2] I cannot succeed in finding the idea of international arbitration in fragment 296 of Pascal, where several people claim to have discovered it ; in this paragraph Pascal simply points out the ridiculous aspect of the claim made in his time by every belligerent—to condemn the conduct of his adversary in the name of justice.

The people who believe in natural right are not always implacable enemies of civil struggles, and certainly not of tumultuous rioting ; that has been sufficiently shown in the course of the Dreyfus question.   When the force of the State was in the hands of their adversaries, they acknowledged, naturally enough, that it was being employed to violate justice, and they then proved that one might with a good conscience " step out of the region of legality in order to enter that of justice " (to borrow a phrase of the Bonapartists) ; when they could not over-throw the government, they tried at least to intimidate it.   But when they attacked the people who for the time being controlled the force of the State, they did not at all desire to suppress that force, for they wished to utilise it some day for their own profit ; all the revolu-tionary disturbances of the nineteenth century have ended in reinforcing the power of the State.

Proletarian violence entirely changes the aspect of all the conflicts in which it intervenes, since it disowns the force organised by the middle class, and claims to suppress the State which serves as its central nucleus. Under such conditions, it is no longer possible to argue about the primordial rights of man.   That is why our parliamentary socialists, who spring from the middle classes and who know nothing outside the ideology of the State, are so bewildered when they are confronted with working-class violence.   They cannot apply to it the commonplaces which generally serve them when they speak about force, and they look with terror on movements which may result in the ruin of the institutions by which they live.   If revolutionary syndicalism triumphs, there will be no more brilliant speeches on immanent Justice, and the parliamentary regime, so dear to the intellectuals, will be finished with—it is the abomination of desolation ! We must not be astonished, then, that they speak about violence with so much anger.

Giving evidence on June 5, 1907, before the Cours
d'Assises de la Seine, in the Bousquet-Levy case, Jaurès
said, " I have no superstitious belief in legality, it has
already received too many blows; but I always advise
workmen to have recourse to legal means, *for violence is
the sign of temporary weakness.*" This is clearly a reminiscence of the Dreyfus question. Jaurès remembered
that his friends were obliged to have recourse to revolutionary manifestations, and it is easy to understand that,
as a result of this affair, he had not retained very great
respect for legality. He probably likened the present
position of the syndicalists to the former position of the
Dreyfusards ; for the moment they are weak, but they
are destined ultimately to have the force of the
State at their own disposal ; they would then be
very imprudent to destroy by violence a force which
is destined to become theirs. He may even regret at
times that the State has been so severely shaken by
the Dreyfus agitation, just as Gambetta regretted that
the administration had lost its former prestige and
discipline.

One of the most elegant of Republican ministers [1] has
made a speciality of high-sounding phrases directed against
the upholders of violence. Viviani charms deputies,
senators, and the employés assembled to admire his
excellency on his official tours, by telling them that
violence is the caricature, or rather " the fallen and
degenerate daughter," of force. After boasting that he
has, by a magnificent gesture, extinguished the lamps of

---

[1] The *Petit Parisien*, that one always quotes with pleasure as the
barometer of democratic stupidity, tells us that " this scornful definition
of the elegant and *immoral* M. de Morny—*Republicans are people who
dress badly*—seems to-day altogether without any foundation." I
borrow this philosophical observation from an enthusiastic description
of the marriage of the charming minister Clémentel (October 22, 1905).
This well-informed newspaper has accused me of giving the workers
hooligan advice (April 7, 1907).

Heaven, he assumes the attitudes of a matador, at whose
feet a furious bull has fallen.[1]

If I were more vain about my literary efforts than I
am, I should like to imagine that he was thinking of me
when he said in the Senate, on November 16, 1906, that
" one must not mistake a fanatic for a party, nor rash
statements for a system of doctrine." There is only one
pleasure greater than that of being appreciated by intelligent people, and that is the pleasure of not being
understood by blunderheads, who are only capable of
expressing in a kind of jargon what serves them in the
place of thought. But I have every reason to suppose
that, in the brilliant set which surrounds this *charlatan*,[2]
there is not one who has ever heard of the *Mouvement
Socialiste*. It is quite within the comprehension of Viviani
and his companions in the Cabinet that people may
attempt an insurrection when they feel themselves
solidly organised enough to take over the State ; but

[1] " I have seen violence myself," he told the Senate on November
16, 1906, " face to face. I have been, day after day, in the midst of
thousands of men who bore on their faces the marks of a terrifying
exaltation. I have remained in the midst of them, face to face and
shoulder to shoulder." He boasted that in the end he had triumphed
over the strikers in the Creusot workshops.

[2] In the course of the same speech, Viviani strongly insisted on his
own Socialism, and declared that he intended " to remain faithful to
the ideal of his first years of public life." If we are to judge by a
brochure in 1897 by the *Allemanistes*, under the title *La Vérité sur
l'union socialiste*, this ideal was opportunism ; when he left Algeria
for Paris, Viviani was transformed into a Socialist, and the brochure
then asserts that his new attitude is a lie. Evidently this work was
edited by fanatics with no understanding of the manners of polite
society.

[*Allemanistes* : this was the name given to the members of the
" Revolutionary Socialist Workmen's Party " because Allemane was
the best-known member of the group. They did not wish (in principle
at any rate) to admit any but workmen into the party ; they were for
a long time very hostile to the parliamentary Socialists. During the
Dreyfus affair they went with the rest and demanded a retrial ; to-day
they have disappeared, but they had some influence in the formation
of the Syndicalist idea.—*Trans. Note.*]

working-class violence which has no such aim, seems to them only folly and an odious caricature of revolution. Do what you like, but don't kill the goose.

III

In the course of this study one thing has always been present in my mind, which seemed to me so evident that I did not think it worth while to lay much stress on it—that men who are participating in a great social movement always picture their coming action as a battle in which their cause is certain to triumph. These constructions, knowledge of which is so important for historians, I propose to call myths ; [1] the syndicalist " general strike " and Marx's catastrophic revolution are such myths. As remarkable examples of such myths, I have given those which were constructed by primitive Christianity, by the Reformation, by the Revolution and by the followers of Mazzini. I now wish to show that we should not attempt to analyse such groups of images in the way that we analyse a thing into its elements, but that they must be taken as a whole, as historical forces, and that we should be especially careful not to make any comparison between accomplished fact and the picture people had formed for themselves before action.

I could have given one more example which is perhaps still more striking : Catholics have never been discouraged even in the hardest trials, because they have always pictured the history of the Church as a series of battles between Satan and the hierarchy supported by Christ ; every new difficulty which arises is only an episode in a war which must finally end in the victory of Catholicism.

---

[1] In the *Introduction à l'économie moderne*, I have given the word *myth* a more general sense, which closely corresponds to the narrower meaning given to it here.

At the beginning of the nineteenth century the revolutionary persecutions revived this myth of the struggle with Satan, which inspired so many of the eloquent pages in Joseph de Maistre ; this rejuvenation explains to a large extent the religious renascence which took place at that epoch. If Catholicism is in danger at the present time, it is to a great extent owing to the fact that the myth of the Church militant tends to disappear. Ecclesiastical literature has greatly contributed to rendering it ridiculous ; thus in 1872, a Belgian writer recommended a revival of exorcisms, as they seemed to him an efficacious means of combating the revolutionaries.[1] Many educated Catholics are horrified when they discover that the ideas of Joseph de Maistre have helped to encourage the ignorance of the clergy, which did not attempt to acquire an adequate knowledge of a science which it held to be accursed ; to these educated Catholics the myth of the struggle with Satan then appears dangerous, and they point out its ridiculous aspects ; but they do not in the least understand its historical bearing. The gentle, sceptical, and, above all, pacific, habits of the present generation are, moreover, unfavourable to its continued existence ; and the enemies of the Church loudly proclaim that they do not wish to return to a regime of persecution which might restore their former power to warlike images.

In employing the term myth I believed that I had made a happy choice, because I thus put myself in a position to refuse any discussion whatever with the people who wish to submit the idea of a general strike to a detailed criticism, and who accumulate objections

[1] P. Bureau, *La Crise morale des temps nouveaux*, p. 213. The author, a professor of the Institut Catholique de Paris, adds: " This recommendation can only excite hilarity nowadays. We are compelled to believe that the author's curious proposition was then accepted by a large number of his correligionists, when we remember the astonishing success of the writings of Léo Taxil after his pretended conversion."

against its practical possibility. It appears, on the contrary, that I had made a most unfortunate choice, for while some told me that myths were only suitable to a primitive state of society, others imagined that I thought the modern world might be moved by illusions analogous in nature to those which Renan thought might usefully replace religion.[1] But there has been a worse misunderstanding than this even, for it has been asserted that my theory of myths was only a kind of lawyer's plea, a falsification of the real opinions of the revolutionaries, the *sophistry of an intellectualist.*

If this were true, I should not have been exactly fortunate, for I have always tried to escape the influence of that intellectualist philosophy, which seems to me a great hindrance to the historian who allows himself to be dominated by it. The contradiction that exists between this philosophy and the true understanding of events has often struck the readers of Renan. Renan is continually wavering between his own intuition, which was nearly always admirable, and a philosophy which cannot touch history without falling into platitudes ; but, alas, he too often believed himself bound to think in . accordance with the *scientific opinions* of his day.

The intellectualist philosophy finds itself unable to explain phenomena like the following—the sacrifice of his life which the soldier of Napoleon made in order to have had the honour of taking part in " immortal deeds " and of living in the glory of France, knowing all the time that " he would always be a poor man " ; then, again, the extraordinary virtues shown by the Romans who resigned themselves to a frightful inequality and who suffered so much to conquer the world ; [2] " the belief in

[1] The principal object of these illusions seems to me to have been the calming of the anxieties that Renan had retained on the subject of the *beyond* (cf. an article by Mgr. d'Hulst in the *Correspondant* on October 25, 1892, pp. 210, 224-225).

[2] Renan, *Histoire du peuple d'Israël,* vol. iv. p. 191.

glory (which was) a value without equal," created by
Greece, and as a result of which " a selection was made
from the swarming masses of humanity, life acquired
an incentive and there was a recompense here for those
who had pursued the good and the beautiful." [1] The
intellectualist philosophy, far from being able to explain
these things, leads, on the contrary, to an admiration for
the fifty-first chapter of Jeremiah, " the lofty though
profoundly sad feeling with which the peaceful man
contemplates these falls of empires, and the pity excited
in the heart of the wise man by the spectacle of the
nations *labouring for vanity*, victims of the arrogance of
the few." Greece, according to Renan, did not experience
anything of that-kind, and I do not think that we need
complain about that.[2] Moreover, he himself praises the
Romans for not having acted in accordance with the
conceptions of the Jewish thinker. " They laboured,
they wore themselves out for nothing, said the Jewish
thinker—yes, doubtless, but those are the virtues that
history rewards." [3]

Religions constitute a very troublesome problem for
the intellectualists, for they can neither regard them as
being without historical importance nor can they explain
them. Renan, for example, has written some very strange
sentences on this subject. " Religion is a necessary
imposture. Even the most obvious ways of throwing
dust in people's eyes cannot be neglected when you are
dealing with a race as stupid as the human species, a
race created for error, which, when it does admit the
truth, never does so for the right reasons. It is necessary
then to give it the wrong ones." [4]

Comparing Giordano Bruno, who " allowed himself
to be burnt at Champ - de - Flore " with Galileo, who

[1] Renan, *loc. cit.* p. 267.   [2] Renan, *loc. cit.* pp. 199-200.
[3] Renan, *op. cit.* vol. iii. pp. 458-459.
[4] Renan, *op. cit.* vol. v. pp. 105-106.

submitted to the Holy See, Renan sides with the second, because, according to him, the scientist need not bring anything to support his discoveries beyond good arguments. He considered that the Italian philosopher wished to supplement his inadequate proofs by his sacrifice, and he puts forward this scornful maxim : " A man suffers martyrdom only for the sake of things about which he is not certain." [1] Renan here confuses *conviction*, which must have been very powerful in Bruno's case, with that particular kind of *certitude* about the accepted theories of science, which instruction ultimately produces ; it would be difficult to give a more misleading idea of the forces which really move men.

The whole of this philosophy can be summed up in the following phrase of Renan's: " Human affairs are always an approximation lacking gravity and precision " ; and as a matter of fact, for an intellectualist, what lacks precision must also lack gravity. But in Renan the conscientious historian was never entirely asleep, and he at once adds as a corrective : " To have realised this truth is a great result obtained by philosophy ; but it is an abdication of any active rôle. The future lies in the hands of those who are not disillusioned." [2] From this we may conclude that the intellectualist philosophy is entirely unable to explain the great movements of history.

The intellectualist philosophy would have vainly endeavoured to convince the ardent Catholics, who for

[1] Renan, *Nouvelles Études d'histoire religieuse*, p. vii.   Previously he had said, speaking of the persecutions: " People die for *opinions*, and not for *certitudes*, because they believe and not because they know . . . whenever beliefs are in question the greatest testimony and the most efficacious demonstration is to die for them " (*L'Église chrétienne*, p. 317).   This thesis presupposes that martyrdom is a kind of ordeal, which was partly true in the Roman epoch, by reason of certain special circumstances (G. Sorel, *Le Système historique de Renan*, p. 335).

[2] Renan, *Histoire du peuple d'Israël*, vol. iii. p. 497.

so long struggled successfully against the revolutionary traditions, that the myth of the Church militant was not in harmony with the scientific theories formulated by the most learned authors according to the best rules of criticism ; it would never have succeeded in persuading them.   It would not have been possible to shake the faith that these men had in the promises made to the Church by any argument ; and so long as this faith remained, the myth was, in their eyes, incontestable.   Similarly, the objections urged by philosophy against the revolutionary myths would have made an impression only on those men who were anxious to find a pretext for abandoning any active rôle, for remaining revolutionary in words only.

I can understand the fear that this myth of the general strike inspires in many *worthy progressives*,[1] on account of its character of *infinity* ;[2] the world of to-day is very much inclined to return to the opinions of the ancients and to subordinate ethics to the smooth working of public affairs, which results in a definition of virtue as the golden mean ; as long as socialism remains a *doctrine expressed only in words*, it is very easy to deflect it towards this doctrine of the golden mean ; but this transformation is manifestly impossible when the myth of the " general strike " is introduced, as this implies an absolute revolution.   You know as well as I do that all that is best in the modern mind is derived from this " torment of the infinite " ;

[1] Translator's Note.—In French, "*braves gens.*" Sorel is using the words ironically to indicate those naïve, philanthropically disposed people who believe that they have discovered the solution to the problem of social reform—whose attitude, however, is often complicated by a good deal of hypocrisy, they being frequently rapacious when their own personal interests are at stake.

[2] Parties, as a rule, *define* the reforms that they wish to bring about ; but the general strike has a character of *infinity*, because it puts on one side all discussion of definite reforms and confronts men with a catastrophe.   People who pride themselves on their practical wisdom are very much upset by such a conception, which puts forward no definite project of future social organisation.

you are not one of those people who look upon the tricks
by means of which readers can be deceived by words, as
happy discoveries.   That is why you will not condemn
me for having attached great worth to a myth which
gives to socialism such high moral value and such great
sincerity.   It is because the theory of myths tends to
produce such fine results that so many seek to dispute it.

IV

The mind of man is so constituted that it cannot remain
content with the mere observation of facts, but always
attempts to penetrate into the inner reason of things.   I
therefore ask myself whether it might not be desirable to
study this theory of myths more thoroughly, utilising the
enlightenment we owe to the Bergsonian philosophy.
The attempt I am about to submit to you is doubtless
very imperfect, but I think that it has been planned in
accordance with the only method which can possibly
throw light on the problem.   In the first place, we should
notice that the discussions of the moralists hardly ever
come into contact with what is truly fundamental in our
individuality.   As a rule, they simply try to appraise
our already completed acts with the help of the moral
valuations formulated in advance by society, for the
different types of action commonest in contemporary
life.   They say that in this way they are determining
motives ; but these motives are of the same nature as
those which jurists take account of in criminal justice ;
they are merely social valuations of facts known to
everybody.   Many philosophers, especially the ancients,
have believed that all values could be deduced from
utility, and if any social valuation does exist, it is surely
this latter,—theologians estimate transgressions by the
place they occupy on the road which, according to average
human experience, leads to mortal sin ;   they are thus

able to ascertain the degree of viciousness of any given sin,—while the moderns usually teach that we act after having established a particular maxim (which is, as it were, an abstraction or generalisation of our projected conduct), and justify this maxim by deducing it (more or less sophistically) from general principles which are, to a certain extent, analogous to the Declaration of the Rights of Man ; and, as a matter of fact, this theory was probably inspired by the admiration excited by the Bill of Rights placed at the head of each American constitution.[1]

We are all so extremely concerned in knowing what the world thinks of us that, sooner or later, considerations analogous to those the moralists speak of do pass through our mind ; as a result of this the moralists have been able to imagine that they have really made an appeal to experience for the purpose of finding out what exists at the bottom of the creative conscience, when, as a matter of fact, all they have done is to consider already accomplished acts from the point of view of its social effects.

Bergson asks us, on the contrary, to consider the inner depths of the mind and what happens there during a creative moment. " There are," he says, " two different selves, one of which is, as it were, the external projection of the other, its spatial and, so to speak, social representation. We reach the former by deep introspection, which leads us to grasp our inner states as living things, constantly *becoming*, as states not amenable to measure. . . . But the moments at which we thus grasp ourselves are

[1] The Constitution of Virginia dates from June 1776. The American constitutions were known in Europe by two French translations, in 1778 and 1789. Kant had published the *Foundations of the Metaphysic of Custom* in 1785 and the *Critique of Practical Reason* in 1788. One might say that the utilitarian system of the ancients has certain analogies with economics, that of the theologians with law, and that of Kant with the political theory of growing democracy (cf. Jellinck, *La Déclaration des droits de l'homme et du citoyen*, trad. franc., pp. 18-25 ; pp. 49-50 ; p. 89).

rare, and that is just why we are rarely free. The greater part of our time we live outside ourselves, hardly perceiving anything of ourselves but our own ghost, a colourless shadow. . . . Hence we live for the external world rather than for ourselves ; we speak rather than think ; we are acted rather than act ourselves. To act freely is to recover possession of oneself, and to get back into pure duration." [1]

In order to acquire a real understanding of this psychology we must " carry ourselves back in thought to those moments of our life, when we made some serious decision, moments unique of their kind, which will never be repeated—any more than the past phases in the history of a nation will ever come back again." [2] It is very evident that we enjoy this liberty pre-eminently when we are making an effort to create a new individuality in ourselves, thus endeavouring to break the bonds of habit which enclose us. It might at first be supposed that it would be sufficient to say that, at such moments, we are dominated by an overwhelming emotion ; but everybody now recognises that movement is the essence of emotional life, and it is, then, in terms of movement that we must speak of creative consciousness.

It seems to me that this psychology of the deeper life must be represented in the following way. We must abandon the idea that the soul can be compared to something moving, which, obeying a more or less mechanical law, is impelled in the direction of certain given motive forces. To say that we are acting, implies that we are creating an imaginary world placed ahead of the present world and composed of movements which depend entirely on us. In this way our freedom becomes perfectly

[1] Bergson, *Time and Free Will*, Eng. trans., pp. 231-232. In this philosophy a distinction is made between duration which flows, in which our personality manifests itself, and mathematical time, which science uses to measure and space out accomplished facts.

[2] Bergson, *op. cit.*, Eng. trans., pp. 238-239.

intelligible. Starting from a study of these artificial constructions which embrace everything that interests us, several philosophers, inspired by Bergsonian doctrines, have been led to formulate a rather startling theory. Edouard Le Roy, for example, says: " Our real body is the entire universe in as far as it is experienced by us. And what common sense more strictly calls our body is only the region of least unconsciousness and greatest liberty in this greater body, the part which we most directly control and by means of which we are able to act on the rest." [1] But we must not, as this subtle philosopher constantly does, confuse a passing state of our willing activity with the stable affirmations of science.[2]

These artificial worlds generally disappear from our minds without leaving any trace in our memory ; but when the masses are deeply moved it then becomes possible to trace the outlines of the kind of representation which constitutes a social myth.

This belief in " glory " which Renan praised so much quickly fades away into rhapsodies when it is not supported by myths ; these myths have varied greatly in different epochs : the citizen of the Greek republics, the Roman legionary, the soldier of the wars of Liberty, and the artist of the Renaissance did not picture their conception of glory by the help of the same set of images. Renan complained that " the faith in glory " is compromised by the *limited historical outlook* more or less prevalent at the present day. " Very few," he said, " act with a view to immortal fame. . . . Every one wants to enjoy his own glory ; they eat it in the green blade, and do not gather the sheaves after death." [3] In my opinion, this limited historical outlook is, on the contrary,

[1] E. Le Roy, *Dogme et critique*, p. 239.
[2] It is easy to see here how the sophism creeps in ; the *universe experienced by us* may be either the real world in which we live or the world invented by us for action.
[3] Renan, *op. cit.* vol. iv. p. 329.

not a cause but a consequence ; it results from the weakening of the heroic myths which had such great popularity
at the beginning of the nineteenth century ; the belief in
" glory " perished and a limited historic outlook became
predominant at the time when these myths vanished.[1]

As long as there are no myths accepted by the masses,
one may go on talking of revolts indefinitely, without
ever provoking any revolutionary movement ; this is
what gives such importance to the general strike and
renders it so odious to socialists who are afraid of a
revolution ; they do all they can to shake the confidence
felt by the workers in the preparations they are making
for the revolution ; and in order to succeed in this they
cast ridicule on the idea of the general strike—the only
idea that could have any value as a motive force. One
of the chief means employed by them is to represent it
as a Utopia ; this is easy enough, because there are very
few myths which are perfectly free from any Utopian
element.

The revolutionary myths which exist at the present
time are almost free from any such mixture ; by means
of them it is possible to understand the activity, the
feelings and the ideas of the masses preparing themselves
to enter on a decisive struggle ; the myths are not descriptions of things, but expressions of a determination to act.
A Utopia is, on the contrary, an intellectual product ;

[1] " Assent," said Newman, " however strong, and accorded to images
however vivid, is not therefore necessarily practical. Strictly speaking,
it is not imagination that causes action ; but hope and fear, likes and
dislikes, appetite, passion, affection, the stirrings of selfishness and
self-love. What imagination does for us is to find a means of stimulating
those motive powers ; and it does so by providing a supply of objects
strong enough to stimulate them " (*op. cit.* p. 82). It may be seen from
this that the illustrious thinker adopts an attitude which strongly
resembles that of the theory of myths. It is impossible to read Newman
without being struck by the analogies between his thought and that of
Bergson : people who like to make the history of ideas depend on
ethnical traditions will observe that Newman was descended from
Israelites.

it is the work of theorists who, after observing and discussing the known facts, seek to establish a model to which they can compare existing society in order to estimate the amount of good and evil it contains.[1] It is a combination of imaginary institutions having sufficient analogies to real institutions for the jurist to be able to reason about them ; it is a construction which can be taken to pieces, and certain parts of it have been shaped in such a way that they can (with a few alterations by way of adjustment) be fitted into approaching legislation. Whilst contemporary myths lead men to prepare themselves for a combat which will destroy the existing state of things, the effect of Utopias has always been to direct men's minds towards reforms which can be brought about by patching up the existing system ; it is not surprising, then, that so many makers of Utopias were able to develop into able statesmen when they had acquired a greater experience of political life. A myth cannot be refuted, since it is, at bottom, identical with the convictions of a group, being the expression of these convictions in the language of movement ; and it is, in consequence, unanalysable into parts which could be placed on the plane of historical descriptions. A Utopia, on the contrary, can be discussed like any other social constitution ; the spontaneous movements it presupposes can be compared with the movements actually observed in the course of history, and we can in this way evaluate its verisimilitude ; it is possible to refute Utopias by showing that the economic system on which they have been made to rest is incompatible with the necessary conditions of modern production.

Liberal political economy is one of the best examples of a Utopia that could be given. A state of society

[1] It was evidently a method of this kind that was adopted by those Greek philosophers who wished to be able to argue about ethics without being obliged to accept the customs which historical necessity had imposed at Athens.

was imagined which could contain only the types produced by commerce, and which would exist under the
law of the fullest competition ; it is recognised to-day
that this kind of ideal society would be as difficult to
realise as that of Plato ; but several great statesmen of
modern times have owed their fame to the efforts they
made to introduce something of this ideal of commercial
liberty into industrial legislation.

We have here a Utopia free from any mixture of myth ;
the history of French democracy, however, presents a very
remarkable combination of Utopias and myths. The
theories that inspired the authors of our first constitutions
are regarded to-day as extremely chimerical ; indeed,
people are often loth to concede them the value which
they have been so long recognised to possess—that of
an ideal on which legislators, magistrates, and administrators should constantly fix their eyes, in order to secure
for men a little more justice. With these Utopias were
mixed up the myths which represented the struggle
against the ancient regime ; so long as the myths survived,
all the refutations of liberal Utopias could produce no
result ; the myth safeguarded the Utopia with which it
was mixed.

For a long time Socialism was scarcely anything but
a Utopia ; the Marxists were right in claiming for
their master the honour of bringing about a change
in this state of things ; Socialism has now become the
preparation of the masses employed in great industries
for the suppression of the State and property ; and it
is no longer necessary, therefore, to discuss how men must
organise themselves in order to enjoy future happiness ;
everything is reduced to the *revolutionary apprenticeship* of the proletariat. Unfortunately Marx was not
acquainted with facts which have now become familiar
to us ; we know better than he did what strikes are,
because we have been able to observe economic conflicts

of considerable extent and duration ; the myth of the
" general strike " has become popular, and is now firmly
established in the minds of the workers ; we possess
ideas about violence that it would have been difficult
for him to have formed ; we can then complete his
doctrine, instead of making commentaries on his text,
as his unfortunate disciples have done for so long.

In this way Utopias tend to disappear completely
from Socialism ; Socialism has no longer any need to
concern itself with the organisation of industry since
capitalism does that. I think, moreover, that I have
shown that the general strike corresponds to a kind of
feeling which is so closely related to those which are
necessary to promote production in any very progressive
state of industry, that a revolutionary apprenticeship
may at the same time be considered as an apprenticeship which will enable the workmen to occupy a high
rank among the best workmen of his own trade.

People who are living in this world of " myths," are
secure from all refutation ; this has led many to assert
that Socialism is a kind of religion. For a long time
people have been struck by the fact that religious convictions are unaffected by criticism, and from that they
have concluded that everything which claims to be
beyond science must be a religion. It has been observed
also that Christianity tends at the present day to be less
a system of dogmas than a Christian life, *i.e.* a moral
reform penetrating to the roots of one's being ; consequently, a new analogy has been discovered between
religion and the revolutionary Socialism which aims at
the apprenticeship, preparation, and even reconstruc-
tion of the individual,—a gigantic task. But Bergson
has taught us that it is not only religion which occupies
the profounder region of our mental life ; revolutionary
myths have their place there equally with religion. The
arguments which Yves Guyot urges against Socialism on

the ground that it is a religion, seem to me, then, to be founded on an imperfect acquaintance with the new psychology.

Renan was very surprised to discover that Socialists are beyond discouragement. " After each abortive experiment they recommence their work : the solution is not yet found, but it will be. The idea that no solution exists never occurs to them, and in this lies their strength."[1] The explanation given by Renan is superficial ; it regards Socialism as a Utopia, that is, as a thing which can be compared to observed realities ; if this were true, it would be scarcely possible to understand how confidence can survive so many failures. But by the side of the Utopias there have always been myths capable of urging on the workers to revolt. For a long time these myths were founded on the legends of the Revolution, and they preserved all their value as long as these legends remained unshaken. To-day the confidence of the Socialists is greater than ever since the myth of the general strike dominates all the truly working-class movement. No failure proves anything against Socialism since the latter has become a work of preparation (for revolution) ; if they are checked, it merely proves that the apprenticeship has been insufficient; they must set to work again with more courage, persistence, and confidence than before ; their experience of labour has taught workmen that it is by means of patient apprenticeship that a man may become a true comrade, and it is also the only way of becoming a true revolutionary.[2]

[1] Renan, *op. cit.* vol. iii. p. 497.

[2] It is extremely important to notice the analogy between the revolutionary state of mind and that which corresponds to the *morale* of the producers. I have indicated some remarkable resemblances at the end of these reflections, but there are many more analogies to be pointed out.

V

The works of my friends have been treated with great contempt by the Socialists who mix in politics, but at the same time with much sympathy by people who do not concern themselves with parliamentary affairs. We cannot be suspected of seeking to carry on a kind of *intellectual industry*, and we protest every time people profess to confuse us with the intellectuals, who do, as a matter of fact, make the exploitation of thought their profession. The old stagers of democracy cannot understand why people should take so much trouble unless they secretly aim at the leadership of the working classes. However, we could not act in any other way.

The man who has constructed a Utopia designed to make mankind happy is inclined to look upon the invention as his own personal property ; he believes that no one is in a better position than he is to apply his system. He thinks it very unreasonable that his writings do not procure him some post in the government. But we, on the contrary, have invented nothing at all, and even assert that nothing can be invented ; we have limited ourselves to defining the historical bearing of the notion of a general strike. We have tried to show that a new culture might spring from the struggle of the revolutionary trades unions against the employers and the State ; our greatest claim to originality consists in our having maintained that the proletariat can emancipate itself without being compelled to seek the guidance of that section of the middle classes which concerns itself professionally with matters of the intellect. We have thus been led to regard as essential in contemporary phenomena what was before regarded as accessory, and what is indeed really educative for a revolutionary proletariat that is serving its apprenticeship in struggle. It would be impossible for us to exercise any direct influence on such a work of formation.

We may play a useful part if we limit ourselves to attacking middle-class thought in such a way as to put the proletariat on its guard against an invasion of ideas and customs from the hostile class.

Men who have received an elementary education are generally imbued with a certain reverence for print as such, and they readily attribute genius to the people who attract the attention of the literary world to any great extent ; they imagine that they must have a great deal to learn from authors whose names are so often mentioned with praise in the newspapers ; they listen with singular respect to the commentaries that these literary prize-winners present to them. It is not easy to fight against these prejudices, but it is a very useful work ; we regard this task as being absolutely of the first importance, and we can carry it to a profitable conclusion without ever attempting to direct the working-class movement. The proletariat must be preserved from the experience of the Germans who conquered the Roman Empire ; the latter were ashamed of being barbarians, and put themselves to school with the rhetoricians of the Latin decadence ; they had no reason to congratulate themselves for having wished to be civilised.

In the course of my career I have touched on many subjects which might be considered to be outside the proper range of a Socialist writer. I have endeavoured to show that the science whose marvellous results the middle class constantly boasts of is not as infallible as those who live by its exploitation would have us believe ; and that a study of the phenomena of the Socialist world would often furnish philosophers with an enlightenment which they do not find in the works of the learned. I do not believe, then, that I am labouring in vain, for in this way I help to ruin the prestige of middle-class culture, a prestige which up to now has been opposed to the complete development of the principle of the " class war."

In the last chapter of my book, I have said that art is an anticipation of the kind of work that ought to be carried on in a highly productive state of society. It seems that this observation has been very much misunderstood by some of my critics, who have been under the impression that I wished to propose as the socialist solution — an aesthetic education of the proletariat under the tutelage of modern artists. This would have been a singular paradox on my part, for the art that we possess to-day is a *residue* left to us by an aristocratic society, a residue which has, moreover, been greatly corrupted by the middle class. According to the most enlightened minds, it is greatly to be desired that contemporary art could renew itself by a more intimate contact with craftsmen; academic art has used up the greatest geniuses without succeeding in producing anything which equals what has been given us by generations of craftsmen. I had in view something altogether different from such an imitation when I spoke of an anticipation. I wished to show how one found in art (practised by its best representatives, and, above all, in its best periods) analogies which make it easier for us to understand what the qualities of the workers of the future would be. Moreover, so little did I think of asking the *École des Beaux-Arts* to provide a teaching suitable to the proletariat, that I based the *morale* of the producers not on an aesthetic education transmitted by the middle class, but on the feelings developed by the struggles of the workers against their masters.

These observations lead us to recognise the enormous difference which exists between the *new school* and the anarchism which flourished twenty years ago in Paris. The middle class itself had much less admiration for its

literary men and its artists than the anarchists of that
time felt for them ; their enthusiasm for the celebrities
of a day often surpassed that felt by disciples for the
greatest masters of the past. We need not then be
astonished that by a kind of compensation the novelists
and the poets thus adulated have shown a sympathy
for the anarchists which has often astonished people who
do not know what a force vanity is in the artistic
world.

Intellectually, then, this kind of anarchism was *entirely
middle class*, and the Guesdistes attacked it for this reason.
They said that their adversaries, while proclaiming themselves the irreconcilable enemies of the past, were themselves the servile pupils of this cursed past; they observed,
moreover, that the most eloquent dissertations on revolt
could produce nothing, and that literature cannot change
the course of history. The anarchists replied by showing
that their adversaries had entered on a road which could
not lead to the revolution they announced ; by taking
part in political debates, Socialists, they said, will become
merely reformers of a more or less radical type, and will
lose the sense of their revolutionary formulas. Experience
has quickly shown that the anarchists were right in this
view, and that in entering into middle-class institutions,
revolutionaries have been transformed by adopting the
spirit of these institutions. All the deputies agree
that there is very little difference between a middle-
class representative and a representative of the proletariat.

Many anarchists, tired at last of continually reading
the same grandiloquent maledictions hurled at the
capitalist system, set themselves to find a way which
would lead them to acts which were really revolutionary.
They became members of syndicates which, thanks to
violent strikes, realised, to a certain extent, the social war
they had so often heard spoken of. Historians will one

day see in this entry of the anarchists into the syndicates one of the greatest events that has been produced in our time, and then the name of my poor friend Fernand Pelloutier will be as well known as it deserves to be.[1]

The anarchist writers who remained faithful to their former revolutionary literature do not seem to have looked with much favour upon the passage of their friends into the syndicates ; their attitude proves that the anarchists who became syndicalists showed real originality, and had not merely applied theories which had been fabricated in philosophical coteries.

Above all, they taught the workers that they need not be ashamed of acts of violence. Till that time it had been usual in the Socialist world to attenuate or to excuse the violence of the strikers ; the new members of the syndicates regarded these acts of violence as normal manifestations of the struggle, and as a result of this, the tendencies at work in the syndicates, pushing them towards trades unionism, were abandoned. It was their revolutionary temperament which led them to this conception of violence, for it would be a gross error to suppose that these former anarchists carried over into the workers' associations any of their ideas about propaganda by deed.

Revolutionary syndicalism is not then, as many believe, the first confused form of the working-class movement, which is bound, in the end, to free itself from this youthful error ; it has been, on the contrary, the produce of an improvement brought about by men who had just arrested a threatened deviation towards middle-class ideas. It might be compared to the Reformation, which wished to prevent Christianity submitting to the influence

---

[1] I believe that Léon de Seilhac was the first to render justice to the high qualities of Fernand Pelloutier (*Les Congres ouvriers en France*, p. 272).

of the humanists ; like the Reformation, revolutionary syndicalism may prove abortive, if it loses, as did the latter, the sense of its own originality ; it is this which gives such great interest to inquiries on proletarian violence.

July 15th, 1907.

INTRODUCTION TO THE FIRST
PUBLICATION [1]

THE reflections that I submit to the readers of the *Mouvement Socialiste* on the subject of violence have been inspired by some simple observations about very evident facts, which play an increasingly marked rôle in the history of contemporary classes.

For a long time I had been struck by the fact that the *normal development* of strikes is accompanied by an important series of acts of violence ; [2] but certain learned sociologists seek to disguise a phenomenon that every one who cares to use his eyes must have noticed. Revolutionary syndicalism keeps alive in the minds of the masses the desire to strike, and only prospers when important strikes, accompanied by violence, take place. Socialism tends to appear more and more as a theory of revolutionary syndicalism—or rather as a philosophy of modern history, in as far as it is under the influence of this syndicalism. It follows from these incontestable data, that if we desire to discuss Socialism with any benefit, we must first of all investigate the functions of violence in actual social conditions. [3]

[1] These Reflections were first published in the *Mouvement Socialiste* (first six months, 1906).

[2] Cf. " *Les Grèves* " in the *Science sociale*, October-November 1900.

[3] In the *Insegnamenti sociali della economia contemporanea* (written in 1903, but not published till 1906) I had already, but in a very inadequate manner, pointed out what seemed to me to be the function of violence, in maintaining the division between the proletariat and the middle classes (pp. 53-55).

I do not believe that this question has yet been approached with the care it admits of ; I hope that these reflections will lead a few thinkers to examine the problems of proletarian violence more closely.   I cannot too strongly recommend this investigation to the *new school* which, inspired by the principles of Marx rather than by the formulas taught by the official proprietors of Marxism, is about to give to Socialist doctrines a sense of reality and a gravity which it certainly has lacked for several years. Since the *new school* calls itself Marxist, syndicalist, revolutionary, it should have nothing so much at heart as the investigation of the exact historical significance of the spontaneous movements which are being produced in the working classes, movements which may possibly ensure that the future direction of social development will conform to Marx's ideas.

Socialism is a philosophy of the history of contemporary institutions, and Marx has always argued as a philosopher of history when he was not led away by personal polemics to write about matters outside the proper scope of his own system.

The Socialist imagines, then, that he has been transported into a very distant future, so that he can consider actual events as elements of a long and completed development, and he can attribute to them the colour that they might take for a future philosopher. Such a procedure certainly presupposes a considerable use of hypothesis ; but without certain hypotheses about the future there can be no social philosophy, no reflection on evolution, and no important action in the present even. The object of this study is a more thorough investigation of customs, and not a discussion of the merits or faults of certain important people. I want to find out how the feelings by which the masses are moved form themselves into groups ; all the discussions of the moralists about the motives for the actions of prominent men, and all psychological analyses of character are, then, quite secondary in importance, and even altogether negligible.

It seems, however, that it is more difficult to reason in this way, when we are concerned with acts of violence, than with any other set of circumstances. That is due to our habit of looking on conspiracy as the typical example of violence, or as the *anticipation of a revolution* ; we are thus led to ask ourselves whether certain criminal acts could not be considered heroic, or at least meritorious, if we were to take into account the happy consequences for their fellow-citizens anticipated by the perpetrators, as the result of their crimes. Certain individual criminal attempts have rendered such great services to democracy that the latter has often consecrated as great men those who, at the peril of their lives, have tried to rid it of its enemies ; it has done this the more readily since these great men were no longer living when the hour for dividing the spoils of victory arrived, and we know that the dead obtain admiration more easily than the living.

Each time an outrage occurs, the doctors of the ethico-social sciences, who swarm in journalism, indulge in reflections on the question, Can the criminal act be excused, or sometimes even justified, from the point of view of the highest justice ? Then there is an irruption into the democratic press of that casuistry for which the Jesuits have so many times been reproached.

I think it may be useful here to mention a note on the assassination of the Grand Duke Sergius which appeared in *Humanité* of February 18, 1905 ; the author was not one of those vulgar members of the *Bloc* whose intelligence is hardly superior to that of a negrito, he was one of the leading lights of the State universities : Lucien Herr is one of those who ought to know what they are talking about. The title *Just Reprisals* warns us that the question is to be treated from a high ethical standpoint ; it is the *judgment of the world* [1] which is about to be pronounced. The author scrupulously endeavours to assign the responsibility, calculates the equivalence which ought to exist between a crime and its expiation, goes back to the original misdeeds which have engendered this series of acts of violence in Russia ; all this is a philosophy of history strictly in accordance with the pure principles of the Corsican vendetta.   Carried away by the lyricism of his subject, Lucien Herr concludes in the style of a prophet : " The battle will go on in this way, in suffering and in blood, abominable and odious, till that *predestined day*, which cannot be far off, when the throne itself, the *homicidal throne*, the throne which heaps up so many crimes, will fall down into the ditch that has to-day been dug for it." This prophecy has not yet been realised, but the true character of all great prophecies is never to be realised ; the *homicidal throne* is much more secure than the cash-box of *Humanité*.   But, after all, what can we learn from all this ?

It is not the business of the historian to award prizes for virtue, to propose the erection of statues, or to establish any catechism whatever ; his business is to *understand what is least individual* in the course of events ; the questions which interest the chroniclers and excite novelists are those which he most willingly leaves on one side.   And so I am not at all concerned to justify the *perpetrators of violence*, but to inquire into the function of *violence of the working classes* in contemporary Socialism.

It seems to me that the problem of violence has been very badly formulated by many Socialists ; as a proof of this, I instance an article published in the *Socialiste* on October 21, 1905, by Rappoport.   The author, who has written a book on the philosophy of history,[2] ought, it

---

[1] This expression is not too strong, seeing that the author's studies have been mainly confined to Hegel.

[2] Ch. Rappoport, *La Philosophie de l'histoire comme science de l'évolution*.

seems to me, to have discussed the question by examining the remoter consequences of these events ; but, on the contrary, he considered them under their most immediate, most paltry, and, consequently, least historical aspect. According to him, syndicalism tends necessarily to opportunism, and as this law does not seem to be verified in France, he adds : "If in some Latin countries it assumes revolutionary attitudes, that is mere appearance. It shouts louder, but that is always for the purpose of demanding reforms inside the framework of existing society. It is a meliorism by blows, but it is always meliorism."

Thus there would be two kinds of meliorism : the one patronised by the *Musée Social*, the Direction du Travail, and Jaurès, which would work with the aid of maxims, half-lies, and supplication to eternal justice ; the other proceeds by blows—the latter being the only one that is within the scope of uneducated people who have not yet been enlightened by a knowledge of advanced social economics. These worthy people, democrats devoted to the cause of the Rights of man and the Duties of the informer, sociologist members of the Bloc, think that violence will disappear when popular education becomes more advanced ; they recommend, then, a great increase in the numbers of courses and lectures ; they hope to overturn revolutionary syndicalism by the breath of the professors. It is very strange that a revolutionary like Rappoport should agree with these *worthy progressives* [1] and their acolytes in their estimate of the meaning of syndicalism ; this can only be explained by admitting that even for the best-informed Socialists the problems of violence still remain very obscure.

To examine the effects of violence it is necessary to start from its distant consequences and not from its immediate results. We should not ask whether it is more or less directly advantageous for contemporary

[1] See note p. 13. Trans.

workmen than adroit diplomacy would be, but we should inquire what will result from the introduction of violence into the relations of the proletariat with society. We are not comparing two kinds of reformism, but we are endeavouring to find out what contemporary violence is in relation to the future social revolution.

Many will reproach me for not having given any information which might be useful for tactical purposes ; no formulas, no recipes. What then was the use of writing at all ? Clear-headed people will say that these studies are addressed to men who live outside the realities of everyday life and outside the true movement—that is, outside editors' offices, parliamentary lobbies, and the ante-chambers of the Socialist financiers. Those who have become scientists merely by coming into contact with Belgian sociology will accuse me of having a metaphysical rather than a scientific mind.[1] These are opinions which will scarcely touch me, since I have never paid any attention to the views of people who think vulgar stupidity the height of wisdom, and who admire above all men who speak and write without thinking.

Marx also was accused by the great lords of positivism of having, in *Capital*, treated economics metaphysically ; they were astonished " that he had confined himself to a mere critical analysis of actual facts, instead of formulating receipts." [2] This reproach does not seem to have moved him very much ; moreover, in his preface to his book, he had warned the reader that he would not determine the social position of any particular country, and that he would confine himself to an investigation of the laws of capitalist production, " the tendencies working with iron necessity towards inevitable results." [3]

---

[1] This expectation has been realised ; for in a speech in the Chambre des Deputés on May 11, 1907, Jaurès called me " the metaphysician of Syndicalism," doubtless ironically.

[2] *Capital*, Eng. trans., p. xxvi.   [3] *Loc. cit.* p. xvii.

One does not need a great knowledge of history to perceive that the mystery of historical development is only intelligible to men who are far removed from superficial disturbances ; the chroniclers and the actors of the drama do not see at all, what, later on, will be regarded as fundamental ; so that one might formulate this apparently paradoxical rule, " It is necessary to be outside in order to see the inside." When we apply these principles to contemporary events we run the risk of being taken for metaphysicians, but that is of no importance, for this time we are not at Brussels *savez-vous, sais-tu, pour une fois.*[1] If we are dissatisfied with the unsystematic views formed by common sense, we must follow a method altogether opposed to that of the sociologists, who found their reputation amongst stupid people by means of insipid and confused chatter ; we must firmly resolve to ignore immediate applications, and think only of elaborating generalisations and concepts ; it is necessary to set aside all the favourite preoccupations of the politicians. I hope that in the end it will be recognised that I have never broken this rule.

Though they may lack other qualities, these reflections possess one merit which cannot be questioned ; it is quite evident that they are inspired by a passionate love of truth. Love of truth has become a rare enough quality ; the members of the Bloc despise it profoundly ; official Socialists regard it as having anarchical tendencies ; politicians and their hangers-on cannot sufficiently insult the wretched people who prefer truth to the delights of

[1] Some Belgian comrades have been offended by these innocent jokes, which nevertheless I retain here ; Belgian Socialism is best known in France through Vandevelde, one of the most useless creatures that ever existed, who not being able to console himself for having been born in a country too small to give scope to his genius, came to Paris and gave lectures on all kinds of subjects, and who can be reproached, among other things, for having made an enormous profit on a very small intellectual capital. I have already said what I think of him in the *Introduction à l'économie moderne*, pp. 42-49.

power. But there are still some honest people left in France, and it is for them alone that I have always written.

The greater my experience the more I have recognised that in the study of historical questions a passion for truth is worth more than the most learned methodologies ; it enables one to break through conventional wrappings, to penetrate to the foundations of things, and to grasp reality. There has never been a great historian who has not been altogether carried along by this passion ; and looking at this matter closely, one sees that it is this passion which has given rise to so many happy intuitions.

.   .   .   .   .   .

I do not claim that I have, in this book, said everything that there is to say about violence, and still less to have produced a systematic theory of violence. I have merely reunited and revised a series of articles which appeared in an Italian review, *Il Divenire sociale*,[1] a review which maintains, on the other side of the Alps, the good fight against the exploiters of popular credulity. The articles were written without any fixed plan ; I have not tried to rewrite them, because I did not know how to set about giving a didactic appearance to such an exposition ; it even seemed to me better to preserve their untidy arrangement, since in that form they will perhaps more easily awake thought. We should always be careful in opening up a little-known subject, not to trace its boundaries too rigorously, for in this way the door is closed to the many new facts which arise from unforeseen circumstances. Time after time the theorists of Socialism have been embarrassed by contemporary history. They had constructed magnificent formulas, clear - cut and

---

[1] The last four chapters have been much more developed than they were in the Italian text. I have thus been able to give more space to philosophic considerations. The Italian articles have been collected in a brochure under the title *Lo Sciopero generale e la violenza* with a preface by Enrico Leone.

symmetrical, but they could not make them fit the facts. Rather than abandon their theories, they preferred to declare that the most important facts were mere anomalies, which science must ignore if it is to obtain a real understanding of the whole.

CHAPTER I

CLASS WAR AND VIOLENCE

I. *War of the poorer groups against the rich groups—Opposition of democracy to the division into classes—Methods of buying social peace—The corporative mind.*

II. *Illusions relating to the disappearance of violence—The mechanism of conciliation and the encouragement which it gives to strikers—Influence of fear on social legislation and its consequences.*

I

EVERYBODY complains that discussions about Socialism are generally exceedingly obscure. This obscurity is due, for the most part, to the fact that contemporary Socialists use a terminology which no longer corresponds to their ideas. The best known among the people who call themselves *revisionists* do not wish to appear to be abandoning certain phrases, which have served for a very long time as a label to characterise Socialist literature. When Bernstein, perceiving the enormous contradiction between the language of social democracy and the true nature of its activity, urged his German comrades to have the courage to appear what they were in reality,[1] and to revise a doctrine that had become mendacious, there was a universal outburst of indignation at his audacity; and

[1] Bernstein complains of the pettifoggery and *cant* which reigns among the social democrats (*Socialisme théorique et socialdémocratie pratique*, French translation, p. 277). He addresses these words from Schiller to social democracy : " Let it dare to appear what it is " (p. 238).

the reformists themselves were not the least eager of the defenders of the ancient formula. I remember hearing well-known French Socialists say that they found it easier to accept the tactics of Millerand than the arguments of Bernstein.

This idolatry of words plays a large part in the history of all ideologies ; the preservation of a Marxist vocabulary by people who have become completely estranged from the thought of Marx constitutes a great misfortune for Socialism. The expression " class war," for example, is employed in the most improper manner ; and until a precise meaning can be given to this term, we must give up all hope of a reasonable exposition of Socialism.

A. To most people the class war is the *principle of Socialist tactics*. That means that the Socialist party founds its electoral successes on the clashing of interests which exist in an acute state between certain groups, and that, if need be, it would undertake to make this hostility still more acute ; their candidates ask the poorest and most numerous class to look upon themselves as forming a corporation, and they offer to become the advocates of this corporation ; they promise to use their influence as representatives to improve the lot of the disinherited. Thus we are not very far from what happened in the Greek states ; Parliamentary Socialists are very much akin to the demagogues who clamoured constantly for the abolition of debts, and the division of landed property, who put all public charges upon the rich, and invented plots in order to get large fortunes confiscated. " In the democracies in which the crowd is above the law," says Aristotle, " the demagogues, by their continual attacks upon the rich, always divide the city into two camps . . . the oligarchs should abandon all swearing of oaths like those they swear to-day ; for there are cities in which they have taken this oath—I will be the constant enemy of the people, and I will do them all the evil that lies in my power." [1] Here, certainly, is a war between two classes as clearly defined as it can be ; but it seems to me absurd to assert that it was in this way that Marx understood the class war, which, according to him, was the essence of Socialism.

I believe that the authors of the French law of August 11, 1848, had their heads full of these classical reminiscences when they decreed punishment against all those who, by speeches and newspaper articles, sought " to trouble the public peace by stirring up hatred and contempt amongst the citizens." The terrible insurrection of the month of June was just over, and it was firmly believed that the victory of the Parisian workmen would have brought on, if not an attempt to put communism into practice, at least a series of formidable requisitions on the rich in favour of the poor ; it was hoped that an end would be put to civil wars by increasing the difficulty of propagating *doctrines of hatred*, which might raise the proletariat against the middle class.

Nowadays Parliamentary Socialists no longer entertain the idea of insurrection ; if they still occasionally speak of it, it is merely to give themselves airs of importance ; they teach that the ballot-box has replaced the gun ; but the means of acquiring power may have changed without there being any change of mental attitude. Electoral literature seems inspired by the purest demagogic doctrines ; Socialism makes its appeal to the discontented without troubling about the place they occupy in the world of production ; in a society as complex as ours, and as subject to economic upheavals, there is an enormous number of discontented people in all classes—that is why Socialists are often found in places where one would least expect to meet them. Parliamentary Socialism speaks as many languages as it has types of clients. It makes

[1] Aristotle, *Politics*, v. 9, §§ 10, 11.

its appeal to workmen, to small employers of labour, to peasants ; and in spite of Engels, it aims at reaching the farmers ; [1] it is at times patriotic ; at other times it declares against the Army. It is stopped by no contradiction, experience having shown that it is possible, in the course of an electoral campaign, to group together forces which, according to Marxian conceptions, should normally be antagonistic. Besides, cannot a Member of Parliament be of service to electors of every economic situation ?

In the end the term " proletariat " became synonymous with oppressed ; and there are oppressed in all classes : [2] German Socialists have taken a great interest in the adventures of the Princess of Coburg.[3] One of our most distinguished reformers, Henri Turot, for a long time one of the editors of the *Petite République* [4] and municipal councillor of Paris, has written a book on the " proletariat of love," by which title he designates the lowest class of prostitutes. If one of these days the suffrage is granted to women, he will doubtless be called upon

[1] Engels, *La Question agraire et le socialisme. Critique du programme du parti ouvrier français*, translated in the *Mouvement socialiste*. October 15, 1900, p. 453. It has often been pointed out that certain Socialist candidates had separate bills for the town and the country.

[2] Hampered by the monopoly of the licensed stockbrokers (*agents de change*), the other brokers (*coulissiers*) of the Bourse thus form a financial proletariat, and among them more than one Socialist admirer of Jaurès may be found. [*Trans. Note.*—The *coulissiers* are only allowed to deal in certain markets—the Kaffir, Argentine, etc. They are constantly conducting press campaigns against the privileged brokers. Many of them are naturalised German Jews, and the licensed brokers utilise this fact in defending their own position.]

[3] The Socialist deputy Sudekum, *the best-dressed man in Berlin*, played a large part in the abduction of the Princess of Coburg ; let us hope that he had no financial interest in this *affaire*. At that time he represented Jaurès's newspaper at Berlin.

[4] H. Turot was for some considerable time one of the editors of the nationalist paper *L'Eclair*, and of the *Petite République* at the same time. When Judet took over the management of *L'Eclair* he dismissed his Socialist contributor.

to draw up a statement of the claims of this special proletariat.

B. Contemporary democracy in France finds itself somewhat bewildered by the tactics of the class war. This explains why Parliamentary Socialism does not mingle with the main body of the parties of the extreme left.

In order to understand this situation, we must remember the important part played by revolutionary war in our history ; an enormous number of our political ideas originated from war ; war presupposes the union of national forces against the enemy, and our French historians have always severely criticised those insurrections which hampered the defence of the country. It seems that our democracy is harder on its rebels than monarchies are ; the Vendéens are still denounced daily as infamous traitors. All the articles published by Clémenceau to combat the ideas of Hervé are inspired by the purest revolutionary tradition, and he says so himself clearly : " I stand by and shall always stand by the old-fashioned patriotism of our fathers of the Revolution," and he scoffs at people who would " suppress international wars in order to hand us over *in peace to the amenities of civil war*" (*Aurore*, May 12, 1905).

For some considerable time the Republicans denied that there was any struggle between the classes in France ; they had so great a horror of revolt that they would not recognise the facts. Judging all things from the abstract point of view of the Declaration of the Rights of Man, they said that the legislation of 1789 had been created in order to abolish all distinction of class in law ; for that reason they were opposed to proposals for social legislation, which, nearly always, reintroduced the idea of class, and distinguished certain groups of citizens as being unfitted for the use of liberty. " The revolution

was supposed to have suppressed class distinction,"
wrote Joseph Reinach sadly in the *Matin* of April 19,
1895 ; " but they spring up again at every step. . . .
It is necessary to point out these aggressive returns
of the past, but they must not be allowed to pass unchallenged ; they must be resisted." [1]

Electoral dealing led many Republicans to recognise
that the Socialists obtain great successes by utilising the
passions of jealousy, of deception, or of hate, which exist
in the world ; thenceforward they became aware of the
class war, and many have borrowed the jargon of the
Parliamentary Socialists : in this way the party that is
called Radical Socialist came into being. Clémenceau
asserts even that he knows *moderates* who became Socialists
in twenty-four hours. " In France," he says, " the
Socialists that I know [2] are excellent Radicals who, thinking
that social reforms do not advance quickly enough to
please them, conceive that it would be good tactics to
claim the greater in order to get the less. How many
names and how many secret avowals I could quote to
support what I say ! But that would be useless, for
nothing could be less mysterious " (*Aurore*, August 14,
1905).

Léon Bourgeois—who was not willing to adapt himself
completely to the new methods, and who, for that reason
perhaps, left the Chamber of Deputies for the Senate—
said, at the congress of his party in July 1905 : " The
class war is a fact, but a cruel fact. I do not believe that
it is by prolonging this war that the solution of the problem
will be attained ; I believe that the solution rather lies in its
suppression ; men must be brought to look upon themselves
as partners in the same work." It would therefore seem
to be a question of creating social peace by legislation, thus

---

[1] J. Reinach, *Démagogues et socialistes*, p. 198.
[2] Clémenceau knows the Socialists in Parliament exceedingly well,
and from long experience.

demonstrating to the poor that the Government has no greater care than that of improving their lot, and by imposing the necessary sacrifices on people who possess a fortune judged to be too great for the harmony of the classes.

Capitalist society is so rich, and the future appears to it in such optimistic colours, that it endures the most frightful burdens without complaining overmuch : in America politicians waste large taxes shamelessly ; in Europe, the expenditure in military preparation increases every year ; [1] social peace might very well be bought by a few supplementary sacrifices.[2] Experience shows that the middle classes allow themselves to be plundered quite easily, provided that a little pressure is brought to bear, and that they are intimidated by the fear of revolution ; that party will possess the future which can most skilfully manipulate the spectre of revolution ; the radical party is beginning to understand this ; but, however clever its clowns may be, it will have some difficulty in finding any who can dazzle the big Jew bankers as well as Jaurès and his friends do.

C. The Syndicalist organisation gives a third value to the class war. In each branch of industry employers and workmen form antagonistic groups, which have continual discussions, which negotiate and make agreements. Socialism brings along its terminology of class

[1] At The Hague Conference the German delegate declared that his country bore the expense of armed peace with ease ; Léon Bourgeois held that France bore " quite as lightly the personal and financial obligations which the national defence imposed on its citizens." Ch. Guieysse, who quotes this speech, thinks that the Tsar had asked for the limitation of military expenditure because Russia was not rich enough yet to maintain herself at the level of the great capitalist countries (*La France et la paix armée*, p. 45).

[2] That is why Briand told on June 9, 1907, his constituents at Saint-Etienne that the Republic had made a *sacred pledge* to the workers about old-age pensions.

war, and thus complicates conflicts which might have remained of a purely private order ; corporative exclusiveness, which resembles the local or the racial spirit, is thereby consolidated, and those who represent it like to imagine that they are accomplishing a higher duty and are doing excellent work for Socialism.

It is well known that litigants who are strangers in a town are generally very badly treated by the judges of commercial courts sitting there, who try to give judgment in favour of their fellow-townsmen. Railway companies pay fantastic prices for pieces of ground, the value of which is fixed by juries recruited from among the neighbouring landowners. I have seen Italian sailors overwhelmed with fines, for pretended infractions of the law, by the fishing arbitrators with whom they had come to compete on the strength of ancient treaties. Many workmen are in the same way inclined to assert that in all their contests with the employers, the worker has morality and justice on his side ; I have heard the secretary of a syndicate (so fanatically a reformer as distinct from a revolutionary that he denied the oratorical talent of Guesde) declare that nobody had class feeling so strongly developed as he had,—because he argued in the way I have just indicated,—and he concluded that the revolutionaries did not possess the monopoly of the just conception of the class war.

It is quite understandable that many people have considered this corporative spirit as no better than the parish spirit, and also that they should have attempted to destroy it by employing methods very analogous to those which have so much weakened the jealousies which formerly existed in France between the various provinces. A more general culture and the intermixing with people of another region rapidly destroy provincialism : would it not be possible to destroy the corporative feeling by frequently bringing the important men in the syndicates

into connection with the employers, and by furnishing
them with opportunities of taking part in discussions of
a general order in mixed commissions ?   Experience has
shown that this is feasible.

II

The efforts which have been made to remove the
causes of hostility which exist in modern society have
undoubtedly had some effect, although the peacemakers
may be much deceived about the extent of their work.
By showing a few of the officials of the syndicates that
the middle classes are not such terrible men as they had
believed, by loading them with politeness in commissions
set up in ministerial offices or at the *Musée social*, and by
giving them the impression that there is a *natural and
Republican equity*, above class prejudices and hatreds, it
has been found possible to change the attitude of a few
former revolutionaries.[1]   These conversions of a few of
their old chiefs have caused great confusion in the mind
of the working classes ;   the former enthusiasm of more
than one Socialist has given place to discouragement ;
many working men have wondered whether the trades
union organisation was not becoming a kind of politics,
a means of getting on.

But simultaneously with this evolution, which filled
the heart of the peacemakers with joy, there was a re-
crudescence of the revolutionary spirit in a large section
of the proletariat. Since the Republican Government and
the philanthropists have taken it into their heads to
exterminate Socialism by developing social legislation,

[1] In the matter of social " clowneries " there are very few new
things under the sun.   Aristotle had already laid down the rules of
social peace : he says that demagog   " should in their harangues
appear to be concerned only with the n erest of the rich, just as in
oligarchies the government should only s em to have in view the
interests of the people " (*loc. cit.*).   That is   text which should be
inscribed on the door of the offices of the Directieu du Travail.

and by moderating the resistance of the employers in strikes, it has been observed that, more than once, the conflicts have become more acute than formerly.[1] This is often explained away by saying that it was an accident, the result simply of the survival of old usages ; people like to lull themselves with the hope that everything will go perfectly well on the day when manufacturers have a better understanding of the usages of social peace.[2] I believe, on the contrary, that we are in the presence of a phenomenon which flows quite naturally from the conditions in which this pretended pacification is carried out.

I observe, first of all, that both the theories and action of the peacemakers are founded on the notion of duty, and that duty is something entirely indefinite—while law seeks rigid definition. This difference is due to the fact that the latter finds a real basis in the economics of production, while the former is founded on sentiments of resignation, goodness, and of sacrifices ; and who can judge whether the man who submits to duty has been sufficiently resigned, sufficiently good, sufficiently self-sacrificing ? The Christian is convinced that he will never succeed in doing all that the gospel enjoins on him ; when he is free from economic ties (in a monastery) he invents all sorts of pious obligations, so that he may bring his life nearer to that of Christ, who loved men to such an extent that he accepted an ignominious fate that they might be redeemed.

In the economic world everybody limits his duty by his unwillingness to give up certain profits. While the employer will be always convinced that he has done the

---

[1] Cf. G. Sorel, *Insegnamenti sociali*, p. 343.

[2] In his speech of May 11, 1907, Jaurès said that nowhere had there been such violence as there was in England during the period when both the employers and Government refused to recognise the trade unions. " They have given way ; there is now vigorous and strong action, but which is at the same time legal, firm, and wise."

whole of his duty, the worker will be of a contrary opinion, and no argument could possibly settle the matter : the first will believe that he has been heroic, and the second will treat this pretended heroism as shameful exploitation.

Our great pontiffs of duty refuse to look upon a contract to work as being of the nature of a sale ; nothing is so simple as a sale ; nobody troubles himself to find out whether the grocer or his customer is right when they do not agree on the price of cheese ; the customer goes where he can buy more cheaply, and the grocer is obliged to change his prices when his customers leave him. But when a strike takes place it is quite another thing. All the well-intentioned people, all the " progressives " and the friends of the Republic, begin to discuss which of the two parties is in the right : *to be in the right is to have accomplished one's whole social duty.* Le Play has given much advice on the means of organising labour with a view to the strict fulfilment of duty ; but he could not fix the extent of the mutual obligations ; he left it to the tact of each, to the just estimation of the duties attaching to one's place in the social hierarchy, to the master's intelligent appreciation of the real needs of the workmen.[1]

The employers generally agree to discuss disputes on these lines ; to the claims of the workers they reply that they have already reached the limit of possible concessions—while the philanthropists wonder whether the selling price will not permit of a slight rise in wages. Such a discussion presupposes that it is possible to ascertain the exact extent of a man's social duty, and what sacrifices an employer must continue to make in order to *carry out the duties of his social position.* As there is

---

[1] Le Play, *Organisation du travail*, chap. ii. § 21. According to this writer, more attention should be paid to moral forces than to the systems that are invented in order to regulate wages in a more or less automatic manner.

no process of reasoning which can resolve such a problem, wiseacres suggest recourse to arbitration ; Rabelais would have suggested recourse to the chance of the dice. When the strike is important, deputies loudly demand an inquiry, with the object of discovering whether the industrial leaders are properly fulfilling their *duties as good masters.*

Certain results are obtained in this way—which nevertheless seem absurd—because on the one hand the large employers of labour have been brought up with religious, philanthropic, and civic ideas ; [1] and on the other hand because they cannot show themselves too stubborn, when certain demands are made by people occupying a high position in the country. Conciliators stake their vanity on succeeding, and they would be extremely hurt if industrial leaders prevented them from making social peace. The workmen are in a much more favourable position, because the prestige of the peacemakers is very much less with them than with the capitalists ; the latter give way, therefore, much more easily than the workers, in order to allow these well-intentioned folk the glory of ending the conflict. It is noticeable that these proceedings very rarely succeed when the matter is in the hands of workmen who have become rich : literary, moral, or sociological considerations have very little effect upon people born outside the ranks of the middle classes.

People who are called upon to intervene in disputes in this way are misled by what they have seen of certain secretaries of syndicates, whom they find much less irreconcilable than they expected, and who seem to them to be ripe for a recognition of the idea of social peace. In the course of conciliation meetings more than one revolutionary has shown that he aspires to become a member of the middle class, and there are many intelligent

[1] About the forces which tend to maintain sentiments of moderation, cf. *Insegnamenti sociali*, part iii. chap. v.

people who imagine that socialistic and revolutionary conceptions are only accidents that might be avoided by establishing better relations between the classes. They believe that the working-class world looks at the economic question entirely from the standpoint of duty, and they imagine that harmony would be established if a better social education were given to the citizens.

Let us see what influences are behind the other movement that tends to make conflicts more acute.

Workmen quickly perceive that the labour of conciliation or of arbitration rests on no economico-judicial basis, and their tactics have been conducted—instinctively perhaps—in accordance with this datum. Since the feelings, and, above all, the vanity of the peacemakers are in question, a strong appeal must be made to their imaginations, and they must be given the idea that they have to accomplish a titanic task : demands are piled up, therefore, figures fixed in a rather haphazard way, and there are no scruples about exaggerating them ; often the success of the strike depends on the cleverness with which a syndicalist (who thoroughly understands the spirit of *social diplomacy*) has been able to introduce claims, in themselves very minor, but capable of giving the impression that the employers are not fulfilling their social duty.   It often happens that writers who concern themselves with these questions are astonished that several days pass before the strikers have settled what exactly they have to demand, and that in the end demands are put forward which had not been mentioned in the course of the preceding negotiations. This is easily understood when we consider the bizarre conditions under which the discussion between the interested parties is carried on.

I am surprised that there are no strike professionals who would undertake to draw up lists of the workers' claims ; they would obtain all the more success in conciliation councils as they would not let themselves be dazzled by fine words so easily as the workers' delegates.[1]

When the strike is finished the workmen do not forget that the employers at first declared that no concession was possible ; they are led thus to the belief that the employers are either ignorant or liars. This result is not conducive to the development of social peace !

So long as the workers submitted without protest to the exactions of the employers, they believed that the will of their masters was completely dominated by economic necessities ; they perceived, after the strike, that this necessity is not of a very rigid kind, and that if energetic pressure from below is brought to bear on the masters, the latter will find some means of liberating themselves from the pretended fetters of economic necessity ; thus within practical limits capitalism appears to the workers to be *unfettered*, and they reason as if it were entirely so. What in their eyes restrains this liberty is not the necessities of competition but the ignorance of the employers. Thus is introduced the notion of the *inexhaustibility of production*, which is one of the postulates of the theory of class war in the Socialism of Marx.[2]

Why then speak of social duty ? Duty has some meaning in a society in which all the parts are intimately connected and responsible to one another ; but if capitalism is inexhaustible, joint responsibility is no longer founded on economic realities, and the workers think they would be dupes if they did not demand all they can obtain ; they look upon the employer as an adversary with whom one comes to terms after a war. *Social duty no more exists than does international duty.*

---

[1] The French law of December 27, 1892, seems to have foreseen this possibility ; it lays down that delegates on conciliation boards should be chosen among the interested parties ; it thus keeps out these professionals whose presence would render the prestige of the authorities and of philanthropists precarious.

[2] G. Sorel, *Insegnamenti sociali*, p. 390.

These ideas are somewhat confused, I admit, in many
minds ; but they exist in a much more stable manner
than the partisans of social peace imagine ; the latter are
deluded by appearances, and never penetrate to the
hidden roots of the existing tendencies of Socialism.

Before passing to other considerations, it must be
noticed that our Latin countries present one great obstacle
to the formation of social peace ; the classes are more
sharply separated by external characteristics than they
are in Saxon countries ; these separations very much
embarrass Syndicalist leaders when they abandon their
former manners and take up a position in the official or
philanthropic circles.[1] These circles have welcomed
them with great pleasure, since it has been perceived that
the gradual transformation of trades union officials into
members of the middle classes might produce excellent
results ; but their comrades distrust them. In France
this distrust has become much more definite since a great
number of anarchists have entered the Syndicalist movement ; because the anarchist has a horror of everything
which recalls the proceedings of politicians—a class of
people devoured by the desire to climb into superior
classes, and having already the capitalist mind while yet
poor.[2]

Social politics have introduced new elements which
must now be taken into account. First of all, it must be

[1] Everybody who has seen trades union leaders close at hand is
struck with the extreme difference which exists between France and
England from this point of view ; the English trades union leaders
rapidly become gentlemen, without anybody blaming them for it
(P. de Rousiers, *Le Trade-unionisme en Angleterre*, p. 309 and p. 322).
While correcting this proof, I read an article by Jacques Bardaux,
pointing out that a carpenter and a miner had been made knights by
Edward VII. (*Débats*, December 16, 1907).

[2] Some years ago Arsène Dumont invented the term *social capillarity*
to express the slow climbing of the classes. If Syndicalism submitted to
the influence of the pacifists, it would be a powerful agent of social
capillarity.

noticed that the workers *count* to-day in the world by the same right as the different productive groups which demand to be protected ; they must be treated with solicitude just as the vine-growers or the sugar manufacturers.[1] There is nothing settled about Protectionism ; the custom duties are fixed so as to satisfy the desires of very influential people who wish to increase their incomes ; social politics proceed in the same manner. The Protectionist Government professes to have knowledge which permits it to judge what should be granted to each group so as to defend the producers without injuring the consumers ; similarly, in social politics it declares that it will take into consideration the interests of the employers and those of the workers.

Few people, outside the faculties of law, are so simple as to believe that the State can carry out such a programme : in actual fact, the Parliamentarians decide on a compromise that partially satisfies the interests of those who are most influential in elections without provoking too lively protests from those who are sacrificed. There is no other rule than the true or presumed interest of the electors ; every day the customs commission recasts its tariffs, and it declares that it will not stop recasting them until it succeeds in securing prices which it considers remunerative to the people for whom it has undertaken the part of providence : it keeps a watchful eye on the operations of importers ; every lowering of price attracts its attention and provokes inquiries with the object of discovering whether it would not be possible to raise values again artificially. Social politics are carried on in exactly the

[1] It has often been pointed out that the workers' organisation in England is a simple union of interests, for the purposes of immediate material advantages. Some writers are very pleased with this situation because, quite rightly, they see in it an obstacle to Socialistic propaganda. *To embarrass the Socialists*, even at the price of economic progress and of the safety of the culture of the future, that is the great aim of certain great *idealists* dear to the philanthropic middle classes.

same way; on June 27, 1905, the *rapporteur* [1] of a law on the length of the hours of work in the mines said, in the Chamber of Deputies : " Should the application of the law give rise to disappointment among the workmen, *we have undertaken* to lay a new bill before the house." This worthy man spoke exactly like the *rapporteur* of a tariff law.

There are plenty of workmen who understand perfectly well that all the trash of Parliamentary literature only serves to disguise the real motives by which the Government is influenced. The Protectionists succeed by subsidising a few important party leaders or by financing newspapers which support the politics of these party leaders ; the workers have no money, but they have at their disposal a much more efficacious means of action ; they can inspire *fear*, and for several years past they have availed themselves of this resource.

At the time of the discussion of the law regulating labour in mines, the question of the threats addressed to the Government cropped up several times : on February 5, 1902, the president of the commission told the Chamber that those in power had " lent an attentive ear to clamourings from without ; that they had been inspired by a sentiment of benevolent generosity in allowing themselves to be moved (*despite the tone* in which they were couched), by the claims of the working classes and the long cry of suffering of the workers in the mines." A little later he added: " We have accomplished a work of social justice, . . . a work of benevolence also, in going to those who toil and suffer, like friends solely desirous of working in peace and under honourable conditions, and we must not by a brutal and too egotistic refusal to unbend, allow them to give way to impulses which, *while not actual revolts*, would yet have as many victims." All these confused phrases served

[1] See Translator's Note, p. 162.

to hide the terrible fear which clutched this grotesque depu'y.[1] In the sitting of November 6, 1904, at the Senate, the minister declared that the Government was incapable of giving way to threats, but that it was necessary to open not only ears and mind, but also the heart " to respectful claims " (!) ; a good deal of water had passed under the bridges since the day when the Government had promised to pass the law under the threat of a general strike.[2]

I could choose other examples to show that the most decisive factor in social politics is the cowardice of the Government. This was shown in the plainest possible way in the recent discussions on the suppression of registry offices, and on the law which sent to the civil courts appeals against the decisions of the arbitrators in industrial disputes. Nearly all the Syndicalist leaders know how to make excellent use of this situation, and they teach the workers that it is not at all a question of demanding favours, but that they must profit by *middle-class cowardice* to impose the will of the proletariat. These tactics are supported by so many facts that they were bound to take root in the working-class world.

One of the things which appear to me to have most astonished the workers during the last few years has been the timidity of the forces of law and order in the presence of a riot ; magistrates who have the right to demand the services of soldiers dare not use their power to the utmost, and officers allow themselves to be abused and struck with a patience hitherto unknown in them. It is

[1] This imbecile has become Minister of Commerce. All his speeches on this question are full of balderdash ; he has been a lunacy doctor, and has perhaps been influenced by the logic and the language of his clients.

[2] The Minister declared that he was creating " real democracy," and that it was demagogy " to give way to external pressure, to haughty summonses, which, for the most part, are only higher bids and baits addressed to the credulity of people whose life is laborious."

becoming more and more evident every day that working-class violence possesses an extraordinary efficacity
in strikes: prefects, fearing that they may be obliged
to use force against insurrectionary violence, bring pressure to bear on employers in order to compel them to
give way; the safety of factories is now looked upon as
a favour which the prefect may dispense as he pleases;
consequently he arranges the use of his police so as to
intimidate the two parties, and skilfully brings them to
an agreement.

Trades union leaders have not been long in grasping
the full bearing of this situation, and it must be admitted
that they have used the weapon that has been put into
their hands with great skill. They endeavour to intimidate the prefects by popular demonstrations which might
lead to serious conflicts with the police, and they com-
mend violence as the most efficacious means of obtaining
concessions. At the end of a certain time the obsessed
and frightened administration nearly always intervenes
with the masters and forces an agreement upon them,
which becomes an encouragement to the propagandists
of violence.

Whether we approve or condemn what is called *the
revolutionary and direct method*, it is evident that it is not
on the point of disappearing; in a country as warlike
as France there are profound reasons which would assure
a considerable popularity for this method, even if its
enormous efficacy had not been demonstrated by so many
examples. This is the one great social fact of the present
hour, and we must seek to understand its bearing.

I cannot refrain from noting down here a reflection
made by Clemenceau with regard to our relations with
Germany, which applies equally well to social conflicts
when they take a violent aspect (which seems likely to
become more and more general in proportion as a cowardly

middle class continues to pursue the chimera of social
peace) : " There is no better means," he said (than the
policy of perpetual concessions), " of making the opposite
party ask for more and more. Every man or every power
whose action consists solely in surrender can only finish
by self - annihilation. Everything that lives resists ;
that which does not resist allows itself to be cut up
piecemeal " (*Aurore*, August 15, 1905).

A social policy founded on middle - class cowardice,
which consists in always surrendering before the threat
of violence, cannot fail to engender the idea that the
middle class is condemned to death, and that its disappearance is only a matter of time. Thus every conflict which
gives rise to violence becomes a vanguard fight, and
nobody can foresee what will arise from such engagements ;
although the great battle never comes to a head, yet
each time they come to blows the strikers hope that it
is the beginning of the great *Napoleonic battle* (that which
will definitely crush the vanquished) ; in this way the
practice of strikes engenders the notion of a catastrophic
revolution.

A keen observer of the contemporary proletarian
movement has expressed the same ideas : " They, like
their ancestors (the French revolutionaries), are for struggle,
for conquest ; they desire to accomplish great works by
force. Only, the war of conquest interests them no
longer. Instead of thinking of battles, they now think
of strikes ; instead of setting up as their ideal a battle
against the armies of Europe, they now set up the general
strike in which the capitalist régime will be annihilated.[1]

The theorists of social peace shut their eyes to these
embarrassing facts ; they are doubtless ashamed to
admit their cowardice, just as the Government is ashamed
to admit that its social politics are carried out under the
threat of disturbances. It is curious that people who

[1] Ch. Guieysse, *op. cit.* p. 125.

boast of having read Le Play have not observed that his
conception of the conditions of social peace was quite
different from that of his imbecile successors. He supposed
the existence of a middle class of serious moral habits,
imbued with the feelings of its own dignity, and having
the energy necessary to govern the country without recourse to the old traditional bureaucracy. To those men,
who held riches and power in their hands, he professed
to teach their *social duty towards their subjects*. His
system supposed an undisputed authority ; it is well
known that he deplored the licence of the press under
Napoleon III. as scandalous and dangerous ; his reflections on this subject seem somewhat ludicrous to those
who compare the newspaper of that time with those of
to-day.[1] Nobody in his time would have believed that
a great country would accept peace at any price ; his
point of view in this matter did not differ greatly from
that of Clemenceau. He would never have admitted
that any one could be cowardly and hypocritical enough
to decorate with the name of social duty the cowardice
of a middle class incapable of defending itself.

Middle-class cowardice very much resembles the
cowardice of the English Liberal party, which constantly
proclaims its absolute confidence in arbitration between
nations : arbitration nearly always gives disastrous results
for England.[2] But these *worthy progressives* prefer to

[1] Speaking of the elections of 1869, he said that there had been
" violences of language which France had not till then heard, even in
the worst days of the Revolution " (*Organisation du Travail*, 3rd ed.
p. 340). Evidently, the revolution of 1848 was meant. In 1873 he
declared that the Emperor could not congratulate himself on having
abrogated the system of restraint on the press, before having reformed
the morals of the country (*Réforme sociale en France*, 5th ed. tome iii.
p. 356).

[2] Sumner Maine observed a long while ago that it was England's
fate to have advocates who aroused very little sympathy (*Le Droit
international*, French translation, p. 279). Many Englishmen believe
that by humiliating their country they will rouse more sympathy
towards themselves ; but this supposition is not borne out by the facts.

pay, or even to compromise the future of their country, rather than face the horrors of war. The English Liberal party has the word *justice* always on its lips, absolutely like our middle class ; we might very well wonder whether all the high morality of our great contemporary thinkers is not founded on a degradation of the sentiment of honour.

CHAPTER II

VIOLENCE AND THE DECADENCE OF THE MIDDLE CLASSES

I. *Parliamentarians, who have to inspire fear—Parnell's methods —Casuistry ; fundamental identity of the Parliamentary Socialist groups.*

II. *Degeneration of the middle class brought about by peace— Marx's conceptions of necessity—Part played by violence in the restoration of former social relationships.*

III. *Relation between revolution and economic prosperity—The French Revolution—The Christian conquest—Invasion of the Barbarians—Dangers which threaten the world.*

I

It is very difficult to understand proletarian violence as long as we think in terms of the ideas disseminated by middle-class philosophers ; according to their philosophy, violence is a relic of barbarism which is bound to disappear under the influence of the progress of enlightenment. It is therefore quite natural that Jaurès, who has been brought up on middle-class ideology, should have a profound contempt for people who favour proletarian violence ; he is astonished to see educated Socialists hand in hand with the Syndicalists ; he wonders by what miracle men who have proved themselves thinkers can accumulate *sophistries* in order to give a semblance of reason to the dreams of stupid people who are incapable of thought.[1] This question worries the friends of Jaurès considerably, and they are only too ready to treat the representatives of the *new school* as demagogues, and accuse them of seeking the applause of the impulsive masses.

Parliamentary Socialists cannot understand the ends pursued by the *new school* ; they imagine that ultimately all Socialism can be reduced to the pursuit of the means of getting into power. Is it possible that they think the followers of the *new school* wish to make a higher bid for the confidence of simple electors and cheat the Socialists of the seats provided for them ? Again, the apologia of violence might have the very unfortunate result of disgusting the workers with electoral politics, and this would tend to destroy the chances of the Socialist candidates by multiplying the abstentions from voting ! Do you wish to revive civil war ? they ask. To our great statesmen that seems mad.

Civil war has become very difficult since the discovery of the new firearms, and since the cutting of rectilinear streets in the capital towns.[2] The recent troubles in Russia seem even to have shown that Governments can count much more than was supposed on the energy of their officers. Nearly all French politicians had prophesied the imminent fall of Czarism at the time of the Manchurian defeats, but the Russian army in the presence of rioting did not manifest the weakness shown by the French army during our revolutions ; nearly everywhere repression was rapid, efficacious, and even pitiless. The discussions

[1] This is apparently the way in which the proletarian movement is spoken of in the fashionable circles of refined Socialism.

[2] Cf. the reflections of Engels in the preface to the new edition of articles by Marx which he published in 1895 under the title, *Struggles of the Classes in France from 1848 to 1850.* This preface is wanting in the French translation. In the German edition a passage has been left out, the social democratic leaders considering certain phrases of Engels not politic enough.

which took place at the congress of social democrats at
Jena show that the Parliamentary Socialists no longer
rely upon an armed struggle to obtain possession of the
State.

Does this mean that they are utterly opposed to
violence ?   It would not be in their interest for the
people to be quite calm ;   a certain amount of agitation
suits them, but this agitation must be contained within
well-defined limits and controlled by politicians.   When
he considers it useful for his own interests, Jaurès makes
advances to the Confédération Générale du Travail ; [1]
sometimes he instructs his peaceable clerks to fill his paper
with revolutionary phrases ;   he is past master in the art
of utilising popular anger.   A cunningly conducted
agitation is extremely useful to Parliamentary Socialists,
who boast before the Government and the rich middle
class of their ability to moderate revolution ;   they can
thus arrange the success of the financial affairs in which
they are interested, obtain minor favours for many
influential electors, and get social laws voted in order to
appear important in the eyes of the blockheads who
imagine that these Socialists are great reformers of the
law.   In order that all this may come off there must
always be a certain amount of movement, and the middle
class must always be kept in a state of fear.

It is conceivable that a regular system of diplomacy
might be established between the Socialist party and the
State each time an economic conflict arose between
workers and employers ;   the *two powers* would settle the
particular difference.   In Germany the Government
enters into negotiations with the Church each time the
clericals stand in the way of the administration. Socialists
have even been urged to imitate Parnell, who so often

---

[1] According to the necessities of the moment he is for or against
the general strike.   According to some he voted for the general strike
at the International Congress of 1900 ;   according to others he abstained.

found a means of imposing his will on England. This resemblance is all the greater in that Parnell's authority did not rest only on the number of votes at his disposal, but mainly upon the terror which every Englishman felt at the bare announcement of agrarian troubles in Ireland. A few acts of violence controlled by a Parliamentary group were exceedingly useful to the Parnellian policy, just as they are useful to the policy of Jaurès. In both cases a Parliamentary group *sells peace of mind to the Conservatives*, who dare not use the force they command.

This kind of diplomacy is difficult to conduct, and the Irish after the death of Parnell do not seem to have succeeded in carrying it on with the same success as in his time. In France it presents particular difficulty, because in no other country perhaps are the workers more difficult to manage : it is easy enough to arouse popular anger, but it is not easy to stifle it. As long as there are no very rich and strongly centralised trade unions whose leaders are in continuous relationship with political men,[1] so long will it be impossible to say exactly to what lengths violence will go. Jaurès would very much like to see such associations of workers in existence, for his prestige will disappear at once when the general public perceives that he is not in a position to moderate revolution.

Everything becomes a question of valuation, accurate estimation, and opportunism ; much skill, tact, and calm audacity are necessary to carry on such a diplomacy, *i.e.* to make the workers believe that you are carrying the flag of revolution, the middle class that you are arresting the danger which threatens them, and the country that

---

[1] Gambetta complained because the French clergy was " acephalous " ; he would have liked a select body to have been formed in its midst, with which the Government could discuss matters (Garilhe, *Le clergé séculier français au XIX* *siècle*, pp. 88-89). Syndicalism has no head with which it would be possible to carry on diplomatic relations usefully.

you represent an irresistible current of opinion. The great mass of the electors understands nothing of what passes in politics, and has no intelligent knowledge of economic history ; they take sides with the party which seems to possess power, and you can obtain everything you wish from them when you can prove to them that you are strong enough to make the Government capitulate. But you must not go too far, because the middle class might wake up and the country might be given over to a resolutely conservative statesman. A proletarian violence which escapes all valuation, all measurement, and all opportunism, may jeopardise everything and ruin socialistic diplomacy.

This diplomacy is played both on a large and small scale ; with the Government, with the heads of the groups in Parliament, and with influential electors. Politicians seek to draw the greatest possible advantage from the discordant forces existing in the political field.

Parliamentary Socialists feel a certain embarrassment from the fact that at its origin Socialism took its stand on absolute principles and appealed for a long time to the same sentiments of revolt as the most advanced Republican Party. These two circumstances prevent them from following a party policy like that which Charles Bonnier often recommended : this writer, who has long been the principal theorist of the Guesdist party, would like the Socialists to follow closely the example of Parnell, who used to negotiate with the English parties without allowing himself to become the vassal of any one of them ; in the same way it might be possible to come to an agreement with the Conservatives, if the latter pledged themselves to grant better conditions to the proletariat than the Radicals (*Socialiste*, August 27, 1905). This policy seemed scandalous to many people. Bonnier was obliged to dilute his thesis. He then contented himself with asking that the party should act in the best interests of the proletariat (September 17, 1905) ; but how is it possible to know where these interests lie when the principle of the class war is no longer taken as your unique and absolute rule ?

Parliamentary Socialists believe that they possess special faculties which enable them to take into account, not only the material and immediate advantages reaped by the working classes, but also the moral reasons which compel Socialism to form part of the great Republican family. Their congresses spend their energies in putting together formulas designed to regulate Socialist diplomacy, in settling what alliances are permitted and what for- bidden, in reconciling the abstract principle of the class war (which they are anxious to retain verbally) with the reality of the agreements with politicians. Such an undertaking is madness, and therefore leads to equivoca- tions, when it does not force deputies into attitudes of deplorable hypocrisy. Each year problems have to be rediscussed, because all diplomacy requires a flexibility which is incompatible with the existence of perfectly clear statutes.

The casuistry which Pascal scoffed at so much was not more subtle and more absurd than that which is to be found in polemics between what are called the *Socialist schools*. Escobar would have some difficulty in finding his bearings amid the distinctions of Jaurès ; the moral theology of *responsible* Socialists is not one of the least of the buffooneries of our time.

All moral theology can be split up into two tendencies : there are casuists who say that we must be content with opinions having a slight probability, others that we should always adopt those that are strictest and most certain. This distinction was bound to be met with among our Parliamentary Socialists. Jaurès prefers the soft and conciliatory method, provided that means are found to make it agree, somehow or other, with first principles, and that it has behind it a few respectable authorities ; he is a *probabilist* in the strongest sense of the term—or even a *latitudinarian* (*laxist*).[1] Vaillant recommends the strong and belligerent method, which a!one, in his opinion, is in accordance with the class war, and which has in its favour the unanimous sanction of all the old authorities ; he is a *tutiorist* and a kind of Jansenist.

Jaurès no doubt believes that he is acting for the greatest good of Socialism, just as the more easy going type of casuists believed themselves the best and most useful defenders of the Church ; they did, as a matter of fact, prevent weak Christians from falling into irreligion, and led them to practise the sacraments—exactly as Jaurès prevents the rich intellectuals who have come to Socialism by way of Dreyfusism from drawing back in horror before the class war, and induces them to take up the shares of the party journals. In his eyes, Vaillant is a dreamer who does not see the reality of the world, who intoxicates himself with the chimeras of an insurrection which has now become impossible, and who does not understand the great advantages which may be got from universal suffrage by a boastful politician.

Between these two methods there is only a difference of degree, and not one of kind as is believed by those Parliamentary Socialists who call themselves revolutionary. On this point Jaurès has a great intellectual superiority over his adversaries, for he has never cast any doubt upon the fundamental identity of the two methods.

Both of these methods suppose an entirely dislocated middle - class society — rich classes who have lost all sentiment of their class interest, men ready to follow blindly the lead of people who have taken up the business

[1] [The writers on moral theology who maintain that our actions should be guided only by absolutely sure maxims were called *tutiorists*; opposed to them were the *laxists*. In the *Provinciales* Pascal defends the *tutiorist* position, the Jesuits he attacks are *laxists.—Trans. Note.*]

of directing public opinion. The Dreyfus affair showed that the enlightened middle class was in a strange mental state ; people who had long and loudly served the Conservative party co-operated with anarchists, took part in violent attacks on the army, or even definitely enrolled themselves in the Socialist party ; on the other hand, newspapers, which make it their business to defend traditional institutions, dragged the magistrates of the Court of Cassation in the mire. This strange episode in our contemporary history brought to light the state of dislocation of the classes.

Jaurès, who was very much mixed up in all the ups and downs of Dreyfusism, had rapidly judged the mentality of the upper middle class, into which he had not yet penetrated. He saw that this upper middle class was terribly ignorant, gapingly stupid, politically absolutely impotent ; he recognised that with people who understand nothing of the principles of capitalist economics it is easy to contrive a policy of compromise on the basis of an extremely broad Socialism ; he calculated the proportions in which it is necessary to mix together flattery of the superior intelligence of the imbeciles whose seduction was aimed at, appeals to the disinterested sentiments of speculators who pride themselves on having invented the ideal, and threats of revolution in order to obtain the leadership of people void of ideas. Experience has shown that he had a very remarkable intuition of the forces which exist at this present moment in the middle-class world. Vaillant, on the contrary, is very little acquainted with this world ; he believes that the only weapon that can be employed to move the middle class is fear ; doubtless fear is an excellent weapon, but it might provoke obstinate resistance if you went beyond a certain limit. Vaillant does not possess those remarkable qualities of suppleness of mind, and perhaps even of peasant duplicity, which shine in Jaurès, and which have often caused people to say that he would have made a wonderful cattle-dealer.

The more closely the history of these last years is examined, the more the discussions concerning the two methods will be recognised as puerile : the partisans of the two methods are equally opposed to proletarian violence, because it escapes from the control of the people engaged in Parliamentary politics. Revolutionary Syndicalism cannot be controlled by the so-called revolutionary Socialists of Parliament.

II

The two methods favoured by official Socialism presuppose this same historical datum. The ideology of a timorous humanitarian middle class professing to have freed its thought from the conditions of its existence is grafted on the degeneration of the capitalist system ; and the race of bold captains who made the greatness of modern industry disappears to make way for an ultra-civilised aristocracy which asks to be allowed to live in peace. This degeneration fills our Parliamentary Socialists with joy. Their rôle would vanish if they were confronted with a middle class which was energetically engaged on the paths of capitalistic progress, a class that would look upon timidity with shame, and which would find satisfaction in looking after its class interests. In the presence of a middle class which has become almost as stupid as the nobility of the eighteenth century, their power is enormous. If the stultifying of the upper middle class progresses in a regular manner at the pace it has taken for the last few years, our official Socialists may reasonably hope to reach the goal of their dreams and sleep in sumptuous mansions.

Two accidents alone, it seems, would be able to stop this movement : a great foreign war, which might renew lost energies, and which in any case would doubtless bring into power men with the will to govern ; [1] or a great extension of proletarian violence, which would make the revolutionary reality evident to the middle class, and would disgust them with the humanitarian platitudes with which Jaurès lulls them to sleep. It is in view of these two great dangers that the latter displays all his resources as a popular orator. European peace must be maintained at all costs ; some limit must be put to proletarian violence.

Jaurès is persuaded that France will be perfectly happy on the day on which the editors of his paper, and its share-holders, can draw freely on the coffers of the public Treasury ; it is an illustration of the celebrated proverb : " Quand Auguste avait bu, la Pologne était ivre." A socialist government of this kind would without doubt ruin any country, if it was administered with the same care for financial order as *l'Humanité* has been administered ; but what does the future of the country matter, provided that the new régime gives a good time to a few professors, who imagine that they have invented Socialism, and to a few Dreyfusard financiers ?

Before the working class also could accept this *dictatorship of incapacity*, it must itself become as stupid as the middle class, and must lose all revolutionary energy, at the same time that its masters will have lost all capitalistic energy. Such a future is not impossible ; and a great deal of hard work is being done to stupefy the worker for this purpose. The *Direction du Travail* and the *Musée Social* are doing their best to carry on this marvellous work of idealistic education, which is decorated with the most pompous names, and which is represented as a means of civilising the proletariat. Our professional idealists are very much disturbed by the Syndicalists, and experience

[1] Cf. G. Sorel, *Insegnamenti sociali*, p. 388. The hypothesis of a great European war seems very far fetched at the moment.

shows that a strike is sometimes sufficient to ruin all
the *work of education* which these manufacturers of social
peace have patiently built by years of labour.

In order to understand thoroughly the consequences
of the very singular régime in the midst of which we are
living, we must hark back to Marx's conceptions of the
passage from capitalism to Socialism. These conceptions
are well known, yet we must continually return to them,
because they are often forgotten, or at least undervalued
by official Socialist writers ; it is necessary to insist on
them strongly each time that we have to argue about the
anti-Marxist transformation which contemporary Socialism is undergoing.

According to Marx, capitalism, by reason of the innate
laws of its own nature, is hurrying along a path which
will lead the world of to-day, with the inevitability of the
evolution of organic life, to the doors of the world of to-
morrow. This movement comprises a long period of
capitalistic construction, and it ends by a rapid destruction,
which is the work of the proletariat. Capitalism creates
the heritage which Socialism will receive, the men who
will suppress the present régime, and the means of bringing
about this destruction, at the same time that it preserves
the results obtained in production.[1] Capitalism begets
new ways of working ; it throws the working class into
revolutionary organisations by the pressure it exercises
on wages ; it restricts its own political basis by competition, which is constantly eliminating industrial leaders.
Thus, after having solved the great problem of the
organisation of labour, to effect which Utopians have
brought forward so many naïve or stupid hypotheses,
capitalism provokes the birth of the cause which will

---

[1] This notion of *revolutionary preservation* is very important; I
have pointed out something analogous in the passage from Judaism
to Christianity (*Le Système historique de Renan*, pp. 72-73, 171-172,
467).

overthrow it, and thus renders useless everything that Utopians have written to induce enlightened people to make reforms ; and it gradually ruins the traditional order, against which the critics of the idealists had proved themselves to be so deplorably incompetent. It might therefore be said that capitalism plays a part analogous to that attributed by Hartmann to The Unconscious in nature, since it prepares the coming of social reforms which it did not intend to produce. Without any co-ordinated plan, without any directive ideas, without any ideal of a future world, it is the cause of an inevitable evolution ; it draws from the present all that the present can give towards historical development ; it performs in an almost mechanical manner all that is necessary, in order that a new era may appear, and that this new era may break every link with the idealism of the present times, while preserving the acquisitions of the capitalistic economic system.[1]

Socialists should therefore abandon the attempt (initiated by the Utopians) to find a means of inducing the enlightened middle class to prepare the *transition to a more perfect system of legislation* ; their sole function is that of explaining to the proletariat the greatness of the revolutionary part they are called upon to play. By ceaseless criticism the proletariat must be brought to perfect their organisations ; they must be shown how the embryonic forms which appear in their unions [2] may be developed, so that, finally, they may build up institutions without any parallel in the history of the middle class ; that they may form ideas which depend solely on their position as producers in large industries, and which owe nothing to middle-class thought ; and that they may acquire *habits of*

[1] Cf. what I have said on the transformation which Marx wrought in Socialism, *Insegnamenti sociali*, pp. 179-186.

[2] [The French is *sociétés de résistance*. What is meant is the syndicate, considered principally as a means of combining workmen against the employers.—*Trans. Note*.]

liberty with which the middle class nowadays are no longer acquainted.

This doctrine will evidently be inapplicable if the middle class and the proletariat do not oppose each other implacably, with all the forces at their disposal ; the more ardently capitalist the middle class is, the more the proletariat is full of a warlike spirit and confident of its revolutionary strength, the more certain will be the success of the proletarian movement.

The middle class with which Marx was familiar in England was still, as regards the immense majority, animated by their conquering, insatiable, and pitiless spirit, which had characterised at the beginning of modern times the creators of new industries and the adventurers launched on the discovery of unknown lands. When we are studying the modern industrial system we should always bear in mind this similarity between the capitalist type and the warrior type ; it was for very good reasons that the men who directed gigantic enterprises were named *captains of industry*. This type is still found to-day in all its purity in the United States : there are found the indomitable energy, the audacity based on a just appreciation of its strength, the cold calculation of interests, which are the qualities of great generals and great capitalists.[1] According to Paul de Rousiers, every American feels himself capable of " trying his luck " on the battlefield of business,[2] so that the general spirit of the country is in complete harmony with that of the multi-millionaires ; our men of letters are exceedingly surprised to see these latter condemning themselves to lead to the end of their days a galley-slave existence,

---

[1] I will come back to this resemblance in Chapter VII. iii.

[2] P. de Rousiers, *La Vie américaine, l'éducation et la société*, p. 19. " Fathers give very little advice to their children, and let them learn for themselves, as they say over there " (p. 14). " Not only does (the American) wish to be independent, but he wishes to be powerful " (*La Vie américaine : ranches, fermes et usines*, p. 6).

without ever thinking of leading a nobleman's life for themselves, as the Rothschilds do.

In a society so enfevered by the passion for the success which can be obtained in competition, all the actors walk straight before them like veritable automata, without taking any notice of the great ideas of the sociologists; they are subject to very simple forces, and not one of them dreams of escaping from the circumstances of his condition. Then only is the development of capitalism carried on with that inevitableness which struck Marx so much, and which seemed to him comparable to that of a natural law. If, on the contrary, the middle class, led astray by the *chatter* of the preachers of ethics and sociology, return to an *ideal of conservative mediocrity*, seek to correct the *abuses* of economics, and wish to break with the barbarism of their predecessors, then one part of the forces which were to further the development of capitalism is employed in hindering it, an arbitrary and irrational element is introduced, and the future of the world becomes completely indeterminate.

This indetermination grows still greater if the proletariat are converted to the ideas of social peace at the same time as their masters, or even if they simply consider everything from the corporative point of view; while Socialism gives to every economic contest a general and revolutionary colour.

Conservatives are not deceived when they see in the compromises which lead to collective contracts, and in corporative particularism,[1] the means of avoiding the Marxian revolution;[2] but they escape one danger only to

[1] [This refers to the conduct of former syndicates which limited their ambitions to the interests of their own handicraft without concerning themselves with the general interests of the working classes.— *Trans. Note*.]

[2] There is constant talk nowadays of organising labour, *i.e.* of utilising the corporative spirit by giving it over to the management of well-intentioned, *very serious* and responsible people, and liberating the

fall into another, and they run the risk of being devoured by Parliamentary Socialism.[1]   Jaurès is as enthusiastic as the clericals about measures which turn away the working classes from the idea of the Marxian revolution ; I believe he understands better than they do what the result of social peace will be ; he founds his own hopes on the simultaneous ruin of the capitalistic and the revolutionary spirit.

It is often urged, in objection to the people who defend the Marxian conception, that it is impossible for them to stop the movement of degeneration which is dragging both the middle class and the proletariat far from the paths assigned to them by Marx's theory.   They can doubtless influence the working classes, and it is hardly to be denied that strike violences do keep the revolutionary spirit alive ; but how can they hope to give back to the middle class an ardour which is spent ?

It is here that the rôle of violence in history appears to us as singularly great, for it can, in an indirect manner, so operate on the middle class as to awaken them to a sense of their own class sentiment.   Attention has often been drawn to the danger of certain acts of violence which compromised *admirable social works*, disgusted employers who were disposed to arrange the happiness of their workmen, and developed egoism where the most noble sentiments formerly reigned.

To repay with *black ingratitude* the *benevolence* of those who would protect the workers,[2] to meet with insults the homilies of the defenders of human fraternity, and to

---

workers from the yoke of *sophists*.   The responsible people are de Mun, Charles Benoist (the amusing specialist in constitutional law), Arthur Fontaine, and the band of democratic *abbés*, . . . and lastly Gabriel Hanotaux !

[1] Vilredo Pareto laughs at the simple middle class who are happy, because they are no longer threatened by intractable Marxians, and who have fallen into the snare of the conciliatory Marxians (*Systèmes socialistes*, tome ii. p. 453).

[2] Cf. G. Sorel, *Insegnamenti sociali*, p. 53.

reply by blows to the advances of the propagators of social peace—all that is assuredly not in conformity with the rules of the fashionable Socialism of M. and Mme. Georges Renard,[1] but it is a very practical way of indicating to the middle class that they must mind their own business and only that.

I believe also that it may be useful to thrash the orators of democracy and the representatives of the Government, for in this way you insure that none shall retain any illusions about the character of acts of violence. But these acts can have historical value only if they are the *clear and brutal expression of the class war* : the middle classes must not be allowed to imagine that, aided by cleverness, social science, or high-flown sentiments, they might find a better welcome at the hands of the proletariat.

The day on which employers perceive that they have nothing to gain by works which promote social peace, or by democracy, they will understand that they have been ill-advised by the people who persuaded them to abandon their trade of creators of productive forces for the noble profession of educators of the proletariat. Then there is some chance that they may get back a part of their energy, and that moderate or conservative economics may appear as absurd to them as they appeared to Marx. In any case, the separation of classes being more clearly accentuated, the proletarian movement will have some chance of developing with greater regularity than to-day.

The two antagonistic classes therefore influence each other in a partly indirect but decisive manner. Capitalism drives the proletariat into revolt, because in daily

---

[1] Mme. G. Renard has published in the *Suisse* of July 26, 1900, an article full of lofty psychological considerations about the workers' fête given by Millerand (Léon de Seilhac, *Le Monde socialiste*, pp. 307-309). Her husband has solved the grave question as to who will drink Clos-Vougeot in the society of the future (G. Renard, *Le Régime socialiste*, p. 175).

life the employers use their force in a direction opposed
to the desire of their workers ; but the future of the proletariat is not entirely dependent on this revolt ; the working classes are organised under the influence of other
causes, and Socialism, inculcating in them the revolutionary idea, prepares them to suppress the hostile class.
Capitalist force is at the base of all this process, and its
action is automatic and inevitable.[1]   Marx supposed that
the middle class had no need to be incited to employ
force, but we are to-day faced with a new and very unforeseen fact—a middle class which seeks to weaken its
own strength.   Must we believe that the Marxian conception is dead ?   By no means, for proletarian violence
comes upon the scene just at the moment when the
conception of social peace is being held up as a
means of moderating disputes ; proletarian violence
confines employers to their rôle of producers, and tends
to restore the separation of the classes, just when they
seemed on the point of intermingling in the democratic
marsh.

Proletarian violence not only makes the future revolution certain, but it seems also to be the only means by
which the European nations—at present stupefied by
humanitarianism—can recover their former energy.   This
kind of violence compels capitalism to restrict its attentions
solely to its material rôle and tends to restore to it the
warlike qualities which it formerly possessed.   A growing

[1] In an article written in September 1851 (the first of the series
published under the title : *Revolution and Counter-revolution*), Marx
established the following parallelism between the development of the
middle class and of the proletariat : To a numerous, rich, concentrated,
and powerful middle class corresponds a numerous, strong, concentrated and intelligent proletariat.   Thus he seems to have thought
that the intelligence of the proletariat depends on the historical conditions which secured power in society to the middle classes.   He says,
again, that the true characters of the class war only exist in countries
where the middle class has recast the Government in conformity with
its needs.

and solidly organised working class can compel the capitalist class to remain firm in the industrial war ; if a united and revolutionary proletariat confronts a rich middle class, eager for conquest, capitalist society will have reached its historical perfection.

Thus proletarian violence has become an essential factor of Marxism. Let us add once more that, if properly conducted, it will suppress the Parliamentary Socialists, who will no longer be able to pose as the leaders of the working classes and the guardians of order.

III

The Marxian theory of revolution supposes that capitalism, while it is still in full swing, will be struck to the heart, when—having attained complete industrial efficiency—it has finally achieved its historical mission, and whilst the economic system is still a progressive one. Marx does not seem to have asked himself what would happen if the economic system were on the down grade ; he never dreamt of the possibility of a revolution which would take a return to the past, or even social conservation, as its ideal.

We see nowadays that such a revolution might easily come to pass : the friends of Jaurès, the clericals, and the democrats all take the Middle Ages as their ideal for the future ; they would like competition to be tempered, riches limited, production subordinated to needs. These are dreams which Marx looked upon as reactionary,[1] and consequently negligible, because it seemed to him that

---

[1] " Those who, like Sismondi, would return to the just proportion of production, while preserving the existing bases of society, are *reactionary*, since, to be consistent, they should also desire to re-establish all the other conditions of past times. . . . In existing society, in the industry based on individual exchanges, the anarchy of production, which is the *source of so much poverty* is at the same time the *source of all progress* " (Marx, *The Poverty of Philosophy*, Eng. trans., p. 41).

capitalism was embarked on an irresistible progress ; but nowadays we see considerable forces grouped together in the endeavour to reform the capitalist economic system by bringing it, with the aid of laws, nearer to the medieval ideal. Parliamentary Socialism would like to combine with the moralists, the Church, and the democracy, with the common aim of impeding the capitalist movement ; and, in view of middle-class cowardice, that would not perhaps be impossible.

Marx compared the passage from one historical era to another to a civil inheritance ; the new age inherits prior acquisitions. If the revolution took place during a period of economic decadence, would not the inheritance be very much compromised, and in that case could there be any hope of the speedy reappearance of progress in the economic system ? The ideologists hardly trouble themselves at all with this question ; they affirm that the decadence will stop on the day that the public Treasury is at their disposal ; they are dazzled by the immense reserve of riches which would be delivered up to their pillage ; what banquets there would be, what women, and what opportunities for self-display ! We, on the other hand, who have no such prospect before our eyes, have to ask whether history can furnish us with any guidance on this subject, which will enable us to guess what would be the result of a revolution accomplished in times of decadence.

The researches of Tocqueville enable us to study the French Revolution from this point of view. He very much astonished his contemporaries when, a half-century ago, he showed them that the Revolution had been much more conservative than had been supposed till then. He pointed out that most of the characteristic institutions of modern France date from the Old Régime (centralisation, the issue of regulations on every possible pretext,

administrative tutelage of the communes, exemption of
civil servants from the jurisdiction of the courts) ; he
found only one important innovation—the coexistence,
which was established in the year VIII., of isolated civil
servants and deliberative ,councils. The principles of
the Old Régime reappeared in 1800, and the old customs
were received back into favour.[1] Turgot seemed to him
to be an excellent type of the Napoleonic administrator,
who had " the ideal of a civil servant, in a democratic
society subject to an absolute government." [2] He was
of the opinion that the partition of the land, which it is
customary to place to the credit of the Revolution, had
begun long before, and had not gone on at an exceptionally
rapid pace under its influence.[3]

It is certain that Napoleon did not have to make any
extraordinary effort to put the country once more on a
monarchical footing. He found France quite ready, and
had only a few corrections of detail to make in order to
profit by the experience acquired since 1789. The
administrative and fiscal laws had been drawn up during
the Revolution by people who had applied the methods
of the Old Régime ; they remain in force to-day, still
almost intact. The men he employed had served their
apprenticeship under the Old Régime and under the
Revolution ; they all resemble one another ; in their
governmental practices they are all men of the preceding
period ; they all work with an equal ardour for the greatness of His Majesty.[4] The real merit of Napoleon lay
in his not trusting too much to his own genius, in not
giving himself up to the dreams which had so often
deluded men of the eighteenth century, and had led them

---

[1] Tocqueville, *L'Ancien Régime et la Révolution* (*édition des œuvres
complètes*), livre ii. chapitres i., iii., iv. pp. 89, 91, 94, 288.

[2] Tocqueville, *Mélanges*, pp. 155-156.

[3] Tocqueville, *L'Ancien Régime et la Révolution*, pp. 35-37.

[4] L. Madelin also comes to this conclusion in an article in the *Débats*
of July 6, 1907, on the prefects of Napoleon I.

to desire to regenerate everything from top to bottom—
in short, in his full recognition of the principle of historical
heredity.   It follows from all this that the Napoleonic
régime may be looked upon as an experiment, showing
clearly the enormous part played by conservation throughout the greatest revolutions.

Indeed, I think that the principle of conservation
might even be extended to things military, and the armies
of the Revolution and the Empire may be shown to be
an extension of former institutions.   In any case, it is
very curious that Napoleon should have made no essential
innovations in military equipment, and that it should
have been the fire-arms of the Old Régime which so
greatly contributed to securing the victories of the revolutionary troops.   It was only under the Restoration that
the artillery was improved.

The ease with which the Revolution and the Empire
succeeded in radically transforming the country while
still retaining such a large number of the acquisitions of
the past, is bound up with a fact to which our historians
have not always called attention, and which Taine does
not seem to have noticed :   industrial production was
making great progress, and this progress was such that,
towards 1780, everybody believed in the dogma of the
indefinite progress of mankind.[1]   This dogma, which was
to exercise so great an influence on modern thought,
would be a bizarre and inexplicable paradox if it were not
considered as bound up with economic progress and with
the feeling of absolute confidence which this economic
progress engendered.   The wars of the Revolution and
of the Empire only stimulated this feeling still further,
not only because they were glorious, but also because
they caused a great deal of money to enter the country,

[1] Tocqueville, *L'Ancien Régime et la Révolution*, pp. 254-262, and
Mélanges, p. 62.   Cf. chapter IV. iv. of my study on *Les Illusions du
Progrès*.

and thus contributed to the development of production.[1]

The triumph of the Revolution astonished nearly all
its contemporaries, and it seems that the most intelligent,
the most deliberate, and the best informed as regards
political matters, were the most surprised ; this was
because reasons drawn from theory could not explain
this paradoxical success. It seems to me that even to-
day the question is scarcely less obscure to historians than
it was to our ancestors. The primary cause of this
triumph must be sought in the economic progress of the
time ; it is because the Old Régime was struck by rapid
blows, while production was making great strides, that
the contemporary world was born with comparatively
little labour, and could so rapidly be assured of a vigorous
life.

We possess, on the other hand, a dreadful historical
experience of a great transformation taking place at a
time of economic decadence ; I mean the victory of
Christianity and the fall of the Roman Empire which
closely followed it.

All the old Christian authors agree in informing us
that the new religion brought no serious improvement
in the situation of the world ; corruption, oppression,
and disasters continued to crush the people as in the past.
This was a great disillusion for the fathers of the Church ;
at the time of the persecutions the Christians had believed
that God would overwhelm Rome with favours on the
day that the Empire ceased to persecute the faithful ;
now the Empire was Christian, and the bishops had
become personages of the first rank, yet everything
continued to go on as badly as in the past. What
was still more disheartening, the immorality, so often

---

[1] Kautsky has dwelt very strongly on the rôle played by the treasures
which the French armies took possession of (*La Lutte des classes en
France en 1789*, French trans., pp. 104-106).

denounced as the result of idolatry, had spread to the adorers of Christ. Far from imposing a far-reaching reform on the profane world, the Church itself had become corrupted by imitating the profane world ; it began to resemble an imperial administration, and the factions which tore it asunder were much more moved by an appetite for power than by religious reasons.

It has often been asked whether Christianity was not the cause, or at least one of the principal causes, of the fall of Rome. Gaston Boissier combats this opinion by endeavouring to show that the decadent movement observed after Constantine is the continuation of a movement which had existed for some time, and that it is not possible to see whether Christianity accelerated or retarded the death of the ancient world.[1] That amounts to saying that the extent of the conservation was enormous ; we can, by analogy, imagine what would follow from a revolution which brought our official Socialists of to-day into power. Institutions remaining almost what they are to-day, all the middle-class ideology would be preserved ; the middle-class state would dominate with its ancient abuses ; if economic decadence had begun, it would be accentuated.

Shortly after the Christian conquest, the barbarian invasions began. More than one Christian wondered whether an order in conformity with the principles of the new religion was not at length to appear ; this hope was all the more reasonable as the barbarians had been converted on coming into the Empire, and because they were not accustomed to the corruption of Roman life. From the economic point of view, a regeneration might be hoped for, since the world was perishing beneath the weight of urban exploitation ; the new masters, who had coarse rural manners, would not live as great lords, but as heads of large demesnes ; perhaps, therefore, the earth would

---

[1] Gaston Boissier, *La Fin du paganisme,* livre iv. chap. iii.

be better cultivated. The illusions of Christian authors contemporary with the invasions may be compared to those of the numerous Utopians who hope to see the modern world regenerated by the virtues which they attribute to the man of average condition; the replacing of the very rich classes by new social strata should bring about morality, happiness, and universal prosperity.

The barbarians did not establish any progressive state of society; there were not many of them, and almost everywhere they simply took the place of the old lords, led the same life as they did, and were devoured by urban civilisation. In France, the Merovingian royalty has been made the subject of particularly thorough investigation; Fustel de Coulanges has-used all his erudition in throwing light on the conservative character which it assumed; its conservatism appeared to him to be so strong that he was even able to say that there had been no real revolution, and he represented the whole of the history of the late Middle Ages as a movement which had carried on the movement of the Roman Empire with a little acceleration.[1] " The Merovingian Government," he said, " is more than three parts the continuation of that which the Roman Empire had given to Gaul." [2]

The economic decadence was accentuated under these barbarian kings; no renascence could take place until very long afterwards, when the world had gone through a long series of trials. At least four centuries of barbarism had to be gone through before a progressive movement showed itself; society was compelled to descend to a state not far removed from its origins, and Vico was to find in this phenomenon an illustration of his doctrine of

[1] Fustel de Coulanges, *Origines du régime féodal,* pp. 566-567. I do not deny that there is a good deal of exaggeration in the thesis of Fustel de Coulanges, but the conservation was undeniable.

[2] Fustel de Coulanges, *La Monarchie franque,* p. 650.

ricorsi.[1] Thus a revolution which took place in a time
of economic decadence had forced the world to pass again
through a period of almost primitive civilisation, and had
stopped all progress for several centuries.

These dreadful events have been many times invoked
by the adversaries of Socialism ; I do not deny the validity
of the argument, but two details must be added which
may perhaps appear of small importance to professional
sociologists. Such events presuppose (1) an economic
decadence ; (2) an organisation which assures a very
perfect conservation of the current system of ideas. The
civilised Socialism of our professors has many times been
presented as a safeguard of civilisation : I believe that
it would produce the same effect as was produced by the
classical education given by the Church to the barbarian
kings. The proletariat would be corrupted and stultified
as the Merovingians were, and economic decadence would
only be more certain under the action of these pretended
civilising agents.

The dangers which threaten the future of the world
may be avoided, if the proletariat hold on with obstinacy
to revolutionary ideas, so as to realise as much as possible
Marx's conception. Everything may be saved, if the
proletariat, by their use of violence, manage to re-establish
the division into classes, and so restore to the middle
class something of its former energy ; that is the great
aim towards which the whole thought of men—who are
not hypnotised by the event of the day, but who think

---

[1] [Vico's doctrine of " reflux " (*ricorsi*). Civilisation comes to an end
in the " barbarism of reflection " which is worse than the primitive
barbarism of sensation. . . . The mind, after traversing its course
of progress, after rising from sensation . . . to the rational, from
violence to equity, is bound, in conformity with its eternal nature,
to retraverse the course, to relapse into violence and sensation, and
thence to renew its upward movement, " to commence a reflux."   See
chap. xi. of *The Philosophy of Giambattista Vico*, by Benedetto Croce.
Eng. trans.—*Trans. Note.*]

of the conditions of to-morrow — must be directed. Proletarian violence, carried on as a pure and simple manifestation of the sentiment of the class war, appears thus as a very fine and very heroic thing ; it is at the service of the immemorial interests of civilisation ; it is not perhaps the most appropriate method of obtaining immediate material advantages, but it may save the world from barbarism.

We have a very effective reply to those who accuse Syndicalists of being obtuse and ignorant people. We may ask them to consider the economic decadence for which they are working. Let us salute the revolutionaries as the Greeks saluted the Spartan heroes who defended Thermopylae and helped to preserve the civilisation of the ancient world. 57831

CHAPTER III

PREJUDICES AGAINST VIOLENCE

I. *Old ideas relative to the Revolution—Change resulting from the year of* 1870 *and from the Parliamentary régime.*

II. *Drumont's observations on middle-class ferocity—The judicial Third Estate and the history of the Law Courts—Capitalism against the cult of the State.*

III. *Attitude of the Dreyfusards—Jaurès's judgments on the Revolution : his adoration of success and his hatred for the vanquished.*

IV. *Antimilitarism as a proof of an abandonment of middle-class traditions.*

I

THE ideas current among the outside public on the subject of proletarian violence are not founded on observation of contemporary facts, and on a rational interpretation of the present Syndicalist movement ; they are derived from a comparison of the present with the past—an infinitely simpler mental process ; they are shaped by the memories which the word *revolution* evokes almost automatically. It is supposed that the Syndicalists, merely because they call themselves revolutionaries, wish to reproduce the history of the revolutionaries of '93. The Blanquists, who look upon themselves as the legitimate owners of the Terrorist tradition, consider that for this very reason they are called upon to direct the proletarian movement ; [1] they display much more condescension to the Syndicalists than the other Parliamentary Socialists ; they are inclined to assert that the workers' organisations will come to understand in the end that they cannot do better than to put themselves under their tuition. It seems to me that Jaurès himself, when writing the *Histoire socialiste* of '93, thought more than once of the teachings which this past, a thousand times dead, might yield to him for the conduct of the present.

Proper attention has not always been given to the great changes which have taken place since 1870 in the way people judge the revolution ; yet these changes must be considered if we wish to understand contemporary ideas relative to violence.

For a very long time the Revolution appeared to be essentially a succession of glorious wars, which a people famished for liberty and carried away by the noblest passions had maintained against a coalition of all the powers of oppression and error. Riots and *coups d'état*, the struggles between parties often destitute of any scruple and the banishment of the vanquished, the Parliamentary debates and the adventures of illustrious men, in a word, all the events of its political history were in the eyes of our fathers only very secondary accessories to the wars of liberty.

For about twenty-five years the form of government in France had been at issue ; after campaigns before which the memories of Cæsar and Alexander paled the

---

[1] The reader may usefully refer to a very interesting chapter of Bernstein's book, *Socialisme théorique et socialdémocratie pratique*, pp. 47-63. Bernstein, who knows nothing of the aims of our present-day syndicalism, has not, in my opinion, drawn from Marxism all that it contains. His book, moreover, was written at a time when it was impossible still to understand the revolutionary movement, in view of which these reflections are written.

charter of 1814 had definitely incorporated in the national tradition, the Parliamentary system, Napoleonic legislation, and the Church established by the Concordat ; war had given an irrevocable judgment whose preambles, as Proudhon said, had been dated from Valmy, from Jemmapes, and from fifty other battlefields, and whose conclusions [1] had been received at Saint-Ouen by Louis XVIII.[2] Protected by the prestige of the wars of liberty, the new institutions had become inviolable, and the ideology which was built up to explain them became a faith which seemed for a long time to have for the French the value which the revelation of Jesus has for the Catholics.

From time to time eloquent writers have thought that they could set up a current of reaction against these doctrines, and the Church had hopes that it might get the better of what it called the *error of liberalism.* A long period of admiration for medieval art and of contempt for the period of Voltaire seemed to threaten the new ideology with ruin ; but all these attempts to return to the past left no trace except in literary history. There were times when those in power governed in the least liberal manner, but the principles of the modern régime were never seriously threatened. This fact could not be explained by the power of reason and by some law of progress ; its cause lies simply in the epic of the wars

---

[1] [The word " conclusions " is employed in two senses in civil proceedings. Each counsel presents his claims and arguments to the court in writing in a document which is called " conclusion." On the other hand, at the end of the case the *ministre public* states what, in his opinion, is the decision the court ought to make for the best administration of Justice ; these are the " conclusions " of the *ministre public.* The judgment always declares that the *ministre public* has been heard in his " conclusion." Proudhon uses the word in the second sense. On the return of the Bourbons, Louis XVIII. issued a proclamation in which he stated the principles on which it seemed to him the government of the country must henceforth rest.—*Trans. Note.*]

[2] Proudhon, *La Guerre et la paix*, livre v. chap. iii.

which had filled the French soul with an enthusiasm analogous to that provoked by religions.

This military epic gave an epical colour to all the events of internal politics ; party struggles were thus raised to the level of an Iliad ; politicians became giants, and the revolution, which Joseph de Maistre had denounced as satanical, was made divine. The bloody scenes of the Terror were episodes without great significance by the side of the enormous hecatombs of war, and means were found to envelop them in a dramatic mythology ; riots were elevated to the same rank as illustrious battles ; and calmer historians vainly endeavoured to bring the Revolution and the Empire down to the plane of common history. The prodigious triumphs of the revolutionary and imperial arms rendered all criticism impossible.

The war of 1870 changed all that. At the moment of the fall of the Second Empire the immense majority in France still firmly believed the legends which had been spread about regarding the armies of volunteers, the miraculous rôle of the representatives of the people, and the improvised generals ; experience produced a cruel disillusion. Tocqueville had written : " The Convention created the policy of the impossible, the theory of furious madness, the cult of blind audacity." [1] The disasters of 1870 brought the country back to practical, prudent, and prosaic conditions ; the first result of these disasters was the development of the conception most opposed to that spoken of by Tocqueville ; this was the idea of opportunism, which has now been introduced even into Socialism.

Another consequence was the change that took place in all revolutionary values, and notably the modification in the opinions which were held on the subject of violence.

After 1871 everybody in France thought only of the

[1] Tocqueville. *Mélanges*, p. 189.

search for the most suitable means of setting the country on its feet again. Taine endeavoured to apply the methods of the most scientific psychology to this question, and he looked upon the history of the Revolution as a social experiment. He hoped to be able to make quite clear the danger presented in his opinion by the Jacobin spirit, and thus to induce his contemporaries to change the course of French politics by abandoning ideas which had seemed incorporated in the national tradition, and which were all the more solidly rooted in people's minds because nobody had ever discussed their origin. Taine failed in his enterprise, as Le Play and Renan failed, as all those will fail who try to found an intellectual and moral reform on investigations, on scientific syntheses, and on demonstrations.

It cannot be said, however, that Taine's immense labour was accomplished to no purpose ; the history of the Revolution was thoroughly overhauled ; the military epic no longer dominates people's judgments about political events. The life of men, the inner workings of factions, the material needs which determine the tendencies of the great masses have now come into the foreground. In the speech which he made on September 24, 1905, at the inauguration of the monument to Taine at Vouziers, the deputy Hubert, while giving all homage to the great and many-sided talent of his illustrious compatriot, expressed a regret that the epic side of the Revolution had been disregarded by him in a systematic manner. These are superfluous regrets ; the epic vision can henceforth no longer govern that political history ; an idea of the grotesque effects to which this constant desire to return to the old methods may lead can be obtained by reading Jaurès's *Histoire socialiste*. In vain does Jaurès revive all the most melodramatic images of the old rhetoric ; the only effect he manages to produce is one of absurdity.

The prestige of the great revolutionary days has been directly hit by the comparison with contemporary civil struggles ; there was nothing during the Revolution which could bear comparison with the battles which ensanguined Paris in 1848 and in 1871 ; July 14 and August 10 seem to us now mere scuffles which would not have made an energetic Government tremble.

There is yet another reason, still hardly recognised by professional writers on revolutionary history, which has contributed a great deal towards taking all the romance out of these events. There can be no national epic about things which the people cannot picture to themselves as reproducible in a near future ; popular poetry implies the future much more than the past ; it is for this reason that the adventures of the Gauls, of Charlemagne, of the Crusades, of Joan of Arc cannot form the subject of a narrative capable of moving any but literary people.[1] Since the people have become convinced that contemporary Governments cannot be overthrown by riots like those of July 14 and August 10, they have ceased to look upon the events of these days as epical. Parliamentary Socialists, who would like to utilise the memory of the Revolution to excite the ardour of the people, and who ask them at the same time to put all their confidence in Parliamentarism, are very inconsistent, for they are themselves helping to ruin the epic, whose prestige they wish to maintain in their speeches.

But then what remains of the Revolution when we have taken away the epic of the wars against the coalition, and of that of the victories of the populace ? What

[1] It is very remarkable that in the seventeenth century Boileau had already pronounced against the supernatural Christian epic ; this was because his contemporaries, however religious they might have been, did not expect that angels would come to help Vauban to capture fortresses ; they did not doubt what was related in the Bible, but they did not see matter in it for epics, because these marvels were not destined to be reproduced.

remains is not very savoury : police operations, proscriptions, and sittings of servile courts of law. The
employment of the force of the State against the vanquished shocks us all the more because so many of the
coryphées of the Revolution were soon to be distinguished
among the servants of Napoleon, and to employ the
same police zeal on behalf of the Emperor as they did
on behalf of the Terror. In a country which had been
convulsed by so many changes of Government, and which
consequently had known so many recantations, political
justice had something particularly odious about it,
because the criminal of to-day might become the judge
of to-morrow : General Malet could say before the
council of war which condemned him in 1812 that had
he succeeded he would have had for his accomplices the
whole of France and his judges themselves.[1]

It is useless to carry these reflections any further ;
the slightest observation will suffice to show that proletarian violence recalls a mass of painful memories of
those past times : instinctively, people start thinking
of the committees of revolutionary inspection, of the
brutalities of suspicious agents, coarsened and frightened
by fear, of the tragedies of the guillotine. You understand, therefore, why Parliamentary Socialists make such
great efforts to persuade the public that they have the
souls of sensitive shepherds, that their hearts are overflowing with good feeling, and that they have only one
passion—*hatred of violence*. They would readily give
themselves out to be the protectors of the middle class

[1] Ernest Hamel, *Histoire de la conspiration du général Malet*, p. 241.
According to some newspapers, Jaurès, in his evidence before the Court
of Assizes of the Seine on June 5, 1907, in the Bousquet-Lévy trial,
said that the police officers would show more consideration for the
accused, Bousquet, when he had become a legislator. [Bousquet was
the secretary of the bakers' syndicate, with whom the police dealt
rather harshly. As he was a good orator Jaurès looked upon him as
a future deputy.—*Trans. Note.*]

against proletarian violence ; and in order to heighten their prestige as humanitarians they never fail to shun all contact with anarchists ; sometimes, even, they shun this contact with an abruptness which is not without a certain mixture of cowardice and hypocrisy.

When Millerand was the unquestioned chief of the Socialist party in Parliament, he advised his party *to be afraid to frighten* ; and, as a matter of fact, Socialist deputies would obtain very few votes if they did not manage to convince the general public that they are very reasonable people, great enemies of the old practices of bloody men, and solely occupied in meditating on the philosophy of future law. In a long speech given on October 8, 1905, at Limoges, Jaurès strove to reassure the middle class much more than had been done hitherto ; he informed them that victorious Socialism would show princely generosity, and that he was studying the different ways in which the former holders of property might be indemnified. A few years ago Millerand promised indemnities to the poor (*Petite République*, March 25, 1898) ; now everybody will be put on the same footing, and Jaurès assures us that Vandervelde has written things on this subject full of profundity. I am quite willing to take his word for it !

The social revolution is conceived by Jaurès as a kind of bankruptcy ; substantial annuities will be given to the middle class of to-day : then from generation to generation these annuities will decrease. These plans must often seem very alluring to financiers accustomed to draw great advantages from bankruptcies ; I have no doubt that the shareholders of *L'Humanité* think these ideas marvellous ; they will be made liquidators of the bankruptcy, and will pocket large fees, which will compensate them for the losses which this newspaper has caused them.

In the eyes of the contemporary middle class everything is admirable which dispels the idea of violence. Our middle class desire to die in peace—after them the deluge.

II

Let us now examine the violence of '93 a little more closely, and endeavour to see whether it can be identified with that of contemporary Syndicalism.

Fifteen years ago Drumont, speaking of Socialism and of its future, wrote these sentences, which then appeared exceedingly paradoxical to many people : " The historian, who is always somewhat of a prophet, might say to the Conservatives, ' Salute the working-men leaders of the Commune, you will never see their like again ! . . . Those who are to come will be malicious, wicked, and vindictive in a different way from the men of 1871. Henceforward, a new feeling takes possession of the French proletariat : hatred.' " [1] These were not the airy words of a man of letters : Drumont learned what he knew of the Commune and the Socialist world from Malon, of whom he gave a very appreciative portrait in his book.

This sinister prediction was founded on the idea that the working man was getting farther and farther away from the national tradition, and nearer to the middle class, which is much more accessible than he is to bad feeling. " It was the middle-class element," said Drumont, " which was most ferocious in the Commune, the vicious and bohemian middle class of the Latin Quarter ; the popular element, amid this dreadful crisis, remained *human*, that is *French*. . . . Among the internationalists who formed part of the Commune four only pronounced themselves in favour of violent measures." [2] As will be seen, Drumont has got no farther than that naïve philo-

[1] Drumont, *La Fin d'un monde*, pp. 137-138.
[2] Drumont, *op. cit.* p. 128.

sophy of the eighteenth century, and of the Utopians prior to 1848, according to which men will follow the injunctions of the moral law all the better for not having been spoiled by civilisation ; in descending from the superior classes to the poorer classes a greater number of good qualities are found ; good is only natural to individuals who have remained close to a state of nature.

This theory about the nature of the classes led Drumont to a rather curious historical speculation : none of our revolutions was so bloody as the first, because it was conducted by the middle class—" in proportion as the people became more intimately mixed up with revolutions, they became less ferocious "—" the proletariat, when, for the first time, it had acquired an effective share of authority, was infinitely less sanguinary than the middle class." [1] We cannot remain content with the easy explanations which satisfied Drumont ; but it is certain that something has changed since '93. We have to ask ourselves whether the ferocity of the old revolutionaries was not due to reasons depending on the past history of the middle class, so that in confusing the abuses of the revolutionary middle-class force of '93 with the violence of our revolutionary Syndicalists a grave error would be committed : the word *revolutionary* would, in this case, have two perfectly distinct meanings.

The Third Estate which filled the assemblies in the revolutionary epoch, what may be called the official Third Estate, was not a body of agriculturists and leaders of industry ; power was never then in the hands of manufacturers, but in the hands of the lawyers (*basochiens*).[2] Taine was very much struck by the fact that out of 577 deputies of the Third Estate in the Constituent Assembly,

[1] Drumont, *op. cit.* p. 136.
[2] *Basoche* was a name given somewhat ironically to all the people employed in the law courts—principally solicitors and ushers.

there were 373 " unknown barristers and lawyers of a minor order, notaries, King's attorneys, court-roll commissioners, judges and recorders of the presidial bench, bailiffs and lieutenants of the bailiwick, simple practitioners shut up since their youth within the narrow circle of a mediocre jurisdiction or the routine of continual scribbling, without any other escape than philosophical wanderings through imaginary spaces under the guidance of Rousseau or of Raynal." [1] We have some difficulty nowadays in understanding the importance which lawyers possessed in ancient France ; but a multitude of jurisdictions existed ; property owners were extremely punctilious in going to law about questions which appear to us nowadays as of very minor importance, but which seemed of enormous importance to them on account of the dovetailing of feudal law with the law of property ; functionaries of a judicial order were found everywhere, and they enjoyed the greatest prestige with the people.

This class brought to the Revolution a great deal of administrative capacity ; it was owing to them that the country was able to pass easily through the crisis which shook it for ten years, and that Napoleon was able to reconstruct regular administrative services so rapidly ; but this class also brought a mass of prejudices which caused those of its representatives who occupied high positions to commit grave errors. It is impossible to understand the character of Robespierre, for example, if we compare him to the politicians of to-day ; we must always see in him the serious lawyer, taken up with his duties, anxious not to tarnish the professional honour of an orator of the bar ; moreover, he had literary leanings and was a disciple of Rousseau. He had scruples about legality which astonish the historians of to-day ; when he was obliged to come to supreme resolutions and to defend himself before the Convention, he showed a sim-

[1] Taine, *La Révolution*, tome i. p. 155.

plicity which bordered on stupidity. The famous law
of the 22nd Prairial, with which he has been so often
reproached and which gave so rapid a pace to the revolutionary courts, is the masterpiece of his type of mind ;
the whole of the Old Régime is found in it, expressed in
clear-cut formulas.

One of the fundamental ideas of the Old Régime had
been the employment of the penal procedure to ruin any
power which was an obstacle to the monarchy. It seems
that in all primitive societies the penal law, at its inception,
was a protection granted to the chief and to a few privileged
persons whom he honoured with special favour ; it is
only much later that the legal power serves to safeguard,
indiscriminately, the persons and goods of all the inhabit-
ants of a country. The Middle Ages being a return to
the customs of very ancient times, it was natural that
they should reproduce exceedingly archaic ideas about
justice, and that the courts of justice should come to
be considered as instruments of royal greatness. An
historical accident happened to favour the extraordinary
development of this theory of criminal administration.
The Inquisition furnished a model for courts which, set
in motion on very slight pretexts, prosecuted people
who embarrassed authority, with great persistence, and
made it impossible for them to harm the latter. The
monarchy borrowed from the Inquisition many of its
procedures, and nearly always followed the same principles.

The king constantly demanded of his courts of justice
that they should work for the enlargement of his terri-
tories ; it seems strange to us nowadays that Louis XIV.
should have had annexations proclaimed by commissions
of magistrates ; but he was following the old tradition ;
many of his predecessors had used Parliament to confiscate
feudal manors for very arbitrary motives. Justice,
which seems to us nowadays created to secure the prosperity of production, and to permit its free and constantly

widening development, seemed created in former days to secure the greatness of the monarchy : *its essential aim was not justice, but the welfare of the State.*

It was very difficult to establish strict discipline in the services set up by royalty for war and administration Enquiries had continually to be made in order to punish unfaithful or disobedient employees ; kings employed, for this purpose, men taken from their courts of law ; thus they came to confuse acts of disciplinary surveillance with the repression of crimes. Lawyers must transform everything according to their habits of mind ; in this way negligence, ill-will, or carelessness became revolt against authority, crime, or treason.

The Revolution piously gathered up this tradition, gave an importance to imaginary crimes which was all the greater because its political courts of law carried on their operations in the midst of a populace maddened by the seriousness of the peril ; it seemed quite natural to explain the defeats of generals by criminal inten- tions, and to guillotine people who had not been able to realise hopes fostered by a public opinion, that had returned to the superstitions of childhood. Our penal code contains not a few paradoxical articles dating from this time ; nowadays it is not easy to understand how a citizen can be seriously accused of plotting or of keeping up a correspondence with foreign powers or their agents in order to induce them to begin hostilities, or to enter into war with France, or to furnish them with the means therefor. Such a crime supposes that the State can be imperilled by the act of one person ; this appears scarcely credible to us.[1]

Actions against enemies of the king were always con- ducted in an exceptional manner ; the procedure was

[1] Yet this was the article which was applied to Dreyfus, without anybody, moreover, having attempted to prove that France had been in danger.

simplified as much as possible ; flimsy proofs which would not have sufficed for ordinary crimes were accepted ; the endeavour was to make a terrible and profoundly intimidating example. All this is to be found in Robespierre's legislation. The law of the 22nd Prairial lays down rather vague definitions of political crime, so as not to let any enemy of the Revolution escape ; and the kind of proofs required are worthy of the purest tradition of the Old Régime and of the Inquisition. " The proof necessary to condemn the *enemies of the people* is any kind of document, material, moral, verbal or written, which can naturally obtain the assent of any just and reasonable mind. Juries in giving their verdict should be guided solely by what love of their country indicates to their conscience ; their aim is *the triumph of the republic and the ruin of its enemies."* We have in this celebrated Terrorist law the strongest expression of the theory of the predominance of the State.[1]

The philosophy of the eighteenth century happened to render these methods still more formidable. It professed, in fact, to formulate a return to natural law ; humanity had been till then corrupted by the fault of a small number of people whose interest it had been to deceive it ; but the true means of returning to the principles of primitive goodness, of truth, and of justice had at last been discovered ; all opposition to so excellent a reform, one so easy to apply and so certain of success, was the most criminal act imaginable ; the innovators were resolved to show themselves inexorable in destroying the evil influence which bad citizens might exercise for the purpose of hindering the regeneration of humanity. Indulgence was a culpable weakness, for it amounted to nothing less than the sacrifice of the happiness of multitudes to the caprices of incorrigible people, who gave

[1] The details themselves of this law can only be explained by comparing them with the rules of the old penal law.

proof of an incomprehensible obstinacy, who refused to recognise evidence, and only lived on lies.

From the Inquisition to the political justice of the monarchy, and from this to the revolutionary courts of justice, there was a constant progress towards greater severity in laws, the extension of the use of force, and the amplification of authority. For a considerable time the Church had felt doubts about the value of the exceptional methods practised by its inquisitors.[1] The monarchy, especially when it had reached its full maturity, was troubled with very few scruples about the matter ; but the Revolution displayed the scandal of its superstitious cult of the State quite openly, in the full light of day.

A reason of an economical order gave to the State at that time a strength which the Church had never possessed. At the beginning of modern times, Governments, by their maritime expeditions and the encouragement they gave to industry, had played a very great part in production ; but in the eighteenth century this part had become exceptionally important in the minds of theorists. People at that time had their heads full of great projects ; they conceived kingdoms as vast companies undertaking to colonise and cultivate new lands, and they made efforts to ensure the good working of these companies. Thus the State was the god of the reformers. " They desire," wrote Tocqueville, " to borrow the authority of the central power and to use it to break up and to remake everything according to a new plan which they have themselves conceived ; the central power alone appears to them capable of accomplishing such a task. The power of the State must be limitless, as its rights,[2] they say ;

[1] Modern authors, by taking literally certain instructions of the papacy, have been able to maintain that the Inquisition had been relatively indulgent, having regard to the customs of the time.

[2] Tocqueville is probably alluding here to the maxims of Blackstone on the unlimited power of the English Parliament. The economists

all that is necessary is to persuade the State to make a
suitable use of this power." [1]   The physiocrats seemed
ready to sacrifice individuals to the common weal ; they
had no great love of liberty, and thought the idea of an
equipoise of powers absurd ; they hoped to convert the
State ; their system is defined by Tocqueville as " a
democratic despotism " ; the Government would have
been in theory the representative of everybody, controlled
by an enlightened public opinion ; practically it was an
absolute master. [2]   One of the things which most astonished
Tocqueville in the course of his studies of the Old Régime
is the admiration felt by the physiocrats for China, which
appeared to them as the type of good government, because
in that country there were only valets and clerks carefully
catalogued and chosen by competition. [3]

Since the Revolution there has been such an upheaval
of ideas that we have considerable difficulty in understanding correctly the conceptions of our fathers. [4]   The
capitalist economic system has thrown full light on the
extraordinary power of the individual unaided by the
State ; the confidence which the men of the eighteenth
century had in the industrial capacities of the State seems
puerile to everybody who has studied production elsewhere than in the insipid books of the sociologists, which
still preserve very carefully the cult for the blunders of
the past ; the law of nature has become an inexhaustible
subject of banter for people who have the slightest

---

of the eighteenth century thought that the State had the right to do
everything, since it was the expression of " reason," and no single force
could oppose the action of this " reason."

[1] Tocqueville, *L'Ancien Régime et la Révolution*, p. 100.
[2] Tocqueville, *op. cit.* pp. 235-240.
[3] Tocqueville, *op. cit.* p. 241.
[4] In the history of judicial ideas in France, full consideration must
be given to the dividing up of landed property, which, by multiplying
the independent heads of productive units, contributed more to the
spread of judicial ideas among the masses than was ever done among
the literate classes by the finest treatises on philosophy.

knowledge of history ; the employment of the courts of law as a means of coercing a political adversary arouses universal indignation, and people with ordinary common sense hold that it ruins all judicial conceptions.

Sumner Maine points out that the relationships of governments and citizens have been completely over-hauled since the end of the eighteenth century ; formerly the State was always supposed to be good and wise, consequently any attempt to hinder its working was looked upon as a grave offence ; the Liberal system supposes, on the contrary, that the citizen, left free, chooses the better part, and that he exercises the first of his rights in criticising the Government, which has passed from the position of master to that of servant.[1] Maine does not say what is the cause of this transformation ; the cause seems to me to be above all of an economic order. In the new state of things political crime is an act of simple revolt which cannot carry with it disgrace of any kind, which is combated for reasons of prudence, but which no longer merits the name of crime, for its author in no way resembles a criminal.

We are not perhaps better, more human, more sensitive to the misfortunes of others than were the men of '93 ; and I should even be rather disposed to assert that the country is probably less moral than it was at that time ; but we are no longer dominated to the same extent that our fathers were by this superstition of the God-State, to which they sacrificed so many victims. The ferocity of the members of the National Convention is easily explained by the influence of the conceptions which the Third Estate derived from the detestable practices of the Old Régime.

[1] Sumner Maine, *Essais sur le gouvernement populaire*, French trans., p. 20.

III

It would be strange if the old ideas were quite dead ;
the Dreyfus case showed us that the immense majority
of the officers and priests still conceived justice in the
manner of the Old Régime and looked upon condemnations
for "State reasons" as quite natural.[1]   That should not
surprise us, for these two types of people, never having
had any direct relationship with production, can understand nothing about law.   The revolt of the enlightened
public against the practices of the Minister of War was so
great that for a moment it might have been believed
that " reasons of State " would no longer be admitted
as a pretext for condemnation (outside the two types
mentioned above), except by the readers of the *Petit
Journal*, whose mentality would thus be characterised
and shown to be much the same as that which existed a
century ago.   We know now, alas ! by cruel experience,
that the State had its high priests and its fervent worshippers even among the Dreyfusards.

The Dreyfus case was scarcely over when the Government of " Republican defence " began another political
prosecution, in the name of state policy, and accumulated
almost as many lies as the Etat-Major (army council)
had accumulated in the Dreyfus trial.   No serious person
nowadays can doubt that the great plot for which Déroulède,
Buffet, and Lur-Saluces were condemned was an invention
of the police ;   the siege of what has been called the Fort
Chabrol was arranged in order to make Parisians believe
that they had been on the eve of a civil war.   The victims
of this judicial crime were granted an amnesty, but the

---

[1] The extraordinary and illegal severity which was brought to bear
in the application of the penalty is explained by the fact that the aim
of the trial was to terrify certain spies who, by their situation, were
out of reach ;   whether Dreyfus was guilty or innocent troubled his
accusers little ;   the essential thing was to protect the State from
treachery and to reassure the French people, who were maddened by
the fear of war.

amnesty should not have sufficed : if the Dreyfusards
had been sincere they should have demanded a recognition by the Senate of the scandalous error which the lies
of the police had caused it to commit ; on the contrary,
they seem to have seen nothing that violated the principles
of eternal justice, in their continued support of a condemnation founded on the most evident fraud.

Jaurès and many other eminent Dreyfusards commended
General André and Combes for having organised a regular
system of secret accusations. Kautsky warmly reproached him for his conduct ; the German writer
demanded that Socialists should not continue to represent " the wretched practices of the middle-class Republic "
as great democratic actions, and that they should remain
" faithful to the principle which declares that the informer is the worst kind of rascal " (*Débats*, November 13,
1904). The saddest thing about this affair was that
Jaurès asserted that Colonel Hartmann, who protested
against the system of *fiches* (secret reports), had himself
employed similar methods ; [1] the latter wrote to him :
" I pity you for this—that you have come to defend to-day,
and by such means, the guilty acts which, with us, you
condemned a few years ago ; I pity you, that you should
believe yourself obliged to make the Republican form of
Government responsible for the vile proceedings of the
police spies who dishonour it " (*Débats*, November 5, 1904).

Experience has always shown us hitherto that revolutionaries plead " reasons of State " as soon as they get
into power, that they then employ police methods and

[1] In *L'Humanité* of November 17, 1904, there is a letter from Paul
Guieysse and from Vazeilles, declaring that nothing of this kind can
be imputed to Colonel Hartmann. Jaurès follows this letter with a
strange commentary ; he considers that the informers acted in perfect
good faith, and he regrets that the colonel should have furnished
" imprudently, further matter for the systematic campaign of the
reactionary newspapers." Jaurès has no suspicion that this commentary made his own case much worse, and that it was not unworthy
of a disciple of Escobar.

look upon justice as a weapon which they may use unfairly against their enemies. Parliamentary Socialists do not escape the universal rule ; they preserve the old cult of the State ; they are therefore prepared to commit all the misdeeds of the Old Régime and of the Revolution.

A fine collection of platitudinous political maxims might be composed by going through Jaurĕs's *Histoire socialiste.* I have never had the patience to read the 1824 pages devoted to the story of the Revolution between August 10, 1792, and the fall of Robespierre ; I have simply turned over the leaves of this tedious book, and seen that it contained a mixture of a philosophy worthy of M. Pantalon and a policy fitting a purveyor to the guillotine. For a long time I had reckoned that Jaurès would be capable of every ferocity against the vanquished ; I saw that I had not been mistaken ; but I should not have thought that he was capable of so much platitude : in his eyes the vanquished are always in the wrong, and victory fascinates our great defender of eternal justice so much that he is ready to consent to every proscription demanded of him : " Revolutions," he says, " claim from a man the most frightful sacrifices, not only of his rest, not only of his life, but of human tenderness and pity." [1] Why write so much, then, about the inhumanity of the executioners of Dreyfus ? They also sacrificed " human tenderness " to what appeared to them to be the safety of the country.

A few years ago the Republicans were extremely indignant with the Vicomte de Vogüé, who, when receiving Hanotaux into the French Academy, called the *coup d'état* of 1851 " a somewhat harsh police exploit." [2]

---

[1] J. Jaurès, *La Convention,* p. 1732.

[2] This was on March 24, 1898, at a particularly critical moment of the Dreyfus case, when the Nationalists were asking that agitators and enemies of the army should be swept away. J. Reinach says that De Vogüé openly invited the army to begin again the work of 1850 (*Histoire de l'affaire Dreyfus,* tome iii. p. 545).

I

Jaurès, taught by revolutionary history, now reasons in exactly the same manner as the jovial vicomte ; [1] he praises, for example, " the policy of vigour and of wisdom " which consisted in forcing the Convention to expel the Girondins " with a certain appearance of legality." [2]

The massacres of September 1792 embarrass him somewhat ; legality is not very apparent here, but he has big words and bad reasons for every ugly cause ; Danton's conduct was not very worthy of admiration at the time of these melancholy happenings, but Jaurès must excuse him, since Danton was triumphant during this period. " He did not think it was his duty as a revolutionary and patriotic minister to enter upon a struggle with these *misguided popular forces*. How can we refine the metal of the bells when they are sounding the alarm of imperilled liberty ? " [3]   It seems to me that Cavaignac might have explained his conduct in the Dreyfus case in the same way. To the people who accused him of being hand in hand with the Anti-Semites, he might have answered that his duty as a patriotic minister did not compel him to enter upon a struggle with the misguided populace, and that on the days when the safety of national defence is at stake we cannot refine the metal of the bells which are sounding the alarm of the country in danger.

When he comes to the period when Camille Desmoulins sought to stir up a movement of opinion strong enough to stop the Terror, Jaurès speaks energetically against this attempt. He acknowledges, however, a few pages farther on, that the guillotine system could not last for ever ; but Desmoulins, having succumbed, is wrong in the eyes of our *humble* worshipper of success.   Jaurès

---

[1] De Vogüé has the habit in his polemics of thanking his adversaries for having given him much amusement ; that is why I take the liberty of calling him jovial, although his writings are rather soporific.

[2] J. Jaurès, *op. cit.* p. 1434.

[3] J. Jaurès, *op. cit.* p. 77.

accuses the author of the *Vieux Cordelier* of forgetting
the conspiracies, the treasons, the corruptions, and all
the dreams with which the Terrorists fed their infatuated
imaginations ; he is even ironical enough to speak of
" free France ! " and he brings forth this sentence, worthy
of a Jacobin pupil of Joseph Prudhomme : " The knife
of Desmoulins was chiselled with an incomparable art ;
but he planted it in the heart of the Revolution." [1]
When Robespierre no longer commands the majority in
the Convention he is, as a matter of course, put to death
by the other Terrorists, in virtue of the legitimate working
of the Parliamentary institutions of that time ; but to
appeal to *mere public opinion* against the Government
leaders, that was the " crime." of Desmoulins. His
crime was also that committed by Jaurès at the time he
defended Dreyfus against the great leaders of the army
and the Government ; how many times has not Jaurès
been accused of compromising the national defence ?
But that time is already a long way off ; and our orator
at that period, not having yet tasted the advantages of
power, did not possess a theory of the State as ferocious
as that which he possesses to-day.

I think that I have said sufficient to enable me to conclude that if by chance our Parliamentary Socialists get
possession of the reins of Government, they will prove to
be worthy successors of the Inquisition, of the Old Régime,
and of Robespierre ; political courts will be at work on
a large scale, and we may even suppose that the *unfortunate* law of 1848, which abolished the death penalty in
political matters, will be repealed. Thanks to this *reform,*
we might again see the State triumphing by the hand of
the executioner.

Proletarian acts of violence have no resemblance to these
proscriptions ; they are purely and simply acts of war ;

[1] J. Jaurès, *op. cit.* p. 1731.

they have the value of military demonstrations, and serve to mark the separation of classes. Everything in war is carried on without hatred and without the spirit of revenge : in war the vanquished are not killed ; non-combatants are not made to bear the consequences of the disappointments which the armies may have experienced on the fields of battle ; [1] force is then displayed according to its own nature, without ever professing to borrow anything from the judicial proceedings which society sets up against criminals.

The more Syndicalism develops, by abandoning the old superstitions which come to it from the Old Régime and from the Church—through the men of letters, professors of philosophy, and historians of the Revolution,— the more will social conflicts assume the character of a simple struggle, similar to those of armies on campaign. We cannot censure too severely those who teach the people that they ought to carry out the highly idealistic decrees of a progressive justice. Their efforts will only result in the maintenance of those ideas about the State which provoked the bloody acts of '93, whilst the idea of a class war, on the contrary, tends to refine the conception of violence.

IV

Syndicalism in France is engaged on an antimilitarist propaganda, which shows clearly the immense distance which separates it from Parliamentary Socialism in its conception of the nature of the State. Many newspapers believe that all this is merely an exaggerated humanitarian movement, provoked by the articles of Hervé ; this is a

[1] I bring to notice here a fact which is perhaps not very well known : the Spanish war in the time of Napoleon was the occasion of innumerable atrocities, but Colonel Lafaille says that in Catalonia the murders and cruelties were never committed by Spanish soldiers who had been enlisted for some time and had become familiar with the usages of war (*Mémoires sur les campagnes de Catalogne de 1808 à 1814*, pp. 164-165).

great error. We should be misconceiving the nature of
the movement if we supposed that it was merely a protest
against harshness of discipline, against the length of
military service, or against the presence, in the higher
ranks, of officers hostile to the existing institutions of
the country ; [1] these are the reasons which led many
middle-class people to applaud declamations against the
army at the time of the Dreyfus case, but they are not the
Syndicalists' reasons.

The army is the clearest and the most tangible of all
possible manifestations of the State, and the one which is
most firmly connected with its origins and traditions.
Syndicalists do not propose to reform the State, as the
men of the eighteenth century did ; they want to destroy
it,[2] because they wish to realise this idea of Marx's that
the Socialist revolution ought not to culminate in the
replacement of one governing minority by another
minority.[3] The Syndicalists outline their doctrine still
more clearly when they give it a more ideological aspect,
and declare themselves antipatriotic — following the
example of the *Communist Manifesto*.

It is impossible that there should be the slightest
understanding between Syndicalists and official Socialists
on this question ; the latter, of course, speak of breaking
up everything, but they attack men in power rather than
power itself ; they hope to possess the State forces, and

[1] According to Joseph Reinach, an error was committed after the
war in choosing as generals former pupils of the military schools
(Saint-Cyr and the Polytechnique). He said that the Jesuit colleges
had sent many clericals to the School, and it would have been better
to choose instead officers who had risen from the ranks ; the generals
would have then been less clerical. *Loc. cit.* pp. 555-556 (I believe that
his system would not have had the result he imagined it would).

[2] " The society which will organise production on the basis of a free
and equal association of producers will transport the whole machinery
of State to where its place will be henceforward—in the museum of
antiquities, by the side of the spinning wheel and the bronze axe "
(Engels, *Les Origines de la Société*, French trans. p. 281).

[3] *Manifeste communiste*, translated, Andler, tome i. p. 39.

they are aware that on the day when they control the Government they will have need of an army ; they will carry on foreign politics, and consequently they in their turn will have to praise the feeling of devotion to the fatherland.

Parliamentary Socialists perceive that antipatriotism is deeply rooted in the minds of Socialist workmen, and they make great efforts to reconcile the irreconcilable ; they are anxious not to oppose too strongly ideas to which the proletariat has become attached, but at the same time they cannot abandon their cherished State, which promises them so many delights. They have stooped to the most comical oratorical acrobatics in order to get over the difficulty.   For instance, after the sentence of the Court of Assizes of the Seine, condemning Hervé and the antimilitarists, the National Council of the Socialist party passed a resolution branding this " verdict, due to hatred and fear," declaring that a class justice could not " respect liberty of opinion," protesting against the employment of troops in strikes, and affirming " resolutely the necessity for action, and for an international understanding among the workers, for the suppression of war " (*Socialiste*, January 20, 1906).   All this is very clever, but the fundamental question is avoided.

Thus it cannot any longer be contested that there is an absolute opposition between revolutionary Syndicalism and the State ; this opposition takes in France the particularly harsh form of antipatriotism, because the politicians have devoted all their knowledge and ability to the task of spreading confusion in people's minds about the essence of Socialism.   On the plane of patriotism there can be no compromises and half-way positions ; it is therefore on this plane that the Syndicalists have been forced to take their stand when middle-class people of every description employed all their powers of seduction to corrupt Socialism and to alienate the workers from the revolutionary idea. They have been led to deny the idea of patriotism by one of those necessities which are met with at all times in the course of history,[1] and which philosophers have sometimes great difficulty in explaining —because the choice is imposed by external conditions, and not freely made for reasons drawn from the nature of things. This character of historical necessity gives to the existing antipatriotic movement a strength which it would be useless to attempt to dissimulate by means of sophistries.[2]

We have the right to conclude from the preceding analysis that Syndicalist violence, perpetrated in the course of strikes by proletarians who desire the overthrow of the State, must not be confused with those acts of savagery which the superstition of the State suggested to the revolutionaries of '93, when they had power in their hands and were able to oppress the conquered—following the principles which they had received from the Church and from the Monarchy. We have the right to hope that a Socialist revolution carried out by pure Syndicalists would not be defiled by the abominations which sullied the middle-class revolutions.

[1] After the trial of Hervé, Léon Daudet wrote : " Those who followed this case were thrilled by the testimonies, by no means theatrical, of the trade union secretaries " (*Libre Parole*, December 31, 1905).

[2] Yet Jaurès had the audacity to declare in the Chamber on May 11, 1907, that there was only " on the surface of the working-class movement a few paradoxical and outrageous formulas, which originated, not from the negation of the fatherland, but from condemnation of the abuse to which word and idea were so often put." Language like this could only have been used before an assembly which was entirely ignorant of the working-class movement.

CHAPTER IV

THE PROLETARIAN STRIKE

I. *The confusion in Parliamentary Socialism and the clearness of the general strike—Myths in history—The value of the general strike proved by experience.*

II. *Researches made to perfect Marxism—Means of throwing light upon it, starting from the point of view of the general strike : class war ; preparation for the revolution and absence of Utopias ; irrevocable character of the revolution.*

III. *Scientific prejudices against the general strike ; doubts about science—The clear and the obscure parts in thought—Economic incompetence of Parliaments.*

I

EVERY time that we attempt to obtain an exact conception of the ideas behind proletarian violence we are forced to go back to the notion of the general strike ; and this same conception may render many other services, and throw an unexpected light on all the obscure parts of Socialism. In the last pages of the first chapter I compared the general strike to the Napoleonic battle which definitely crushes an adversary ; this comparison will help us to understand the part played by the general strike in the world of ideas.

Military writers of to-day, when discussing the new methods of war necessitated by the employment of troops infinitely more numerous than those of Napoleon, equipped with arms much more deadly than those of his time, do not for all that imagine that wars will be decided in any other way than that of the Napoleonic battle. The new tactics proposed must fit into the drama Napoleon had conceived ; the detailed development of the combat will doubtless be quite different from what it used to be, but the end must always be the catastrophic defeat of the enemy. The methods of military instruction are intended to prepare the soldier for this great and terrible action, in which everybody must be ready to take part at the first signal. From the highest to the lowest, the members of a really solid army have always in mind this catastrophic issue of international conflicts.

The revolutionary Syndicates argue about Socialist action exactly in the same manner as military writers argue about war ; they restrict the whole of Socialism to the general strike ; they look upon every combination as one that should culminate in this catastrophe ; they see in each strike a reduced facsimile, an essay, a preparation for the great final upheaval.

The *new school*, which calls itself Marxist, Syndicalist, and revolutionary, declared in favour of the idea of the general strike as soon as it became clearly conscious of the true sense of its own doctrine, of the consequences of its activity, and of its own originality. It was thus led to leave the old official, Utopian, and political tabernacles, which hold the general strike in horror, and to launch itself into the true current of the proletarian revolutionary movement ; for a long time past the proletariat had made adherence to the principle of the general strike the *test* by means of which the Socialism of the workers was distinguished from that of the amateur revolutionaries.

Parliamentary Socialists can only obtain great influence if they can manage, by the use of a very confused language, to impose themselves on very diverse groups ; for example, they must have working-men constituents simple enough to allow themselves to be duped by high-sounding phrases

about future collectivism ; they are compelled to represent themselves as profound philosophers to stupid middle-
class people who wish to appear to be well informed
about social questions ; it is very necessary also for
them to be able to exploit rich people who think that they
are earning the gratitude of humanity by taking shares
in the enterprises of Socialist politicians.   This influence
is founded on balderdash, and our bigwigs endeavour—
sometimes only too successfully—to spread confusion
among the ideas of their readers ; they detest the general
strike because all propaganda carried on from that point
of view is too socialistic to please philanthropists.

In the mouths of these self-styled representatives of
the proletariat all socialistic formulas lose their real sense.
The class war still remains the great principle, but it must
be subordinated to national solidarity.[1]   Internationalism
is an article of faith about which the most moderate declare
themselves ready to take the most solemn oaths ; but
patriotism also imposes sacred duties.[2]   The emancipation of the workers must be the work of the workers themselves—their newspapers repeat this every day,—but real
emancipation consists in voting for a professional politician, in securing for him the means of obtaining a
comfortable situation in the world, in subjecting oneself
to a leader.   In the end the State must disappear—and

[1] The *Petit Parisien*, which makes a specialty of Socialist and
working-class questions, warned strikers on March 31, 1907, that they
" must never imagine that they are absolved from the observance of
the ordinary social duties and responsibilities."

[2] At the time when the antimilitarists were beginning to occupy
public attention, the *Petit Parisien* was distinguished by its patriotism :
on October 8, 1905, it published an article on " The Sacred Duty "
and on " The Worship of this Tricolor Flag which has carried all over
the World our Glories and our Liberties " ; on January 1, 1906, it congratulated the Jury de la Seine : " The flag has been avenged for the
insults flung by its detractors on this noble emblem.   When it is
carried through the streets it is saluted.   The juries have done more
than bow to it ; they have gathered round it with respect."   This is
certainly very cautious Socialism.

they are very careful not to dispute what Engels has written on this subject—but this disappearance will take place only in a future so far distant that you must prepare yourself for it by using the State meanwhile as a means of providing the politicians with titbits ; and the best means of bringing about the disappearance of the State consists in strengthening meanwhile the Governmental machine. This method of reasoning resembles that of Gribouille, who threw himself into the water in order to escape getting wet in the rain.

Whole pages could be filled with the bare outlines of the contradictory, comical, and quack arguments which form the substance of the harangues of our great men ; nothing embarrasses them, and they know how to combine, in pompous, impetuous, and nebulous speeches, the most absolute irreconcilability with the most supple opportunism. A learned exponent of Socialism has said that the art of reconciling opposites by means of nonsense is the most obvious result which he had got from the study of the works of Marx.[1] I confess my extreme incompetence in these difficult matters ; moreover, I make no claim whatever to be counted among the people upon whom politicians confer the title of learned ; yet I cannot easily bring myself to admit that this is the sum and substance of the Marxian philosophy.

The controversy between Jaurès and Clemenceau demonstrated quite clearly that our Parliamentary Socialists can succeed in deceiving the public only by their equivocation ;

[1] Two motions had been discussed at length by the National Council, one proposing that the departmental federations should be invited to enter the electoral struggle wherever it was possible, the other that candidates should be put forward everywhere. One member got up and said, " I should be glad of your earnest attention, for the argument which I am about to state may at first sight appear strange and paradoxical. (These two motions) are not irreconcilable, if we try to solve this contradiction according to the *natural Marxian method of solving any contradiction*" (*Socialiste*, October 7, 1905). It seems that nobody understood. And, in fact, it was unintelligible.

and that, as the result of continually deceiving their readers, they have finally lost all sense of honest discussion. In the *Aurore* of September 4, 1905, Clemenceau accuses Jaurès of muddling the minds of his partisans " with metaphysical subtleties into which they are incapable of following him " ; there is nothing to object to in this accusation, save the use of the word *metaphysical* ; Jaurès is no more a metaphysician than he is a lawyer or an astronomer. In the number of October 26 Clemenceau proves that his opponent possesses " the art of falsifying his texts," and he ends by saying, " It seemed to me instructive to expose certain polemical practices which we wrongly supposed to be monopoly of the Jesuits."

Against this noisy, garrulous, and lying Socialism, which is exploited by ambitious people of every description, which amuses a few buffoons, and which is admired by decadents—revolutionary Syndicalism takes its stand, and endeavours, on the contrary, to leave nothing in a state of indecision ; its ideas are honestly expressed, without trickery and without mental reservations ; no attempt is made to dilute doctrines by a stream of confused commentaries. Syndicalism endeavours to employ methods of expression which throw a full light on things, which put them exactly in the place assigned to them by their nature, and which bring out the whole value of the forces in play. Oppositions, instead of being glozed over, must be thrown into sharp relief if we desire to obtain a clear idea of the Syndicalist movement ; the groups which are struggling one against the other must be shown as separate and as compact as possible ; in short, the movements of the revolted masses must be represented in such a way that the soul of the revolutionaries may receive a deep and lasting impression.

These results could not be produced in any very certain manner by the use of ordinary language ; use must be made of a body of images which, *by intuition alone*, and before any considered analyses are made, is capable of evoking as an undivided whole the mass of sentiments which corresponds to the different manifestations of the war undertaken by Socialism against modern society. The Syndicalists solve this problem perfectly, by concentrating the whole of Socialism in the drama of the general strike ; there is thus no longer any place for the reconciliation of contraries in the equivocations of the professors ; everything is clearly mapped out, so that only one interpretation of Socialism is possible. This method has all the advantages which " integral " knowledge has over analysis, according to the doctrine of Bergson ; and perhaps it would not be possible to cite another example which would so perfectly demonstrate the value of the famous professor's doctrines.[1]

The possibility of the actual realisation of the general strike has been much discussed ; it has been stated that the Socialist war could not be decided in one single battle. To the people who think themselves cautious, practical, and scientific the difficulty of setting great masses of the proletariat in motion at the same moment seems prodigious ; they have analysed the difficulties of detail which such an enormous struggle would present. It is the opinion of the Socialist-sociologists, as also of the politicians, that the general strike is a popular dream, characteristic of the beginnings of a working-class movement ; we have had quoted against us the authority of Sidney Webb, who has decreed that the general strike is an illusion of youth,[2] of which the English workers—whom the monopolists of sociology have so often presented to us as the

[1] The nature of these articles will not allow of any long discussion of this subject ; but I believe that it would be possible to develop still further the application of Bergson's ideas to the theory of the general strike. Movement, in Bergson's philosophy, is looked upon as an undivided whole ; which leads us precisely to the catastrophic conception of Socialism.

[2] Bourdeau, *Évolution du Socialisme*, p. 232.

depositaries of the true conception of the working-class movement—soon rid themselves.

That the general strike is not popular in contemporary England, is a poor argument to bring against the historical significance of the idea, for the English are distinguished by an extraordinary lack of understanding of the class war ; their ideas have remained very much dominated by medieval influences : the guild, privileged, or at least protected by laws, still seems to them the ideal of working-class organisation; it is for England that the term *working-class aristocracy*, as a name for the trades unionists, was invented, and, as a matter of fact, trades unionism does pursue the acquisition of legal privileges.[1] We might therefore say that the aversion felt by England for the general strike should be looked upon as strong presumptive evidence in favour of the latter by all those who look upon the class war as the essence of Socialism.

Moreover, Sidney Webb enjoys a reputation for competence which is very much exaggerated ; all that can be put to his credit is that he has waded through uninteresting blue-books, and has had the patience to compose an extremely indigestible compilation on the history of trades unionism ; he has a mind of the narrowest description, which could only impress people unaccustomed to reflection.[2] Those who introduced his fame into France knew nothing at all about Socialism ; and if he is really in the first rank of contemporary authors of economic history, as his translator affirms,[3] it is because the

[1] This is seen, for example, in the efforts made by the trade unions to obtain laws absolving them from the civil responsibilities of their acts.

[2] Tarde could never understand the reputation enjoyed by Sidney Webb, who seemed to him to be a worthless scribbler.

[3] Métin, *Le Socialisme en Angleterre*, p. 210. This writer has received from the Government a *certificate of socialism* ; on July 26, 1904, the French Commissioner-General at the St. Louis exhibition said : " M. Métin is animated by the best democratic spirit ; he is an excellent republican ; *he is even a socialist* whom working-class organisa-

intellectual level of these historians is rather low ; moreover, many examples show us that it is possible to be a most illustrious professional historian and yet possess a mind something less than mediocre.

Neither do I attach any importance to the objections made to the general strike based on considerations of a practical order. The attempt to construct hypotheses about the nature of the struggles of the future and the means of suppressing capitalism, on the model furnished by history, is a return to the old methods of the Utopists. There is no process by which the future can be predicted scientifically, nor even one which enables us to discuss whether one hypothesis about it is better than another ; it has been proved by too many memorable examples that the greatest men have committed prodigious errors in thus desiring to make predictions about even the least distant future.[1]

And yet without leaving the present, without reasoning about this future, which seems for ever condemned to escape our reason, we should be unable to act at all. Experience shows that the *framing of a future, in some indeterminate time*, may, when it is done in a certain way, be very effective, and have very few inconveniences ; this happens when the anticipations of the future take the form of those myths, which enclose with them all the strongest inclinations of a people, of a party or of a class, inclinations which recur to the mind with the insistence of instincts in all the circumstances of life ; and which give an aspect of complete reality to the hopes of immediate action by which, more easily than by any other method, men can reform their desires, passions, and mental activity.

---

tion should welcome as a friend " (*Association ouvrière*, July 30, 1904). An amusing study could be made of those persons who possess certificates of this kind, given to them, either by the Government, the *Musée social*, or the *well-informed press*.

[1] The errors committed by Marx are numerous and sometimes enormous (cf. G. Sorel, *Saggi di critica del marxismo*, pp. 51-57).

We know, moreover, that these social myths in no way prevent a man profiting by the observations which he makes in the course of his life, and form no obstacle to the pursuit of his normal occupations.[1]

The truth of this may be shown by numerous examples. The first Christians expected the return of Christ and the total ruin of the pagan world, with the inauguration of the kingdom of the saints, at the end of the first generation. The catastrophe did not come to pass, but Christian thought profited so greatly from the apocalyptic myth that certain contemporary scholars maintain that the whole preaching of Christ referred solely to this one point.[2] The hopes which Luther and Calvin had formed of the religious exaltation of Europe were by no means realised ; these fathers of the Reformation very soon seemed men of a past era ; for present-day Protestants they belong rather to the Middle Ages than to modern times, and the problems which troubled them most occupy very little place in contemporary Protestantism. Must we for that reason deny the immense result which came from their dreams of Christian renovation ? It must be admitted that the real developments of the Revolution did not in any way resemble the enchanting pictures which created the enthusiasm of its first adepts ; but without those pictures would the Revolution have been victorious ? Many Utopias were mixed up with the Revolutionary myth,[3] because it had been formed by a society passionately fond of imaginative literature, full of confidence in the " science," [4] and very little acquainted with the

---

[1] It has often been remarked that English or American sectarians whose religious exaltation was fed by the apocalyptic myths were often none the less very practical men.

[2] At the present time, this doctrine occupies an important place in German exegesis ; it was introduced into France by the Abbé Loisy.

[3] Cf. the Letter to Daniel Halévy, IV.

[4] In French *petite science*. This expression is used to indicate the popular science with which the majority is much more familiar than it

economic history of the past. These Utopias came to
nothing ; but it may be asked whether the Revolution
was not a much more profound transformation than those
dreamed of by the people who in the eighteenth century
had invented social Utopias. In our own times Mazzini
pursued what the wiseacres of his time called a mad
chimera ; but it can no longer be denied that, without
Mazzini, Italy would never have become a great power,
and that he did more for Italian unity than Cavour and
all the politicians of his school.

A knowledge of what the myths contain in the way
of details which will actually form part of the history of
the future is then of small importance ; they are not
astrological almanacs ; it is even possible that nothing
which they contain will ever come to pass,—as was the
case with the catastrophe expected by the first Christians.[1]
In our own daily life, are we not familiar with the fact
that what actually happens is very different from our
preconceived notion of it ? And that does not prevent
us from continuing to make resolutions. Psychologists
say that there is heterogeneity between the ends in view
and the ends actually realised : the slightest experience of
life reveals this law to us, which Spencer transferred into
nature, to extract therefrom his theory of the multiplica-
tion of effects.[2]

The myth must be judged as a means of acting on the
present ; any attempt to discuss how far it can be taken

---

is with the difficult researches of the real scientists. These latter are
generally as modest as the writers on popular science are vain and
boastful.

[1] I have tried to show elsewhere how this social myth, which has
disappeared, was succeeded by a piety which has remained extremely
important in Catholic life ; this evolution from the social to the individual, seems to me quite natural in a religion (*Le Système historique
de Renan*, pp. 374-382).

[2] I believe, moreover, that the whole of Spencer's evolutionism is
to be explained as an application of the most commonplace psychology
to physics.

literally as future history is devoid of sense. *It is the myth in its entirety which is alone important* : its parts are only of interest in so far as they bring out the main idea. No useful purpose is served, therefore, in arguing about the incidents which may occur in the course of a social war, and about the decisive conflicts which may give victory to the proletariat ; even supposing the revolutionaries to have been wholly and entirely deluded in setting up this imaginary picture of the general strike, this picture may yet have been, in the course of the preparation for the Revolution, a great element of strength, if it has embraced all the aspirations of Socialism, and if it has given to the whole body of Revolutionary thought a precision and a rigidity which no other method of thought could have given.

To estimate, then, the significance of the idea of the general strike, all the methods of discussion which are current among politicians, sociologists, or people with pretensions to political science, must be abandoned. Everything which its opponents endeavour to establish may be conceded to them, without reducing in any way the value of the theory which they think they have refuted. The question whether the general strike is a partial reality, or only a product of popular imagination, is of little importance. All that it is necessary to know is, whether the general strike contains everything that the Socialist doctrine expects of the revolutionary proletariat.

To solve this question we are no longer compelled to argue learnedly about the future ; we are not obliged to indulge in lofty reflections about philosophy, history, or economics ; we are not on the plane of theories, and we can remain on the level of observable facts. We have to question men who take a very active part in the real revolutionary movement amidst the proletariat, men who do not aspire to climb into the middle class and whose mind is not dominated by corporative prejudices. These men may be deceived about an infinite number of political, economical, or moral questions ; but their testimony is decisive, sovereign, and irrefutable when it is a question of knowing what are the ideas which most powerfully move them and their comrades, which most appeal to them as being identical with their socialistic conceptions, and thanks to which their reason, their hopes, and their way of looking at particular facts seem to make but one indivisible unity.[1]

Thanks to these men, we know that the general strike is indeed what I have said : the *myth* in which Socialism is wholly comprised, *i.e.* a body of images capable of evoking instinctively all the sentiments which correspond to the different manifestations of the war undertaken by Socialism against modern society. Strikes have engendered in the proletariat the noblest, deepest, and most moving sentiments that they possess ; the general strike groups them all in a co-ordinated picture, and, by bringing them together, gives to each one of them its maximum of intensity ; appealing to their painful memories of particular conflicts, it colours with an intense life all the details of the composition presented to consciousness. We thus obtain that intuition of Socialism which language cannot give us with perfect clearness—and we obtain it as a whole, perceived instantaneously.[2]

We may urge yet another piece of evidence to prove the power of the idea of the general strike. If that idea were a pure chimera, as is so frequently said, Parliamentary Socialists would not attack it with such heat ; I do not remember that they ever attacked the senseless hopes which the Utopists have always held up before the dazzled eyes of the people.[3] In the course of a polemic about realisable

---

[1] This is another application of Bergson's theories.
[2] This is the " global knowledge " of Bergson's philosophy.
[3] I do not remember that the official Socialists have ever shown up

social reforms, Clemenceau brought out the Machiavelian-
ism in the attitude of Jaurès, when he is confronted with
popular illusions : he shelters his conscience beneath
" some cleverly balanced sentence," but so cleverly
balanced that it " will be received without thinking by
those who have the greatest need to probe into its substance, while they will drink in with delight the delusive
rhetoric of terrestrial joys to come " (*Aurore*, December 28,
1905). But when it is a question of the general strike,
it is quite another thing ; our politicians are no longer
content with complicated reservations ; they speak
violently, and endeavour to induce their listeners to
abandon this conception.

It is easy to understand the reason for this attitude :
politicians have nothing to fear from the Utopias which
present a deceptive mirage of the future to the people,
and turn " men towards immediate realisations of
terrestrial felicity, which any one who looks at these
matters scientifically knows can only be very partially
realised, and even then only after long efforts on the part
of several generations." (That is what Socialist politicians
do, according to Clemenceau.) The more readily the
electors believe in the *magical forces of the State*, the more
will they be disposed to vote for the candidate who
promises marvels ; in the electoral struggle each candidate
tries to outbid the others : in order that the Socialist
candidates may put the Radicals to rout, the electors must
be credulous enough to believe every promise of future
bliss ;[1] our Socialist politicians take very good care,

the *ridiculousness* of the novels of Bellamy, which have had so great
a success. These novels needed criticism all the more, because they
presented to the people an entirely middle-class ideal of life. They
were a natural product of America, a country which is ignorant of the
class war ; but in Europe, would not the theorists of the class war have
understood them ?

[1] In the article which I have already quoted, Clemenceau recalls that
Jaurès made use of these outbidding tactics in a long speech which he
made at Beziers.

therefore, not to combat these comfortable Utopias in any very effective way.

They struggle against the conception of the general strike, because they recognise, in the course of their propagandist rounds, that this conception is so admirably adapted to the working-class mind that there is a possibility of its dominating the latter in the most absolute manner, thus leaving no place for the desires which the Parliamentarians are able to satisfy. They perceive that this idea is so effective as a motive force that once it has entered the minds of the people they can no longer be controlled by leaders, and that thus the power of the deputies would be reduced to nothing. In short, they feel in a vague way that the whole Socialist movement might easily be absorbed by the general strike, which would render useless all those compromises between political groups in view of which the Parliamentary régime has been built up.

The opposition it meets with from official Socialists, therefore, furnishes a confirmation of our first inquiry into the scope of the general strike.

II

We must now proceed further, and inquire whether the picture furnished by the general strike is really complete ; that is to say, whether it comprises all those features of the struggle which are recognised by modern Socialism. But, first of all, we must state the problem more precisely ; this will not be difficult if we start from the explanations given above on the nature of the conception. We have seen that the general strike must be considered as an undivided whole ; consequently, no details about ways and means will be of the slightest help to the understanding of Socialism ; it must even be added that there is always a danger of losing something of this understanding, if an attempt is made to split up this whole into parts. We will now endeavour to show that there is a fundamental identity between the chief tenets of Marxism and the co-ordinated aspects furnished by the picture of the general strike.

This affirmation is certain to appear paradoxical to many who have read the publications of the most accredited Marxians ; and, in fact, for a very long time a well-marked hostility to the general strike existed in Marxian circles. This tradition has done a good deal of harm to the progress of Marx's doctrine ; and it is in fact a very good illustration of the way in which, as a rule, disciples tend to restrict the application of their master's ideas. The *new school* has had considerable difficulty in liberating itself from these influences ; it was formed by people who had received the Marxian imprint in a very marked degree ; and it was a long time before the school recognised that the objections brought against the general strike arose from the incapacity of the official representatives of Marxism rather than from the principles of the doctrine itself.[1]

The *new school* began its emancipation on the day when it perceived clearly that the formulas of Socialism were often very far from the spirit of Marx, and when it recommended a return to that spirit. It was not without a certain amount of stupefaction that it discerned that it had credited the master with many so-called inventions which were in reality taken from his predecessors, or which were commonplaces, even, at the time when the *Communist Manifesto* was drawn up. According to an author—who, in the opinion of the Government and the

[1] In an article, *Introduction à la métaphysique,* published in 1903, Bergson points out that disciples are always inclined to exaggerate the points of difference between masters, and that " the master in so far as he formulates, develops, translates into abstract ideas what he brings is already in a way his own disciple." [Eng. trans. by T. E. Hulme.]

Musée Social is considered to be well informed,—" the accumulation (of capital in the hands of a few individuals) is one of the great discoveries of Marx, one of the discoveries of whch he was most proud.[1] With all due deference to the historical science of this notable university light, this theory was one which was in everybody's mouth long before Marx had ever written a word, and it had become a dogma in the Socialist world at the end of the reign of Louis-Philippe. There are many Marxian theories of the same kind.

A decided step towards reform was made when those Marxians who aspired to think for themselves began to study the syndicalist movement; they discovered that "the genuine trade unionists have more to teach us than they have to learn from us." [2] This was the beginning of wisdom ; it was a step towards the realistic method which had led Marx to his real discoveries ; in this way a return might be made to those methods which alone merit the name philosophical, " for true and fruitful ideas are so many close contacts with currents of reality," and they " owe most of their clearness to the light which the facts, and the applications to which they led, have by reflection shed on them—the clearness of a concept being scarcely anything more at bottom than the certainty, at last obtained, of manipulating the concept profitably." [3] And yet another profound thought of Bergson may usefully be quoted : " For we do not obtain an intuition from reality—that is, an intellectual sympathy with the most intimate part of it—unless we have won its confidence by a long fellowship with its superficial manifestations. And it is not merely a question of assimilating the most conspicuous facts ; so immense a mass of facts must be accumulated and fused together, that in this fusion all

[1] A. Métin, *op. cit.* p. 191.
[2] G. Sorel, *Avenir socialiste des syndicats*, p. 12.
[3] Bergson, *loc. cit.*

the preconceived and premature ideas which observers may unwittingly have put into their observations will be certain to neutralize each other. In this way only can the bare materiality of the known facts be exposed to view." Finally, what Bergson calls an *integral experience* is obtained.[1]

Thanks to the new principle, people very soon came to recognise that the propositions which in their opinion contained a complete statement of Socialism were deplorably inadequate, so that they were often more dangerous than useful. It is the superstitious respect paid by social democracy to the mere text of its doctrines that nullified every attempt in Germany to perfect Marxism.

When the *new school* had acquired a full understanding of the general strike, and had thus obtained a profound intuition of the working-class movement, it saw that all the Socialist theories, interpreted in the light of this powerful construction, took on a meaning which till then they had lacked ; it perceived that the clumsy and rickety apparatus which had been manufactured in Germany to explain Marx's doctrines, must be rejected if the contemporary transformation of the proletarian idea was to be followed exactly ; it discovered that the conception of the general strike enabled them to explore profitably the whole vast domain of Marxism, which until then had remained practically unknown to the big-wigs who professed to be guiding Socialism. Thus the fundamental principles of Marxism are perfectly intelligible only with the aid of the picture of the general strike, and, on the other hand, the full significance of this picture, it may be supposed, is apparent only to those who are deeply versed in the Marxian doctrine.

A. First of all, I shall speak of the class war, which is the point of departure for all Socialistic thought, and which stands in such great need of elucidation,

---

[1] Bergson, *loc. cit.*

since sophists have endeavoured to give a false idea of it.

(1) Marx speaks of society as if it were divided into two fundamentally antagonistic groups; observation, it has often been urged, does not justify this division, and it is true that a certain effort of will is necessary before we can find it verified in the phenomena of everyday life.

The organisation of a capitalistic workshop furnishes a first approximation, and piece-work plays an essential part in the formation of the class idea ; in fact, it throws into relief the very clear opposition of interests about the price of commodities ; [1] the workers feel themselves under the thumb of the employers in the same way that peasants feel themselves in the power of the merchants and the money-lenders of the towns ; history shows that no economic opposition has been more clearly felt than the latter ; since civilisation has existed, country and town have formed two hostile camps.[2] Piece-work also shows that in the wage-earning world there is a group of men somewhat analogous to the retail shopkeepers, possessing the confidence of the employer, and not belonging to the proletariat class.

The strike throws a new light on all this ; it separates the interests and the different ways of thinking of the two groups of wage-earners—the foremen clerks, engineers, etc., as contrasted with the workmen who alone go on strike—much better than the daily circumstances of life do ; it then becomes clear that the administrative group has a natural tendency to become a little aristocracy ;

[1] I do not know whether the *learned* (economists and other people who make inquiries on social conditions) have always quite understood the function of piece-work. It is evident that the well-known formula, " the producer should be able to buy back his product," arose from reflections on the subject of piece-work.

[2] " It may be said that the economic history of society turns on this antithesis," — of town and country (*Capital*, vol. i. p. 152, col. 1).

for these people, State Socialism would be advantageous, because they would go up one in the social hierarchy.

But all oppositions become extraordinarily clear when conflicts are supposed to be enlarged to the size of the general strike; then all parts of the economico-judicial structure, in so far as the latter is looked upon from the point of view of the class war, reach the summit of their perfection; society is plainly divided into two camps, and only into two, on a field of battle. No philosophical explanation of the facts observed in practical affairs could throw such vivid light on the situation as the extremely simple picture called up by the conception of the general strike.

(2) It would be impossible to conceive the disappearance of capitalistic dominance if we did not suppose an ardent sentiment of revolt, always present in the soul of the worker; but experience shows that very often the revolts of a day are far from possessing a really specifically socialistic character; more than once the most violent outbursts have depended on passions which could be satisfied inside the middle-class world; many revolutionaries have been seen to abandon their old irreconcilability when they found themselves on the road to fortune.[1]   It is not only satisfactions of a material kind ˙which produce these frequent and scandalous conversions; vanity, much more than money, is the great motive force in transformation of the revolutionary into a bourgeois. All that would be negligible if it were only a question of a few exceptional people, but it has often been maintained that the psychology of the working classes would so easily adapt itself to the capitalistic order of things that social peace would be

[1] It may be remembered that in the eruption at Martinique a governor perished who, in 1879, had been one of the protagonists of the Socialist congress held at Marseilles.   The Commune itself was not fatal to all its partisans; several have had fairly distinguished careers; the ambassador of France at Rome was among the most importunate of those who, in 1871, demanded the death of the hostages.

rapidly obtained if employers on their part would make a few sacrifices of money and *amour propre*.

G. Le Bon says that the belief in the revolutionary instincts of crowds is a very great mistake, that their tendencies are conservative, that the whole power of Socialism lies in the rather muddled state of mind of the middle class ; he is convinced that the masses will always flock to a Cæsar.[1]   There is a good deal of truth in these judgments, which are founded on a very wide knowledge of history, but G. Le Bon's theories must be corrected in one respect : they are only valid for societies which lack the conception of the class war.

Observation shows that this last conception is maintained with an indestructible vitality in every circle which has been touched by the idea of the general strike : the day when the slightest incidents of daily life become symptoms of the state of war between the classes, when every conflict is an incident in the social war, when every strike begets the perspective of a total catastrophe, on that day there is no longer any possibility of social peace, of resignation to routine, or of enthusiasm for philanthropic or successful employers.   The idea of the general strike has such power behind it that it drags into the revolutionary track everything it touches.   In virtue of this idea, Socialism remains ever young ; all attempts made to bring about social peace seem childish ; desertions of comrades into the ranks of the middle class, far from discouraging the masses, only excite them still more to rebellion ; in a word, the line of cleavage is never in danger of disappearing.

(3) The successes obtained by politicians in their attempts to make what they call the proletarian influence

---

[1] G. Le Bon, *Psychologie du socialisme*, 3rd ed. p. 111 and pp. 457-459. The author, who a few years ago was treated as an imbecile by the little bullies of university Socialism, is one of the most original physicists of our time.

felt in middle-class institutions, constitute a very great obstacle to the maintenance of the notion of class war. The world has always been carried on by compromises between opposing parties, and order has always been provisional. No change, however considerable, can be looked upon as impossible in a time like ours, which has seen so many novelties introduced in an unexpected manner. Modern progress has been brought about by successive compromises ; why not pursue the aims of Socialism by methods which have succeeded so well ? Many means of satisfying the more pressing desires of the unfortunate classes can be thought of. For a long time these proposals for improvement were inspired by a conservative, feudal, or Catholic spirit. We wish, said the inventors, to rescue the masses from the influence of the Radicals. The latter, seeing their political influence assailed, not so much by their old enemies as by Socialist politicians, invent nowadays all kinds of projects of a progressive, democratic, free-thinking colour. We are beginning at last to be threatened with socialistic compromises !

Enough attention has not always been paid to the fact that many kinds of political, administrative, and financial systems engender and support the domination of a middle class.[1] We must not always attach too much importance to violent attacks on the middle class ; they may have behind them the desire to reform and perfect capitalism.[2] There are, it seems, quite a number of people about nowadays who, though not in the least desiring the disappear-

[1] The Socialists are mistaken in believing that the existence of a middle class is bound up with the existence of the capitalist industrial system. Any country submitted to a bureaucracy, directing production—either directly or through corporations—would have a middle class.

[2] I know, for instance, a very enlightened Catholic, who gives vent with singular acrimony to his contempt for the French middle class ; but his ideal is Americanism, *i.e.* a very young and very active capitalistic society.

ance of the capitalistic régime, would willingly abolish inheritance like the followers of Saint Simon.[1]

The idea of the general strike destroys all the theoretical consequences of every possible social policy ; its partisans look upon even the most popular reforms as having a middle-class character ; so far as they are concerned, nothing can weaken the fundamental opposition of the class war. The more the policy of social reforms becomes preponderant, the more will Socialists feel the need of placing against the picture of the progress which it is the aim of this policy to bring about, this other picture of complete catastrophe furnished so perfectly by the general strike.

B. Let us now examine, with the aid of the conception of the general strike, certain very essential aspects of the Marxian Revolution.

(1) Marx says that on the day of the Revolution the proletariat will be disciplined, united, and organised by the very mechanism of production. This exceedingly concentrated formula would not be very intelligible if we did not read it in connection with its context ; according to Marx, the working class is bowed beneath a system in which " abject poverty, oppression, slavery, degradation, and exploitation increase," and against which it is organising an ever-increasing resistance until the day when the whole social structure breaks up.[2] The accuracy of this description has been many times disputed ; it seems indeed to be more suited to the *Manifesto* period (1847) than to the time when *Capital* was published (1867) ; but this objection must not stop us, and it may be thrust on

---

[1] P. de Rousiers was very much struck by the way rich fathers in the United States forced their sons to earn their own living ; he often met " Frenchmen who were profoundly shocked by what they called the egoism of American fathers. It seemed revolting to them that a rich man should leave his son to earn his own living, that he did nothing *to set him up in life* " (*La Vie américaine, l'éducation et la société*, p. 9).

[2] *Capital*, vol. i. p. 342, col. 1.

one side by means of the theory of myths. The different terms which Marx uses to describe the preparation for the decisive combat are not to be taken literally as statements of fact about a determined future ; it is the description in its entirety which should engage our attention, and taken in this way it is perfectly clear : Marx wishes us to understand that the whole preparation of the proletariat depends solely on the organisation of a stubborn, increasing, and passionate resistance to the present order of things.

This argument is of supreme importance if we are to have a sound conception of Marxism ; but it is often contested, if not in theory, at least in practice ; the proletariat, it has been held, should prepare for the part it is to play in the future by other ways than those of revolutionary Syndicalism. Thus the exponents of co-operation hold that a prominent place in the work of enfranchisement must be given to their own particular remedy ; the democrats say that it is essential to abolish all the prejudices arising from the old Catholic influence, etc. Many revolutionaries believe that, however useful Syndicalism may be, it is not, in itself, sufficient to organise a society which needs a new philosophy, a new code of laws, etc. ; as the division of labour is a fundamental law of the world, Socialists should not be ashamed to apply to specialists in philosophy and law, of whom there is never any lack. Jaurès never stops repeating this kind of stuff. This expansion of Socialism is contrary to the Marxian theory, as also to the conception of the general strike ; but it is evident that the conception of the general strike makes a much more striking appeal to the mind than any formula.

(2) I have already called attention to the danger for the future of civilisation presented by revolutions which take place in a period of economic decadence ; many Marxists do not seem to have formed a clear idea of Marx's

thought on this subject. The latter believed that the great catastrophe would be preceded by an enormous economic crisis, but the crisis Marx had in mind must not be confused with an economic decadence ; crises appeared to him as the result of a too risky venture on the part of production, which creates productive forces out of proportion to the means of regulation which the capitalistic system automatically brings into play. Such a venture supposes that the future was looked upon as favourable to very large enterprises, and that the conception of economic progress prevailed absolutely at the time. In order that the lower middle classes, who are still able to find tolerable conditions of existence under the capitalist régime, may join hands with the proletariat, it is essential that they shall be able to picture the future of production as bright with hope, just as the conquest of America formerly appeared to the English peasants, who left Europe to throw themselves into a life of adventure.

The general strike leads to the same conclusions. The workers are accustomed to seeing their revolts against the restrictions imposed by capitalism succeed during periods of prosperity ; so that it may be said that if you once identify revolution and general strike it then becomes impossible to conceive this of an essential transformation of the world taking place in a time of economic decadence. The workers are equally well aware that the peasants and the artisans will not join hands with them unless the future appears so rosy-coloured that industrialism will be able to ameliorate the lot not only of the producers, but that of everybody.[1]

It is very important always to lay stress on the high

---

[1] It is not difficult to see that propagandists are obliged to refer frequently to this aspect of the social revolution : this will take place while the intermediary classes are still in existence, but when they become sickened by the farce of social pacification, and when a period of such great economic progress has been reached that the future will appear in colours favourable to everybody.

degree of prosperity which industry must possess in order
that the realisation of Socialism may be possible ; for experience shows us that it is by seeking to stop the progress
of capitalism, and to preserve the means of existence of
classes who are on the down-grade, that the prophets of
social peace chiefly endeavour to capture popular favour.
The dependence of the revolution on the constant and
rapid progress of industry must be demonstrated in a
striking manner.[1]

(3) Too great stress cannot be laid on the fact that
Marxism condemns every hypothesis about the future
manufactured by the Utopists. Professor Brentano of
Munich relates that in 1869 Marx wrote to his friend
Beesly (who had published an article on the future of the
working class) to say that up till then he had looked upon
him as the sole revolutionary Englishman, and that henceforth he looked upon him as a reactionary—for, he said,
" the man who draws up a programme for the future is a
reactionary." [2] He considered that the proletariat had
no need to take lessons from the learned inventors of
solutions to social problems, but simply to take up production where capitalism left it.   There was no need for
programmes of the future ; the programmes were already
worked out in the workshops. The idea of a techno-
logical continuity dominates the whole of the Marxian
position.

[1] Kautsky has often dwelt on this idea, of which Engels was particularly fond.

[2] Bernstein said about this story that Brentano might have exaggerated a little, but that " the phrase quoted by him was not inconsistent with Marx's general line of thought " (*Mouvement socialiste*,
September 1, 1899, p. 270). Of what can Utopias be composed ? Of
the past and often of a very far-off past ; it is probably for this reason
that Marx called Beesly a *reactionary*, while everybody else was
astonished at his revolutionary boldness. The Catholics are not the
only people who are hypnotised by the Middle Ages, and Yves Guyot
pokes fun at the *collectivist troubadourism* of Lafargue (Lafargue and
Y. Guyot, *La Propriété*, pp. 121-122).

Experience gained in strikes leads us to a conception identical with that of Marx. Workmen who put down their tools do not go to their employers with schemes for the better organisation of labour, and do not offer them assistance in the management of their business ; in short, Utopias have no place in economic conflicts. Jaurès and his friends are well aware that this is a very strong argument against their own ideas of the way in which Socialism is to be realised : they would like even now to have fragments of the industrial programmes manufactured by learned sociologists and accepted by the workers introduced into strike negotiations ; they would like to see the creation of what they call *industrial parliamentarism* which, exactly as in the case of political parliamentarism would imply, on the one hand, the masses who are led and, on the other, demagogues to show them the way. This would be the apprentice stage of their sham Socialism, and might begin at once.

With the general strike all these fine things disappear ; the revolution appears as a revolt, pure and simple, and no place is reserved for sociologists, for fashionable people who are in favour of social reforms, and for the Intellectuals who have embraced *the profession of thinking for the proletariat*.

C. Socialism has always inspired terror because of the enormous element of the unknown which it contains ; people feel that a transformation of this kind would permit of no turning back. Utopists have used all their literary art in the endeavour to lull anxiety by pictures of the future, so enchanting that fear might be banished ; but the more they accumulated fine promises, the more did thoughtful people suspect traps, and in this they were not altogether mistaken, for the Utopists would have led the world to disasters, tyranny, and stupidity, if they had been hearkened to.

Marx was firmly convinced that the social revolution

of which he spoke would constitute an *irrevocable trans-formation*, and that it would mark an absolute separation between two historical eras ; he often returned to this idea, and Engels has endeavoured to show, by means of images which were sometimes a little grandiose, how economic enfranchisement would be the point of departure of an era having no relationship with the past.   Rejecting all Utopias, these two founders of modern Socialism renounced all the resources by which their predecessors had rendered the prospect of a great revolution less formidable ; but however strong the expressions which they employed might have been, the effects which they produced are still very inferior to those produced by the evocation of the general strike.   This conception makes it impossible for us to ignore the fact that a kind of irresistible wave will pass over the old civilisation.

There is something really terrifying in all this ; but I believe that it is very essential that this feature of Socialism should be insisted on if the latter is to have its full educational value.   Socialists must be convinced that the work to which they are devoting themselves is a *serious, formidable, and sublime work* ; it is only on this condition that they will be able to bear the innumerable sacrifices imposed on them by a propaganda, which can procure them neither honours, profits, nor even immediate intellectual satisfaction.   Even if the only result of the idea of the general strike was to make the Socialist conception more heroic, it should on that account alone be looked upon as having an incalculable value.

The resemblances which I have just established between Marxism and the general strike might be carried still further and deeper ; if they have been overlooked hitherto, it is because we are much more struck by the form of things than by their content ; a large number of people find great difficulty in believing that there can be any parallelism between a philosophy based on Hegelianism and the constructions made by men entirely devoid of higher culture. Marx had acquired in Germany a taste for very condensed formulas, and these formulas were so admirably suited to the conditions in the midst of which he worked that he naturally made great use of them. When he wrote, there had been none of the great and numerous strikes which would have enabled him to speak with a detailed knowledge of the means by which the proletariat may prepare itself for the revolution. This absence of knowledge gained from experience very much hampered Marx's thought ; he avoided the use of too precise formulas which would have had this inconvenience of giving a kind of sanction to existing institutions, which seemed valueless to him ; he was therefore happy to be able to find in German academic writing a habit of abstract language which allowed him to avoid all discussion of detail.[1]

No better proof perhaps can be given of Marx's genius than the remarkable agreement which is found to exist between his views and the doctrine which revolutionary Syndicalism is to-day building up slowly and laboriously, keeping always strictly to strike tactics.

III

For some time yet, the conception of the general strike will have considerable difficulty in becoming acclimatised in circles which are not specially dominated by strike tactics. I think it might be useful at this point to enquire

[1] I have elsewhere put forward the hypothesis that Marx, in the penultimate chapter of the first volume of *Capital* perhaps wished to demonstrate the difference between the evolution of the proletariat and that of middle-class force. He said that the working class is disciplined, united and organised by the very mechanism of capitalist production. There is perhaps an indication of a movement towards liberty, opposed to the movement towards automatism which will be discussed later when we come to consider middle-class force (*Saggi di critica*. pp. 46-47).

into the motives which explain the repugnance felt by many intelligent and sincere people who are disturbed by the novelty of the Syndicalist point of view. All the members of the *new school* know that they had to make great efforts in order to overcome the prejudices of their upbringing, to set aside the associations of ideas which sprang up spontaneously in their mind, and to reason along lines which in no way corresponded to those which they had been taught.

During the nineteenth century there existed an incredible scientific ingenuousness which was the direct outcome of the illusions that had aroused so much excitement towards the end of the eighteenth century.[1] Because astronomers had managed to calculate the tables of the moon, it was believed that the aim of all science was to forecast the future with accuracy ; because Le Verrier had been able to indicate the probable position of the planet Neptune—which had never been seen, and which accounted for the disturbances of observable planets— it was believed that science could remedy the defects of society, and indicate what measures should be taken to bring about the disappearance of the unpleasant things in the world. It may be said that this was the *middle-class conception of science* : it certainly corresponds very closely to the mental attitude of those capitalists, who, ignorant of the perfected appliances of their workshops, yet direct industry, and always find ingenious inventors to get them out of their difficulties. For the middle class science is a mill which produces solutions to all the problems we are faced with : [2] science is no longer con-

---

[1] The history of scientific superstitions is of the deepest interest to philosophers who wish to understand Socialism. These superstitions have remained dear to our democracy, as they had been dear to the *beaux esprits* of the Old Régime ; I have touched on a few of the aspects of this history in *Les Illusions du progrès*. Engels was often under the influence of these errors, from which Marx himself was not always free.

[2] Marx quotes this curious phrase from Ure, written about 1830 : " This invention supports the doctrine already developed by us : if

sidered as a perfected means to knowledge, but only as a
recipe for procuring certain advantages.[1]

I have said that Marx rejected all attempts to determine
the conditions of a future society ; too much stress cannot
be laid on this point, for it shows that he took his stand
outside middle-class science.   The doctrine of the general
strike also repudiates this science, and many professors
consequently accuse the *new school* of having negative
ideas only ; their own aim, on the other hand, is the noble
one of constructing universal happiness.   The leaders of
social democracy, it seems to me, have not been very
Marxian on this point ; a few years ago, Kautsky wrote
a preface to a somewhat burlesque Utopia.[2]

I believe that among the motives which led Bernstein
to part from his old friends must be counted the horror
which he felt for their Utopias.   If Bernstein had lived
in France and had known our revolutionary Syndicalism,
he would soon have perceived that the latter was on the
true Marxian track ; but neither in England nor in
Germany did he find a working-class movement which
could guide him ; wishing to remain attached to realities,
as Marx had been, he thought that it was better to carry
on a policy of social reform, pursuing practical ends, than
to lull himself to sleep to the sound of fine phrases about
the happiness of future humanity.

The worshippers of this useless pseudo science did not
allow themselves to be stopped by the objection, legitimate
in this case, that their methods of calculation were entirely
inadequate of their means of determination.   Their conception of science, being derived from astronomy, supposes

capital enlists the aid of science, the rebel hand of labour always learns
how to be tractable " (*Capital*, Eng. trans., vol. i. p. 188, col. 2).

[1] To use the language of the *new school*, science was considered from
the point of view of the consumer and not from the point of view of the
producer.

[2] Atlanticus, *Ein Blick in den Zukunftsstaat*.   E. Seillière reviewed
this book in the *Débats* of August 16, 1899.

that everything can be expressed by some mathematical law.   Evidently there are no laws of this kind in sociology ; but man is always susceptible to analogies connected with the forms of expression : it was thought that a high degree of perfection had been attained, and that already something had been accomplished for science when—starting from a few principles not offensive to common sense, which seem confirmed by a few common experiences—it had been found possible to present a doctrine in a simple, clear, and deductive manner.   This so-called science is simply chatter.[1]

The Utopists excelled in the art of exposition in accordance with these prejudices ; the more their exposition satisfied the requirements of a school book, the more convincing they thought their inventions were.   I believe that the contrary of this belief is the truth, and that we should distrust proposals for social reform all the more, when every difficulty seems solved in an apparently satisfactory manner.

I should like to examine here, very briefly, a few of the illusions which have arisen out of what may be called the *little science*,[2] which believes that when it has attained

---

[1] " It has not been enough noticed how feeble is the reach of deduction in the psychological and moral sciences. . . . Very soon appeal has to be made to common sense, that is to say, to the continuous experience of the real, in order to inflect the consequences deduced and bend them along the sinuosities of life.   Deduction succeeds in things moral only metaphorically so to speak " (Bergson, *Creative Evolution*, p. 224).   Newman had already written something similar to this, but in more precise terms : " Thus it is that the logician for his own purposes, and most usefully as far as these purposes are concerned, turns rivers, full, winding and beautiful, into navigable canals. . . . His business is not to ascertain facts in the concrete but to find and dress up middle terms ; and, provided they and the extremes which they go between are not equivocal, either in themselves or in their use.   Supposing he can enable his pupils to show well in a *viva voce* disputation, . . . he has achieved the main purpose of his profession " (*Grammar of Assent*, pp. 261-262).   There is no weakness in this denunciation of small talk.

[2] See note, p. 66.

clarity of exposition that it has attained truth. This *little science* has contributed a great deal towards creating the crisis in Marxism, and every day we hear the *new school* accused of delighting in the obscurities of which Marx has so often been accused, while French Socialists and Belgian Sociologists, on the contrary, . . . !

Perhaps the best way of giving an accurate idea of the error committed by these sham scientists against whom the *new school* is waging war will be to examine the general characteristics of some social phenomena, and to run through some of the achievements of the mind, beginning with the highest.

A. (1) The positivists, who represent, in an eminent degree, mediocrity, pride, and pedantry, had decreed that philosophy was to give way before *their science* ; but philosophy is not dead, and it has acquired a new and vigorous lease of life thanks to Bergson, who far from wishing to reduce everything to science, has claimed for the philosopher the right to proceed in a manner quite opposed to that employed by the scientist. It might be said that metaphysics has reclaimed the lost ground by demonstrating to man the illusion of so-called scientific solutions, and by bringing the mind back to the mysterious region which the *little science* abhors. Positivism is still admired by a few Belgians, the employees of the *Office du Travail*,[1] and General André ; [2] but these are people who count for very little in the world of thought.

(2) Religions do not seem to be on the point of disappearing. Liberal Protestantism is dying because it

---

[1] This is the office of the Minister for Labour, and is principally occupied with the Syndicates. It gives itself a certain socialistic air in the hope of duping the workmen.

[2] A few years ago, this illustrious warrior (?) was instrumental in blocking the candidature for the *Collège de France* of Paul Tennery (whose erudition was universally recognised in Europe) in favour of a positivist. The positivists constitute a lay congregation which is ready for any dirty work.

attempted, at all costs, to give a perfectly rationalistic exposition of Christian theology. Auguste Comte manufactured a caricature of Catholicism, in which he had retained only the administrative, hierarchical, and disciplinary machinery of that Church; his attempt obtained success only with those people who like to laugh at the simplicity of their dupes. In the course of the nineteenth century, Catholicism recovered strength to an extraordinary degree because it would abandon nothing ; it even strengthened its mysteries, and, what is very curious, it gains ground in cultivated circles where the rationalism which was formerly in fashion at the University is scoffed at.[1]

(3) The old claim made by our fathers that they had created a science of art or even that they could describe a work of art in so adequate a manner that the reader could obtain from a book an exact aesthetic appreciation of a picture or of a statue, we look upon nowadays as a perfect example of pedantry. Taine's efforts in the direction first mentioned are very interesting, but only as regards the history of the various schools. His method gives us no useful information about the works themselves. As for the descriptions, they are only of value if the works themselves are of small aesthetic value, and if they belong to what is sometimes called *literary painting*. The poorest photograph of the Parthenon conveys a hundred times as much information as a volume devoted to the praise of the marvels of this monument ; it seems to me that the famous *Prière sur l'Acropole*, so often praised as one of the finest passages in Renan, is a rather remarkable example of rhetoric, and that it is much more likely to render Greek art unintelligible to us than to make us admire the Parthenon. Despite all his enthusiasm for Diderot

[1] Pascal protested eloquently against those who considered obscurity an objection against Catholicism, and Brunetière was right in looking upon him as being one of the most *anticartesian* of the men of his time (*Études critiques*, 4ᵉ série, pp. 144-149).

(which is sometimes comical and expressed nonsensically), Joseph Reinach is obliged to acknowledge that his hero was lacking in artistic feeling in his famous *Salons*, because Diderot appreciated most of all those pictures which offered possibilities of literary dissertation,[1] and Brunetière could say that Diderot's *Salons* were the corruption of criticism, because he discussed works of art in them as if they were books.[2]

The impotence of speech is due to the fact that art flourishes best on mystery, half shades and indeterminate outlines ; the more speech is methodical and perfect, the more likely is it to eliminate everything that distinguishes a masterpiece ; it reduces the masterpiece to the proportions of an academic product.

As a result of this preliminary examination of the three highest achievements of the mind, we are led to believe that it is possible to distinguish in every complex body of knowledge a clear and an obscure region, and to say that the latter is perhaps the more important. The mistake made by superficial people consists in the statement that this second part must disappear with the progress of enlightenment, and that eventually everything will be explained rationally in terms of the *little science*. This error is particularly revolting as regards art, and, above all, perhaps, as regards modern painting, which seeks more and more to render combinations of shades to which no attention was formerly paid on account of their lack of stability and of the difficulty of rendering them by speech.[3]

B. (1) In ethics, the part that can be expressed easily,

[1] J. Reinach, *Diderot*, pp. 116-117, 125-127, 131-132.

[2] Brunetière, *Évolution des genres*, p. 122. Elsewhere he calls Diderot a *philistine*, p. 153.

[3] It is to the credit of the *impressionists* that they showed that these fine shades can be rendered by painting ; but some few among them soon began to paint according to the formulas of a school, and then there appeared a scandalous contrast between their works and their avowed aims.

in clearly reasoned expositions, is that which has reference to the equitable relations between men ; it contains maxims which are to be found in many different civilisations ; consequently it was for a long time believed that a *résumé* of these precepts might form the basis of a natural morality applicable to the whole of humanity. The obscure part of morality is that which has reference to sexual relationships, and this part is not easily expressed in formulas ; to understand it thoroughly you must have lived in a country for a great number of years. It is, moreover, the fundamental part ; when it is known the whole psychology of a people is understood ; the supposed uniformity of the first system in reality then conceals many differences ; almost identical maxims may correspond to very different applications ; their clearness was only a delusion.

(2) In legislation, everybody sees immediately that the law regulating contracts and debts constitutes the obvious part, that which is called scientific ; here again there is great uniformity in the rules adopted by different peoples, and it was believed that it was eminently desirable to draw up a common code founded on a rational revision of those which existed, but in practice it is again found that, in different countries, the courts generally attach different meanings to these supposed common principles ; that is because there is something individual and particular in each maxim.

The mysterious region is the family, which influences all social relationships. Le Play was very much struck by an opinion of Tocqueville on this subject : " I am astonished," said this great thinker, " that ancient and modern publicists have not attributed a greater influence on the progress of human affairs to the laws of inheritance. These laws, it is true, refer to civil private affairs, but they should be placed at the head of all political institutions, for they have an incredible influence on the social state of peoples, of which state the political laws are only the expression." [1] This remark governed all the researches of Le Play.

This division of legislation into a clear and an obscure region has one curious consequence : it is very rare for people who are not members of the legal professions to undertake any discussion of equity ; they know that it is necessary to have an intimate knowledge of certain rules of law, in order to be able to argue about these questions : an outsider would run the risk of making himself ridiculous if he were to venture on an opinion ; but on the question of divorce, of paternal authority, of inheritance, every man of letters believes himself as learned as the cleverest lawyer, because in this obscure region there are no well-defined principles, nor regular deductions.

(3) In economics, the same distinction is, perhaps, still more evident ; questions relative to exchange can be easily expounded ; the methods of exchange are very much alike in the different countries, and it is hardly likely that any very violent paradoxes will be made about monetary circulation. On the other hand, everything relative to production presents a complexity which is sometimes inextricable ; it is in production that local traditions are most strongly maintained ; ridiculous Utopias regarding production may be invented indefinitely without revolting the common sense of readers. Nobody denies that production is the fundamental part of any economic system ; this is a truth which plays a great part in Marxism, and which has been acknowledged even by authors who have been unable to understand its importance.[2]

---

[1] Tocqueville, *Démocratie en Amérique*, tome i. chap. iii.   Le Play, *Réforme sociale en France*, chap. xvii. 4.

[2] In my *Introduction à l'économie moderne* I have shown how this distinction may be used to throw light on many questions which had

C. Let us now examine how Parliamentary assemblies work. For a long time it was believed that their principal function was that of arguing out the most important questions of social organisation, and, above all, those relating to the constitution. In such matters it is possible to proceed from first principles by way of deduction to clear and concise conclusions. Our forefathers excelled in this scholastic type of argument, which forms the luminous part of political discussions. Now that the question of the constitution is scarcely ever discussed, certain great laws still give rise to fine oratorical tournaments ; thus on the question of the separation of the Church and the State, the professional expounders of first principles were heard and even applauded ; it was the opinion of all that the debates had rarely reached so high a level, and this was because the question was one that lent itself to academic discussion. But when, as more frequently happens, commercial laws or social measures are discussed, then we see the stupidity of our representatives displayed in all its splendour ; ministers, presidents, or *rapporteurs de commissions*,[1] specialists, vie with each other in displays of stupidity ; the reason for this is that we are now dealing with economic questions, and the mind is no longer guided by simple rules ; in order to be able to give an opinion worthy of consideration on these questions, one must have had a practical acquaintance with them, and our honourable members cannot be said to possess this kind of knowledge. Among them may be found many representatives of the *little science* ; on July 5, 1905, a well-known specialist in venereal diseases [2]

---

till then remained exceedingly obscure, and notably to show the exact value of certain important arguments used by Proudhon.

[1] [Laws in France are discussed by a committee elected by the Chamber ; they alter the text of the law, and it is the duty of the *rapporteur*, named by the committee, to defend the amended text in open discussion in the Chamber.—*Trans. Note.*]

[2] Doctor Augagneur was for a long time one of the glories of that

declared that he had not studied political economy, having " a certain mistrust for that conjectural science." We must doubtless understand from this that it is more difficult to argue about production than it is to diagnose syphilis.

The *little science* has engendered a fabulous number of sophistries which we continually come across, and which go down very well with the people who possess the stupid and mediocre culture distributed by the University. These sophistries consist in putting very different things on the same plane from a love of logical simplicity ; thus sexual morality is reduced to the equitable relations between contracting parties, the family code to that regulating debts and agreements, and production to exchange.

Because, in nearly every country and in every age, the State has undertaken to regulate circulation, both of money and of banknotes, or has laid down a legal system of measures, it does not by any means follow that there would be the same advantage in entrusting to the State, for mere love of uniformity, the management of great enterprises : yet this argument is one of those which appeal most strongly to many medical students and nurslings of the School of Law. I am convinced that Jaurès is even now unable to understand why industry has been abandoned by lazy legislators to the anarchical tendencies of egotists ; if production is really the base of everything, as Marx says, it is criminal not to place it in the front rank, not to subject it to a great legislative action, conceived on the same lines as those parts of legislation which owe their clearness to their abstract character, *i.e.* not to order and arrange it so that it rests

class of Intellectuals who looked upon Socialism as a variety of Drey-fusism ; his great protests in favour of Justice have brought him to the governorship of Madagascar, which proves that virtue is sometimes rewarded.

on great principles analogous to those which are brought forward when constitutional laws are discussed.

Socialism is necessarily very obscure, since it deals with production, *i.e.* with the most mysterious part of human activity, and since it proposes to bring about a radical transformation of that region which it is impossible to describe with the clearness that is to be found in more superficial regions. No effort of thought, no progress of knowledge, no rational induction will ever dispel the mystery which envelops Socialism ; and it is because the philosophy of Marx recognised fully this feature of Socialism that it acquired the right to serve as the starting-point of Socialist inquiry.

But we must hasten to add that this obscurity lies only in the language by which we endeavour to describe the methods of realising Socialism ; this obscurity may be said to be scholastic only ; it does not in the least prevent us picturing the proletarian movement in a way that is exact, complete, and striking, and this may be achieved by the aid of that powerful construction which the proletarian mind has conceived in the course of social conflicts, and which is called the " general strike." It must never be forgotten that the perfection of this method of representation would vanish in a moment if any attempt were made to resolve the general strike into a sum of historical details ; *the general strike must be taken as a whole and undivided, and the passage from capitalism to Socialism conceived as a catastrophe, the development of which baffles description.*

The professors of the *little science* are really difficult to satisfy. They assert very loudly that they will only admit into thought abstractions analogous to those used in the deductive sciences : as a matter of fact, this is a rule which is insufficient for purposes of action, for we do nothing great without the help of warmly-coloured and clearly-defined images, which absorb the whole of our attention ; now, is it possible to find anything more satisfying from their point of view than the general strike ? But, reply the professors, we ought to rely only on those realities which are given by experience: is, then, the picture of the general strike made up of tendencies which were not obtained directly from observation of the revolutionary movement ? Is it a work of pure reason, manufactured by indoor scientists attempting to solve the social problem according to the rules of logic ? Is it something arbitrary ? Is it not, on the contrary, a spontaneous product analogous to those others which students of history come across in periods of action ? They insist, and say that man ought not to let himself be carried away by his impulses without submitting them to the control of his intelligence, whose rights are unchallenged ; nobody dreams of disputing them ; of course, this picture of the general strike must be tested, and that is what I have tried to do above ; but the critical spirit does not consist in replacing *historical data* by the *charlatanism of a sham science*.

If it is desired to criticise the basis of the idea of the general strike, the attack must be directed against the revolutionary tendencies which it groups together, and shows as in action ; by no other method worthy of attention can you hope to prove to the revolutionaries that they are wrong in giving all their energies to the cause of Socialism, and that their real interests would be better served if they were politicians ; they have known this for a long time, and their choice is made ; as they do not take up a utilitarian standpoint, any advice which you may give will be in vain.

We are perfectly well aware that the historians of the future are bound to discover that we laboured under many illusions, because they will see behind them a finished world. We, on the other hand, must act, and nobody can tell us to-day what these historians will know ;

nobody can furnish us with the means of modifying our motor images in such a way as to avoid their criticisms.

Our situation resembles somewhat that of the physicists who work at huge calculations based on theories which are not destined to endure for ever.   We have nowadays abandoned all hope of discovering a complete science of nature ; the spectacle of modern scientific revolutions is not encouraging for scientists, and has no doubt led many people, naturally enough, to proclaim the bankruptcy of science, and yet we should be mad if we handed the management of industry over to sorcerers, mediums, and wonder-workers.   The philosopher who *does not seek to make a practical application of his theories* may take up the point of view of the future historian of science, and then dispute the absolute character of present - day scientific theses ; but he is as ignorant as the present-day physicist when he is asked how to correct the explanations given by the latter ; must he therefore take refuge in scepticism ?

Nowadays no philosophers worthy of consideration accept the sceptical position ; their great aim, on the contrary, is to prove the legitimacy of a science which, however, makes no claim to know the real nature of things, and which confines itself to discovering relations which can be utilised for practical ends.   It is because sociology is in the hands of people who are incapable of any philosophic reasoning that it is possible for us to be attacked (in the name of the *little science*) for being content with methods founded on the laws that a really thorough psychological analysis reveals as fundamental in the genesis of action, and which are revealed to us in all great historical movements.

To proceed scientifically means, first of all, to know what forces exist in the world, and then to take measures whereby we may utilise them, by reasoning from experience. That is why I say that, by accepting the idea of the general strike, although we know that it is a myth, we are proceeding exactly as a modern physicist does who has complete confidence in his science, although he knows that the future will look upon it as antiquated. It is we who really possess the scientific spirit, while our critics have lost touch both with modern science and modern philosophy ; and having proved this, we are quite easy in our minds.

CHAPTER V

THE POLITICAL GENERAL STRIKE

I

POLITICIANS are people whose wits are singularly sharpened by their voracious appetites, and in whom the hunt for fat jobs develops the cunning of Apaches. They hold purely proletarian organisations in horror, and discredit them as much as they can ; frequently they even deny their efficacity, in the hope of alienating the workers from groups which, they say, have no future. But when they perceive that their hatred is powerless, that their abuse does not hinder the working of these detested organisations, and that these have become strong, then they seek to turn to their own profit the forces which the proletariat has created.

The co-operative societies were for a long time denounced as useless to the workers; since they have prospered, more than one politician has cast languishing eyes on their cash-box, and would like to see the party supported by the income from the bakery and the grocery, as the Israelite consistories in many countries live on the dues from the Jewish butchers.[1]

The syndicates may be very useful in electoral propaganda ; a certain amount of skill is needed to utilise them profitably, but politicians do not lack lightness of finger. Guérard, the secretary of the railway syndicate, was once one of the most ardent revolutionaries in France ; in the end, however, it was borne in upon him that it was easier to play with politics than to prepare for the general strike ;[2] he is to-day one of those men in whom the *Direction du Travail* has most confidence, and in 1902 he went to a great deal of trouble in order to secure the return of Millerand to Parliament. There is a very large railway station in the constituency which the *Socialist minister* sought to represent, and, without the support of Guérard, Millerand would probably have been defeated. In the *Socialiste* of September 14, 1902, a Guesdist denounced this conduct, which seemed to him doubly

[1] In Algeria the scandals in the administration of the consistories (the administrative councils of the Jewish community), which had become sinks of electoral corruption, compelled the Government to reform them ; but the recent law respecting the separation of the Churches and the State will probably bring about a return to the old practices.

[2] An attempt to organise a railway strike was made in 1898 ; Joseph Reinach says this about it : " A very shady individual, Guérard, who had founded an association of railway workers and employees which had a membership of 20,000, intervened (in the conflict with the navvies of Paris) with the announcement of a general strike of his syndicate. . . . Brisson authorised search warrants, had the stations guarded by soldiery, and placed lines of sentinels along the track; nobody came out " (*Histoire de l'affaire Dreyfus*, tome iv. pp. 310-311. Nowadays the Guérard syndicate is in such good odour with the Government that the latter has granted it permission to start a big lottery. On May 14, 1907, Clemenceau spoke of it in the Chamber as a body of " sensible and reasonable people," opposed to the goings-on of the *Confédération du Travail*.

scandalous since, in the first place, the congress of railway workers had decided that the syndicate should not enter into politics and, secondly, because a former deputy, a Guesdist, was Millerand's opponent. The author of the article feared that " the corporative groups were on the wrong track, and that, although they started out to *utilise* politics, they might finally find themselves the *tools* of a party." He was quite right ; in any deals between the representatives of the syndicates and politicians, it will always be the latter who will reap the greater advantage.

Politicians have more than once intervened in strikes, desiring to destroy the prestige of their adversaries and to capture the confidence of the workers. The Longwy dock strikes, in 1905, arose out of the efforts of a *Republican federation* which attempted to organise the syndicates that might possibly serve its policy as against that of the employers ; [1] the business did not quite take the turn desired by the promoters of the movement, who were not familiar enough with this kind of operation. Some Socialist politicians, on the contrary, possess consummate skill in combining instincts of revolt into electoral forces. It was inevitable, therefore, that a few people should be struck by the idea that the great movements of the masses might be used for political ends.

The history of England affords more than one example of a Government giving way when numerous demonstrations against its proposals took place, even though it was strong enough to repel by force any attack on existing institutions. It seems to be an admitted principle of Parliamentary Government that the majority cannot persist in pursuing schemes which give rise to popular demonstrations of too serious a kind. It is one of the applications of the system of compromise on which this régime is founded ; no law is valid when it is looked upon

---

[1] *Mouvement socialiste*, December 1-15, 1905, p. 130.

by a minority as being so oppressive that it rouses them to violent opposition. Great riotous demonstrations are an indication that the moment is not far off when an armed revolt might break out ; Governments which are respectful of the old traditions give way before such demonstrations.[1]

Between the first simple threat of trouble and a riot a general political strike might take place, which might assume any one of a large number of forms : it might be peaceful and of short duration, its aim being to show the Government that it is on the wrong track, and that there are forces which could resist it ; it might also be the first act of a series of bloody riots.

During the last few years Parliamentary Socialists have not been so sure that they would soon come into power, and they have recognised that their authority in the two Houses is not destined to increase indefinitely. When there are no exceptional circumstances to force the Government to buy their support with large concessions, their Parliamentary power is very much reduced. It would therefore be a great advantage to them if they could bring outside pressure to bear on recalcitrant majorities which would appear to threaten the Conservatives with a formidable insurrection.

If there were in existence rich working-class federations, highly centralised and in a position to impose a strict discipline on their members, Socialist deputies would not have very much trouble in inflicting their leadership occasionally on their Parliamentary colleagues. All that they would have to do would be to take advantage of an

[1] The clerical party thought that it would be able to make use of these tactics to block the application of the law regarding the congregations ; it hoped that some show of violence would cause the Government to give way, but the latter stuck to its guns, and it may be said that one of the mainsprings of the Parliamentary system was thus broken, since there are fewer obstacles than formerly to the dictatorship of Parliament.

opportunity that was favourable to a movement of revolt, in order to stop some branch of industry for a few days. It has more than once been proposed that the Government should be brought to a standstill in this fashion by a stoppage in the working of the mines or of the railways.[1] For such tactics to produce the full effect desired, the strike must break out unexpectedly at the word of command of the party, and must stop when the latter has signed a compact with the Government. It is for these reasons that politicians are so very much in favour of the centralisation of the syndicates, and that they talk so much about discipline.[2] It is to be understood, of course, that this discipline is one which must subject the proletariat to their command. Associations which are very decentralised and grouped into *Bourses du Travail* would offer them far fewer guarantees of success ; so that all those who are not in favour of a solid concentration of the proletariat round the party leaders are regarded by the latter as anarchists.

The political general strike has this immense advantage, that it does not greatly imperil the precious lives of the politicians ; it is an improvement on the *moral insurrection* which the " Mountain " made use of in the month of May 1793, in order to force the Convention to expel the Girondists from its midst ; Jaurès, who is afraid of alarming his clients, the financiers (just as the members

[1] In 1890 the National Congress at Lille of the Guesdist party passed a resolution by which it declared that the general strike of the miners was actually possible, and that a general strike of the miners by itself would bring about the results that are expected in vain from a stoppage of every trade.

[2] " There may be room in the party for individual initiative, but the arbitrary fancies of the individual must be put down. The safety of the party lies in its laws ; we must steadfastly abide by them. It is the constitution freely chosen by ourselves which binds us together, and which will enable us to conquer together or to die." Thus spoke a learned exponent of Socialism at the National Council (*Socialiste*, October 7, 1905). If a Jesuit expressed himself thus, there would be an outcry about monkish fanaticism.

of the " Mountain " were afraid of alarming the Departments), admires exceedingly any movement which is free from the violent acts that *distress humanity* ; [1] he is not, therefore, an irreconcilable opponent of the political general strike.

Recent events have given a very great impetus to the idea of the general political strike. The Belgians obtained the reform of the Constitution by a display which has been decorated, perhaps rather ambitiously, with the name of general strike. It now appears that these events did not have the tragic aspect they have been sometimes credited with : the ministry was very pleased to be put in a position to compel the House to accept an electoral bill which the majority disapproved of ; many Liberal employers were very much opposed to this ultra-clerical majority ; what happened, therefore, was something quite contrary to a proletarian general strike, since the workers served the ends of the State and of the capitalists. Since those already far-off times there has been another attempt to bring pressure to bear on the central authority, with a view to establishing a more democratic system of suffrage ; this attempt failed completely ; the ministry, this time, was no longer secretly on the side of the promoters of the bill, and they did not force its adoption. Many Belgians were very much astonished at their failure, and could not understand why the king did not dismiss his ministers to please the Socialists ; he had formerly insisted on the resignation of his clerical ministers in face of a display of Liberal feeling ; in fact, this king in their opinion understood nothing of his duties, and, as was said at the time, he was only a pasteboard king.

This Belgian incident is not without interest, because it brings home to us the fact that the proletarian general

[1] J. Jaurès, *La Convention*, p. 1384.

strike and the political general strike are diametrically opposed to one another. Belgium is one of the countries where the Syndicalist movement is weakest ; the whole Socialist organisation is founded on the bakers', grocers', and haberdashers' shops that are run by committees of the party ; the worker, accustomed from of old to a clerical discipline, remains an *inferior*, who believes himself obliged to follow the leadership of people who sell him the commodities he needs at a slight reduction, and who din catholic or socialistic speeches into his ears. Not only do we find grocery set up as a priestcraft, but it is also from Belgium that we get the well-known theory of public services against which Guesde wrote such a violent pamphlet in 1883, and which Deville called in the same year a Belgian imitation of collectivism.[1] The whole of Belgian Socialism tends towards the development of State industrialism and the constitution of a class of State-workers who would be firmly disciplined under the iron hand of leaders accepted by democracy.[2] It is quite natural, therefore, that in such a country the general strike should be conceived in a political form ; in such conditions the only aim of popular insurrection must be to take the power from one group of politicians and to hand it over to another—the people still remaining the passive beast that bears the yoke.[3]

The recent troubles in Russia have helped to popularise

[1] Deville, *Le Capital*, p. 10.

[2] Paul Leroy-Beaulieu recently proposed to call the whole body of Government employees " the Fourth Estate," and those in private employment " the Fifth Estate " ; he said that the first tended to form hereditary castes (*Débats*, November 28, 1905). As time goes on, the distinction between the two groups will grow more pronounced ; the first group is a great source of support to Socialist politicians, who desire to transform it into a perfectly disciplined corporation capable of taking the lead in the working-class movement; thus, by the intermediacy of the employees of the State, the Parliamentarians would govern the more easily the workers in private industry.

[3] This does not prevent Vandervelde from comparing the future world to the Abbey of Thelema, celebrated by Rabelais, where every-

the idea of the general strike among professional politicians. Many people were surprised at the results produced by great concerted stoppages of work ; but what really happened and what followed from these disturbances is not very well known. People who are acquainted with the country believe that Witte was hand in glove with many of the revolutionaries, and that he was delighted at being able to obtain, by terrifying the Czar, the dismissal of his enemies and the grant of institutions which, in his opinion, would put obstacles in the way of any return to the old régime. It is very remarkable that for a long time the Government seemed paralysed, and in the administration anarchy was at its height, while, from the moment Witte thought it necessary in his personal interests to act vigorously, repression was rapid ; that day arrived (as several people had foreseen) when the financiers needed to revive Russian credit. It seems hardly probable that previous insurrections ever had the irresistible power attributed to them ; the *Petit Parisien*, which was one of the French newspapers that had advertised [1] the fame of Witte, said that the great strike of October 1905 came to an end on account of the hunger of the workers ; according to this newspaper, the strike had even been *prolonged for a day* in the hope that the Poles would take part in the movement, and would obtain concessions as the Finns had done ; then it congratulated the Poles for having been *wise enough not to budge*, and for not having given a pretext for German intervention (*Petit Parisien*, November 7, 1905).

---

body did as he pleased, and from saying that he aspires to an " anarchist community " (Destrée and Vandervelde, *Le Socialisme en Belgique*, p. 289). Oh, the magic of big words !

[1] Many French papers advertised the merits of the Russian minister, Witte, exactly as they advertised cures made by patent medicines. The French press receives at all time large subventions from the Russian embassy, but in this period Witte spent much more than usual, in order to secure his continuance in office by quoting French opinion.

We must not allow ourselves, therefore, to be too much dazzled by certain descriptions, and Ch. Bonnier was right when, in the *Socialiste* of November 18, 1905, he cast doubt on the truth of the account which had been given of the course of events in Russia ; he had always been an irreconcilable opponent of the general strike, and he pointed out that there was no resemblance at all between what had happened in Russia and what the " genuine Syndicalists in France " look forward to. In his opinion, the strike in Russia had merely been the consummation of a very complex process, one method out of the many employed, which had succeeded owing to the exceptionally favourable circumstances in which it had developed.

We have here, then, a criterion which will serve to distinguish two kinds of movement generally designated by the same name. We have studied a proletarian general strike, which is one undivided whole ; now we have to consider the general political strike, which combines the incidents of economic revolt with many other elements depending on systems foreign to the industrial system. In the first case, no detail ought to be considered by itself ; in the second, everything depends on the art with which heterogeneous details are combined. In this case the parts must be considered separately, their importance estimated, and an attempt made to harmonise them. One would think that such a task ought to be looked upon as purely Utopian (or even quite absurd) by the people who are in the habit of bringing forward so many *practical* objections to the proletarian general strike ; but if the proletariat, left to itself, can do nothing, politicians are equal to anything. Is it not one of the dogmas of democracy that the genius of demagogues can overcome all obstacles ?

I will not stop here to discuss what chances of success

these tactics have, and I leave it to the stock-jobbers who read *L'Humanité* to discover how the general political strike may be prevented from degenerating into anarchy. My only concern in the following pages will be to throw full light on the difference between the two conceptions of the general strike.

II

We have seen that the idea of the Syndicalist general strike contains within itself the whole of proletarian Socialism; not only are all its real elements found therein, but they are moreover grouped in the same way as in social struggles, and their movements are exactly those proper to their nature. It would be impossible to find any image which would represent equally well the political form of Socialism, and which could be contrasted with the proletarian conception of it as represented by the general strike; yet, by making the political general strike the pivoting point in the tactics of those Socialists who are at the same time revolutionary and Parliamentary, it becomes possible to obtain an exact notion of what it is that separates the latter from the Syndicalists.

A. To begin with, we perceive immediately that the political general strike does not presuppose a class war concentrated on a field of battle in which the proletariat attacks the middle class; the division of society into two antagonistic armies disappears, for this class of revolt is possible with any kind of social structure. In the past many revolutions were the result of coalitions between discontented groups; Socialist writers have often pointed out that the poorer classes have more than once allowed themselves to be massacred to no purpose, save to place power in the hands of new rulers who, with great astuteness, had managed to utilise for their own advantage a passing discontent of the people against the former authorities.

It seems, indeed, that the Russian Liberals had hoped to see something of the kind happen in 1905 ; they were delighted at the number of peasant and working-class insurrections ; it has even been asserted that they heard with great satisfaction of the reverses of the army in Manchuria.[1]   They believed that the Government, getting alarmed, would have recourse to their enlightenment ; as there is a large number of sociologists among them, the *little science* would thus have obtained a huge success ; but it is probable that the people would have been left to twiddle their thumbs.

It is, I suppose, for much the same kind of reason that the capitalistic shareholders of *L'Humanité* are such ardent admirers of certain strikes ; they look upon the proletariat as a very convenient instrument with which to clear the ground, and they feel certain from their study of history that it will always be possible for a Socialist Government to bring rebels to reason.   Moreover, are not the laws against anarchists, made in an hour of madness, still carefully preserved on the Statute books ?   They are stigmatised as *rascally laws* ; but they may yet serve to protect capitalist-socialists.[2]

B. (1) Further, under the influence of this conception it would no longer be true to say that the whole organisation of the proletariat was contained within revolutionary

[1] The correspondent of the *Débats*, in the issue of November 25, 1906, related how the members of the Duma had congratulated a Japanese journalist on the victories of his compatriots.   (Cf. the *Débats*, December 25, 1907.)

[2] We may also ask how much the old enemies of military justice desire the abolition of the courts martial.   For a long time, the Nationalists were able to maintain with some show of reason that they were retained in order that Dreyfus, if the Court of Cassation ordered a third trial, should not be brought up before a Court of Assizes ; a court martial can be more easily packed than a jury.

Syndicalism. Since the Syndicalist general strike would no longer be the entire revolution, other organisations would have been created side by side with the syndicates ; as the strike could only be one detail cunningly dovetailed into many other incidents which must be set going at the propitious moment, the syndicates would have to await the word of command of the political committees, or at least work in perfect unison with the committees which represent the superior intelligence of the Socialist movement. In Italy Ferri has symbolised this unison in a rather comical manner, by saying that Socialism has need of two legs ; this figure of speech was borrowed from Lessing, who little thought that it might become one of the principles of sociology. In the second scene of *Minna von Barnhelm*, the innkeeper says to Just that a man cannot stand on one glass of brandy any more than he can walk on one leg ; he also adds that all good things are three in number, and that a rope of four strands is all the stronger. I am not aware that sociology has made any use of these other aphorisms, which·are worth just as much as the one Ferri misused.

(2) If the Syndicalist general strike is connected with the idea of an era of great economic progress, the political general strike calls up rather that of a period of decadence. Experience shows that classes on the downgrade are more easily captured by the fallacious harangues of politicians than classes on the upgrade, so that there seems to be a close relation between the political perspicacity of men and the conditions under which they live. Prosperous classes may often act very imprudently, because they have too much confidence in their own strength ; they face the future with too much boldness, and they are overcome for the moment by a frenzied desire for renown. Enfeebled classes habitually put their trust in people who promise them the protection of the State, without ever trying to understand how this protection could possibly

harmonise their discordant interests ; they readily enter into every coalition formed for the purpose of forcing concessions from the Government ; they greatly admire charlatans who speak with a glib tongue. Socialism must be exceedingly careful if it is not to fall to the level of what Engels called bombastic antisemitism,[1] and the advice of Engels on this point has not always been followed.

The political general strike presupposes that very diverse social groups shall possess the same faith in the magical force of the State ; this faith is never lacking in social groups which are on the downgrade, and its existence enables windbags to represent themselves as able to do everything. The political general strike would be greatly helped by the stupidity of philanthropists, and this stupidity is always a result of the degeneration of the rich classes. Its chances of success would be enhanced by the fact that it would have to deal with cowardly and discouraged capitalists.

(3) Under such conditions it would no longer be possible to ignore plans of the future state of society ; these plans on which Marx poured ridicule, and which the Syndicalist general strike ignores, would become an essential element of the new system. A political general strike could not be proclaimed until it was known with absolute certainty that the complete framework of the future organisation

---

[1] Engels feared that the Socialists, in order to gain adherents in the electoral struggles rapidly, would make promises which were contrary to Marxist doctrine. The antisemites told the peasants and the small shopkeepers that they would protect them from the development of capitalism. Engels thought that an imitation of this procedure would be dangerous, since, in his opinion, the social revolution could only be realised when capitalism had almost completely destroyed the small proprietors and small industries ; if the Socialists, then, endeavoured to hinder this evolution, they would ultimately compromise their own cause. Engels did not know that the French Socialists (whose agrarian programme he was criticising) had often made such promises, and that several Socialist deputies were very friendly with Drumont. Engels, "La Question agraire et le Socialisme," in the *Mouvement socialiste,* October 15, 1900, p. 462. Cf. pp. 458-459 and p. 463.

was ready. That is what Jaurès intended to convey in his articles of 1901 when he said that modern society " will recoil from an enterprise as indeterminate and as empty (as the Syndicalist strike) as one draws back from a precipice." [1]

There are plenty of young barristers, briefless and likely to remain so, who have filled enormous note-books with their detailed projects for the social organisation of the future. If we have not yet been favoured with the breviary of the revolution which Lucien Herr announced in 1900, we know at least that regulations have been framed for the establishment of the book-keeping branch of collectivist society, and Tarbouriech has even gone into the question of the printed forms to be recommended for the use of the future bureaucracy.[2] Jaurès is continually bewailing the fact that so many lights are condemned to remain hidden under the capitalist bushel ; and he feels convinced that the revolution depends very much less on the conditions Marx had in mind than on the efforts of unknown geniuses.

C. I have already called attention to the terrible nature of the revolution as conceived by Marx and the Syndicalists, and I have said that it is very important that its character of absolute and irrevocable transformation should be preserved, because it is that which gives Socialism its high educational value. The comfort-loving followers of our politicians could not view with any approval the profoundly serious work which is being carried on by the proletariat ; the former desire to reassure the middle

---

[1] Jaurès, *Études socialistes*, p. 107.

[2] Many idiotically serious things like this may be found in Tarbouriech's *Cité future*. People who call themselves well-informed say that Arthur Fontaine, Directeur du Travail, has some astonishing solutions of the social question in his portfolios, and that he will reveal them on the day he retires. Our successors will bless him for having saved up for them pleasures we shall not know.

class, and promise not to allow the people to give themselves up entirely to their anarchical instincts. They
explain to the middle class that they do not by any means
dream of suppressing the great State machine, but wise
Socialists desire two things : (1) to take possession of this
machine so that they may improve its works, and make
them run to further their friends' interests as much as
possible, and (2) to assure the stability of the Government,
which will be very advantageous for all business men.
Tocqueville had observed that, since the beginning of the
nineteenth century, the administrative institutions of
France having changed very little, revolutions had no longer
produced any very great upheavals.[1] Socialist financiers
have not read Tocqueville, but they understand instinctively
that the preservation of a highly centralised, very authori-
tative and very democratic State puts immense resources
at their disposal, and protects them from proletarian
revolution. The transformations which their friends,
the Parliamentary Socialists, may carry out will always
be of a very limited scope, and it will always be possible,
thanks to the State, to correct any imprudences they may
commit.

The general strike of the Syndicalists drives away from
Socialism all financiers in quest of adventures ; the
political strike rather pleases these gentlemen, because it
would be carried out in circumstances favourable to the
power of politicians, and consequently to the operations
of their financial allies.[2]

[1] Tocqueville, *L'Ancien Régime et la Révolution*, p. 297.

[2] In the *Avant-Garde* of October 29, 1905, may be read the report
of Lucien Rolland to the National Council of the Unified Socialist
Party on the election at Florac of Louis Dreyfus, a speculator in grain
and shareholder of *L'Humanité*. " I was greatly pained," says Rolland,
" to hear one of the *rois de l'époque* (kings of the time) speak in the name
of our Internationale, of our red flag, of our principles, and cry, ' Long
live the social republic ! ' " Those whose only knowledge of this
election has been gained from the *official report* published in the *Socialiste*
of October 28, 1905, will have gained a singularly false idea of it.

Marx supposes, exactly as the Syndicalists do, that the revolution will be absolute and irrevocable, because it will place the forces of production in the hands of *free men*, *i.e.* of men who will be capable of running the workshop created by capitalism without any need of masters. This conception would not at all suit the financiers and the politicians whom they support, for both are only fit to exercise the noble profession of masters. Therefore, the authors of all enquiries into *moderate Socialism* are forced to acknowledge that the latter implies the division of society into two groups : the first of these is a select body, organised as a political party, which has adopted the mission of thinking for the thoughtless masses, and which imagines that, because it allows the latter to enjoy the results of its superior enlightenment, it has done something admirable.[1] The second is the whole body of the producers. The select body of politicians has no other profession than that of using its wits, and they find that it is strictly in accordance with the principles of immanent justice (of which they are sole owners) that the proletariat should work to feed them and furnish them with the means for an existence that only distantly resembles an ascetic's.

This division is so evident that generally no attempt is made to hide it : the officials of Socialism constantly speak of the party as of an organism having a life of its own. At the International Socialist Congress of 1900, the party was warned against the danger it ran in follow-

---

Official Socialist documents should be mistrusted. I do not believe that, during the Dreyfus case, the friends of the general staff ever distorted truth so much as the official Socialists did on this occasion.

The *fourieriste* Tousseil published in the reign of Louis-Philippe a book entitled *Les Juifs rois de l'époque*, in which he attacked the great speculators. Rolland is alluding to this, and wishes to recall the fact that L. Dreyfus was a large speculator in corn.

[1] The *Intellectuals* are not, as is so often said, men who think : they are people *who have adopted the profession of thinking*, and who take an *aristocratic salary* on account of the nobility of this profession.

ing a policy which might separate it too much from the proletariat ; it must inspire the masses with confidence if it desires to have their support on the day of the great battle.[1] The great reproach which Marx levelled at his adversaries in the Alliance was this separation of the leaders and the led, which had the effect of reinstating the State—and which is to-day so marked in Germany— and elsewhere.

III

A. We will now carry our analysis of the ideas grouped round the political strike a little farther, and enquire first of all what becomes of the notion of class.

(1) It will no longer be possible to distinguish the classes by the place occupied by their members in capitalistic production ; we go back to the old distinction between rich groups and poor groups — such was the division between the classes as it appeared to those older Socialists who sought to reform the iniquities of the actual distribution of riches. The " social Catholics " take up this position also, and endeavour to improve the lot of the poor, not only by charity, but also by a large number of institutions which aim at a mitigation of the wretchedness caused by the capitalist industrial system. It seems that even to-day things are considered from this point of view in circles that admire Jaurès as a prophet ; I have been told that the latter sought to convert Buisson to Socialism by making an appeal to the goodness of his heart, and that these two soothsayers had a very ludicrous discussion as to the best way to *remedy the defects* of society.

[1] For example, Vaillant says : " Since we have to fight this great battle, do you think that we can win it if we have not the proletariat behind us ? We must have the proletariat ; and we shall not have it if we have discouraged it, if we have shown it that the Party no longer represents its interests, no longer *represents* the war of the working class against the capitalist class " (*Cahiers de la Quinzaine,* 16ᵉ de la IIᵉ série, pp. 159-160). This number contains the shorthand note of the proceedings at the Congress.

The masses believe that they are suffering from the iniquitous consequences of a past which was full of violence, ignorance, and wickedness ; they are confident that the *genius of their leaders* will render them less unhappy ; they believe that democracy, if it were only free, would replace a malevolent hierarchy by a benevolent hierarchy.

The leaders, who foster this sweet illusion in their men, see the situation from quite another point of view ; the present social organisation revolts them just in so far as it creates obstacles to their ambition ; they are less shocked by the existence of the classes than by their own inability to attain to the positions already acquired by older men ; when they have penetrated far enough into the sanctuaries of the State, into drawing-rooms and places of amusement, they cease, as a rule, to be revolutionary and speak learnedly of " evolution."

(2) The sentiment of revolt which is met with in the poorer classes will henceforth be coloured by a violent jealousy. Our democratic newspapers foster this passion with considerable skill, imagining that this is the best means of dulling the minds of their readers and of keeping up the circulation of the paper ; they exploit the scandals which arise from time to time among the rich ; they lead their readers to feel a savage pleasure when they see shame entering the household of one of the great ones of the earth. With a really astonishing impudence, they pretend that they are thus serving the cause of the superfine morality, which they hold as much at heart, they say, as the well-being and the liberty of the poorer classes ! But it is probable that their own interests are the sole motives for their actions.[1]

---

[1] I note here, in passing, that the *Petit Parisien*, the importance of which as an organ of the policy of social reform is so great, took up strongly the case of the Princess of Saxony and the charming teacher Giron. This newspaper, which is very fond of sermonising the people,

Jealousy is a sentiment which seems to belong, above all, to passive beings. Leaders have active sentiments ; with them, jealousy is transformed into a thirst to obtain, at whatever cost, the most coveted situations, and they employ to this end any means which enables them to set aside people who stand in the way of their onward march. In politics, people are no more held back by scruples than they are in sport, and we hear every day of cases where competitors in all kinds of contests seek to improve their chances by some trickery or other.

(3) The *masses who are led* have a very vague and extremely simple idea of the means by which their lot can be improved ; demagogues easily get them to believe that the best way is to utilise the power of the State to *pester* the rich. We pass thus from jealousy to vengeance, and it is well known that vengeance is a sentiment of extraordinary power, especially with the weak. The history of the Greek cities and of the Italian republics of the Middle Ages is full of instances of fiscal laws which were very oppressive on the rich, and which contributed not a little towards the ruin of governments. In the fifteenth century, Aeneas Sylvius (later Pope Pius II.) noted with astonishment the extraordinary prosperity of the commercial towns of Germany and the great liberty enjoyed therein by the middle class, who, in Italy, were persecuted.[1] If our contemporary social policy were examined closely, it would be seen that it also was steeped in ideas of jealousy and vengeance ; many regulations have been framed more with the idea of pestering employers than of improving the situation of the workers. When the clericals are in a minority, they never fail to

---

cannot understand why the outraged husband obstinately refuses to take back his wife. On September 14, 1906, it said the* " she had broken with the ordinary moral code " ; it may be conclude om this that the moral code of the *Petit Parisien* is something quite out of the ordinary.

[1] Jansen, *L'Allemagne et la Réforme*, French trans., tome i. p. 361.

recommend severe regulations in order to be revenged on free-thinking free-mason employers.[1]

The leaders obtain all sorts of advantages from these methods ; they alarm the rich, and exploit them for their own personal profit ; they cry louder than anybody against the privileges of fortune, and know how to obtain for themselves all the enjoyments which the latter procures ; by making use of the evil instincts and the stupidity of their followers, they realise this curious paradox, that they get the people to applaud the inequality of conditions in the name of democratic equality. It would be impossible to understand the success of demagogues from the time of Athens to contemporary New York, if due account was not taken of the extraordinary power of the idea of vengeance in extinguishing reasonable reflection.

I believe that the only means by which this pernicious influence of the demagogues may be wiped out are those employed by Socialism in propagating the notion of the proletarian general strike ; it awakens in the depths of the soul a sentiment of the sublime proportionate to the conditions of a gigantic struggle ; it forces the desire to satisfy jealousy by malice into the background ; it brings to the fore the pride of free men, and thus protects the worker from the quackery of ambitious leaders, hungering for the fleshpots.

B. The great differences which exist between the two general strikes (*i.e.* between the two kinds of Socialism) become still more obvious when social struggles are compared with war ; in fact, war also may give rise to two

[1] The application of the social laws gives rise—in France, at least—to very singular inequalities of treatment ; judicial proceedings depend on political or financial conditions. The case of the rich tailor may be remembered who was decorated by Millerand and against whom proceedings had so often been taken for infringement of the laws for the protection of work-girls.

opposite systems of ideas, so that quite contradictory things can be said about it, all based on incontestable facts.

War may be considered from its noble side, *i.e.* as it has been considered by poets celebrating armies which have been particularly illustrious ; proceeding thus we find in war :

(1) The idea that the profession of arms cannot compare to any other profession—that it puts the man who adopts this profession in a class which is superior to the ordinary conditions of life,—that history is based entirely on the adventures of warriors, so that the economic life only existed to maintain them.

(2) The sentiment of glory which Renan so justly looked upon as one of the most singular and the most powerful creations of human genius, and which has been of such incomparable value in history.[1]

(3) The ardent desire to try one's strength in great battles, to submit to the test which gives the military calling its claim to superiority, and to conquer glory at the peril of one's life.

There is no need for me to insist on these features of war at any great length ; my readers will understand the part played in ancient Greece by this conception of war. The whole of classical history is dominated by the idea of war conceived heroically : in their origin, the institutions of the Greek republics had as their basis the organisation of armies of citizens ; Greek art reached its apex in the citadels ; philosophers conceived of no other possible form of education than that which fostered in youth the heroic tradition, and they endeavoured to keep the study and practice of music within bounds, because they wished to prevent the development of sentiments foreign to this discipline ; social Utopias were created with a view to maintaining a nucleus of homeric warriors in the cities,

[1] Renan, *Histoire du peuple d'Israël*, tome iv. pp. 199-200.

etc. In our own times, the wars of Liberty have been scarcely less fruitful in ideas than those of the ancient Greeks.

There is another aspect of war which does not possess this character of nobility, and on which the pacificists always dwell.[1] The object of war is no longer war itself ; its object is to allow politicians to satisfy their ambitions : the foreigner must be conquered in order that they themselves may obtain great and immediate material advantages ; the victory must also give the party which led the country during the time of success so great a preponderance that it can distribute great favours to its followers ; finally, it is hoped that the citizens will be so intoxicated by the spell of victory they will overlook the sacrifices which they are called upon to make, and will allow themselves to be carried away by enthusiastic conceptions of the future. Under the influence of this state of mind, the people permit the Government to develop its authority in an improper manner, without any protest, so that every conquest abroad may be considered as having for its inevitable corollary a conquest at home made by the party in office.

The Syndicalist general strike presents a very great number of analogies with the first conception of war : the proletariat organises itself for battle, separating itself distinctly from the other parts of the nation, and regarding itself as the great motive power of history, all other social considerations being subordinated to that of combat ; it is very clearly conscious of the glory which will be attached to its historical rôle and of the heroism of its militant attitude ; it longs for the final contest in which it will give proof of the whole measure of its valour. Pursuing no conquest, it has no need to make plans for utilising its victories : it counts on expelling the capitalists

---

[1] The distinction between the two aspects of war is the basis of Proudhon's book on *La Guerre et la paix*.

from the productive domain, and on taking their place in the workshop created by capitalism.

This conception of the general strike manifests in the clearest manner its indifference to the material profits of conquest by affirming that it proposes to suppress the State. The State has always been, in fact, the organiser of the war of conquest, the dispenser of its fruits, and the *raison d'être* of the dominating groups which profit by the enterprises—the cost of which is borne by the general body of society.

Politicians adopt the other point of view ; they argue about social conflicts in exactly the same manner as diplomats argue about international affairs ; all the actual fighting apparatus interests them very little ; they see in the combatants nothing but instruments. The proletariat is their army, which they love in the same way that a colonial administrator loves the troops which enable him to bring large numbers of negroes under his authority ; they apply themselves to the task of training the proletariat, because they are in a hurry to win quickly the great battles which will deliver the State into their hands ; they keep up the ardour of their men, as the ardour of troops of mercenaries has always been kept up, by promises of pillage, by appeals to hatred, and also by the small favours which their occupancy of a few political places enables them to distribute already. But the proletariat for them is *food for cannon*, and nothing else, as Marx said in 1873.[1]

The reinforcement of power of the State is at the basis of all their conceptions ; in the organisations which they at present control, the politicians are already preparing the framework of a strong, centralised and disciplined authority, which will not be hampered by the criticism of an opposition, which will be able to enforce silence, and which will give currency to its lies.

[1] *L'Alliance de la démocratie socialiste*, p. 15. Marx accused his opponents of modelling their policy on Napoleonic lines.

C. In Socialist literature the question of a future *dictatorship of the proletariat* is constantly cropping up, but nobody likes to explain it ; sometimes this formula is improved and the epithet *impersonal* is added to the substantive *dictatorship*, though this addition does not throw much light on the question. Bernstein pointed out a few years ago that this dictatorship would probably be that " of club orators and of literary men," [1] and he was of opinion that the Socialists of 1848, when speaking of this dictatorship, had had in view an imitation of 1793, " a central, dictatorial and revolutionary authority, upheld by the terrorist dictatorship of the revolutionary clubs " ; he was alarmed by this outlook, and he asserted that all the working men with whom he had had an opportunity of conversing were very mistrustful of the future.[2] Hence he concluded that it would be better to base Socialist policy and propaganda on a conception of modern society more in accordance with the idea of evolution. His analysis seems to me to be inadequate.

In the dictatorship of the proletariat we may first of all notice a reminiscence of the Old Régime. Socialists have for a long time been dominated by the idea that capitalist society must be likened to the feudal system ; I scarcely know any idea more false and more dangerous. They imagine that the new feudalism would disappear beneath the influence of forces analogous to those which

[1] Bernstein evidently had in mind here a well-known article by Proudhon, from which, moreover, he quotes a fragment on page 47 of his book. This article closes with imprecations against the Intellectuals : " Then you will know what a revolution is, that has been set going by lawyers, accomplished by artists, and conducted by novelists and poets. Nero was an artist, a lyric and dramatic artist, a passionate lover of the ideal, a worshipper of the antique, a collector of medals, a tourist, a poet, an orator, a swordsman, a sophist, a Don Juan, a Lovelace, a nobleman full of wit, fancy, and fellow-feeling, overflowing with love of life and love of pleasure. That is why he was Nero " (*Représentant du peuple*, April 29, 1848).

[2] Bernstein, *Socialisme théorique et social-démocratie pratique*, pp. 298 and 226.

ruined the old feudal system. The latter succumbed beneath the attacks of a strong and centralised power, imbued with the conviction that it had received a mandate from God to employ exceptional measures against the evil. The kings of the *new model* [1] who established modern monarchical system were terrible despots, wholly destitute of scruples ; but great historians have absolved them from all blame for the acts of violence they committed, because they lived in times when feudal anarchy, the barbarous manners of the old nobles and their lack of culture, joined to a want of respect for the ideas of the past,[2] seemed crimes against which it was the duty of the royal power to act energetically. It is probably then with a view to treating the leaders of capitalism with a wholly royal energy that there is so much talk nowadays of a dictatorship of the proletariat.

Later on, royalty relaxed its despotism and constitutional government took its place. It is said that the dictatorship of the proletariat will also weaken at length, and will disappear, and that finally an *anarchical society* will take its place ; but how this will come about is not explained. The regal despotism did not fall by itself or by the goodness of sovereigns ; one must be very simple to suppose that the people who would profit by the demagogic dictatorship would willingly abandon its advantages.

Bernstein saw quite plainly that the dictatorship of the proletariat corresponds to a division of society into masters and servants, but it is curious that he did not

---

[1] Cf. Gervinus, *Introduction à l'histoire du XIXe siècle*, French trans., p. 27.

[2] The history of the papacy very much embarrasses modern writers ; some of them are fundamentally hostile to it on account of their hatred of Christianity ; but many are led to condone the greatest faults of the papal policy in the Middle Ages on account of the natural sympathy which inclines them to admire all the efforts made by theorists to tyrannise the world.

perceive that the idea of the political strike (which he now, to a certain extent, accepts) is connected in the closest manner with this dictatorship of politicians which he fears. The men who had managed to organise the proletariat in the form of an army, ever ready to obey their orders, would be generals who would set up a state of siege in vanquished society; we should therefore have, on the day following the revolution, a dictatorship exercised by those politicians who in the society of to-day already form a compact group.

I have already recalled what Marx said about the people who reinstated the State by creating in contemporary society an embryo of the future society of masters. The history of the French Revolution shows us how these things happen. The revolutionaries made arrangements whereby their administrative staff was ready to take possession of authority immediately the old administration decamped, so that there was no break of continuity in the domination of a governing class. There are no bounds to Jaurès's admiration for these operations, which he describes in the course of his *Histoire socialiste*, he does not exactly understand their significance, but he guesses the analogy they bear to his own conceptions of social revolution. The flabbiness of the men of that time was so great that sometimes the substitution of the old by the new officials was accomplished under conditions bordering on farce; we always find a supernumerary state—an *État postiche* [1] (artificial state), to use

---

[1] One of the ludicrous comedies of the Revolution is that related by Jaurès in *La Convention*, pp. 1386–1388. In the month of May 1793 an insurrectionary committee was set up at the Bishop's palace, which formed an *État postiche* (see above), and which on May 31 repaired to the town-hall and declared that the people of Paris withdrew all powers from every constituted authority; the general council of the Commune, having no means of defence, " was forced to give in," but not without assuming an air of high tragedy: pompous speeches, embracings all round, " to prove that there was neither wounded vanity on the one part, nor pride of domination on the other "; finally, this buffoonery was

the expression of that time—which is organised in advance
by the side of the legal State, which considers itself a
legitimate before it has become a *legal* power, and which
profits by some slight incident to take up the reins of
government as they slip from the feeble hands of the
constituted authorities.

The adoption of the red flag is one of the most singular
and the most characteristic episodes of that time.   This
signal was used in times of disaffection to give warning
that martial law was about to be set up ; on August 10,
1792, it became the revolutionary symbol, in order to
proclaim " the martial law of the people against rebels
to the executive power." Jaurès comments on this
incident in these terms : " It is we, the people, who are
now the law. . . . We are not rebels. The rebels are
in the Tuileries, and it is against the factions of the court
and the party of the constitutional monarchy that we
raise, in the name of the country and of liberty, the flag of
legal repressions." [1]   Thus the insurgents began by proclaiming that they held legitimate authority ; they are
fighting against a State which has only the appearance
of legitimacy, and they take the red flag to symbolise
the re-establishment by force of the real order.   As
conquerors, they will treat the conquered as conspirators,
and will demand that their plots be punished.   The real
conclusion to all these fine ideas was to be the massacre
of the prisoners in September.

All this is perfectly simple, and the general political
strike would develop in the same way with similar
occurrences.   In order that this strike should succeed,
the greater part of the proletariat must be members of

---

terminated by an order which reinstated the council which had just been
dismissed.   Jaurès is delightful here : the revolutionary committee,
he says, " freed (the legal authority) from all the fetters of legality."
This happy thought is a reproduction of the well-known phrase of the
Bonapartists : " Sortir de la légalité pour rentrer dans le droit."

[1] Jaurès, *Législative*, p. 1288.

syndicates which are under the thumb of political committees ; there must be a complete organisation made up
of the men who will take over the Government, so that
it will only be necessary to make a simple transmutation
in the personnel of the State. The organisation of the
État postiche would have to be more complete than it was
at the time of the Revolution, because the conquest of
the State by force does not seem so easy to accomplish
as formerly ; but the principle would be the same. It
is even possible that, since the transmission of authority
operates nowadays in a more perfect fashion, thanks
to the new resources at the disposal of the Parliamentary
system, and since the proletariat would be thoroughly
well organised under the official syndicates, we should
see the social revolution culminate in a wonderful system
of slavery.

IV

The study of the political strike leads us to a better
understanding of a distinction we must always have in
mind when we reflect on contemporary social questions.
Sometimes the terms *force* and *violence* are used in speaking of acts of authority, sometimes in speaking of acts of
revolt. It is obvious that the two cases give rise to very
different consequences. I think it would be better to
adopt a terminology which would give rise to no ambiguity,
and that the term *violence* should be employed only for
acts of revolt ; we should say, therefore, that the object
of force is to impose a certain social order in which the
minority governs, while violence tends to the destruction
of that order. The middle class have used force since
the beginning of modern times, while the proletariat now
reacts against the middle class and against the State by
violence.

For a long time I was convinced that it is very

important that the theory of social forces should be thoroughly investigated—in a large measure, the forces may be compared to those acting on matter ; but I was not able to perceive the capital distinction in question here until I had come to consider the problem of the general strike. Moreover, I do not think that Marx had ever examined any other form of social constraint except force.   In my *Saggi di critica del marxismo* I endeavoured, a few years ago, to sum up the arguments of Marx with respect to the adaptation of man to the conditions of capitalism, and I presented these arguments in the following manner, on pages 38-40 :—

" (1) There is a social system which is to a certain extent mechanical, in which man seems subject to true *natural laws* : classical economists place at the beginning of things that automatism which is in reality the last product of the capitalistic régime.   ' But the advance of capitalist production,' says Marx,[1] ' develops a more and more numerous class of workers who, by education, tradition, and habit, look upon the conditions of that mode of production as self-evident laws of nature.'   The intervention of an intelligent will in this mechanism would appear as an exception.

" (2) There is a régime of emulation and of keen competition which impels men to set aside traditional obstacles, to seek constantly for what is new, and to imagine conditions of existence which seem to them to be better. According to Marx, it is in this revolutionary task that the middle class excelled.

" (3) There is a régime of violence, which plays an important part in history, and which assumes several distinct forms :

" (a) On the lowest level, we find a scattered kind of violence, which resembles the struggle for life, which acts through economic conditions, and which carries out a

[1] *Capital*, English translation edit. by Engels, p. 76.

slow but sure expropriation ; violence of this character works especially with the aid of fiscal arrangements.[1]

" (*b*) Next comes the concentrated and organised force of the State, which acts directly on labour, ' *to regulate wages, i.e.* force them within the limits suitable to surplus value making, to lengthen the working day, and to maintain the labourer himself in the normal degree of dependence ; this is an essential element of the so-called primitive accumulation.[2]

" (*c*) We have, finally, violence properly so called, which occupies so great a place in the history of primitive accumulation, and which constitutes the principle subject of history."

A few supplementary observations may be useful here.

We must first of all observe that these different phases are placed in a logical sequence, starting from states which most resemble an organism, and in which no independent will appears, and ending in states in which individual minds bring forward their considered plans ; but the historical order is quite the contrary of this order.

At the origin of capitalist accumulation we find some very distinct historical facts, which appear each in its proper time, with its own characteristics, and under conditions so clearly marked that they are described in the chronicles. We find, for instance, the expropriation of the peasants and the suppression of the old legislation which had constituted " serfdom and the industrial hierarchy." Marx adds : " The history of this

---

[1] Marx points out that in Holland taxation was used to raise the price of necessities artificially ; this was the application of a principle of government : this system had a vicious effect on the working class and ruined the peasant, the artisan, and the other members of the better-paid workers ; but it secured the absolute submission of the workers to their masters, the manufacturers (*Capital*, Eng. trans. p. 781).

[2] *Capital*, Eng. trans. p. 761.

expropriation is not a matter of conjecture ; it is inscribed in the annals of humanity in indelible letters of blood and fire." [1]

Farther on Marx shows how the dawn of modern times was marked by the conquest of America, the enslavement of negroes and the colonial wars : " The different methods of primitive accumulation which the capitalist era brought about are divided in a more or less chronological order first of all [between] Portugal, Spain, France and England, until the latter combined the lot, during the last thirty years of the seventeenth century, into a systematic whole, embracing simultaneously the colonial system, public credit, modern finance and the protectionist system. Some of these methods are backed by the employment of brute force ; but all, without exception, exploit the power of the State, the concentrated and organised force of society, in order to precipitate violently the passage from the feudal economic order to the capitalist economic order, and to shorten the phases of the transition." It is on this occasion that he compared force to a midwife, and says that it multiplies the social movement. [2]

Thus we see that economic forces are closely bound up with political power, and capitalism finally perfects itself to the point of being able to dispense with any direct appeal to the public force, except in very exceptional cases. " In the ordinary run of things, the worker can be left to the action of the *natural laws of production, i.e.* to his dependence on capital, a dependence springing from

---

[1] *Capital,* Eng. trans. p. 738.

[2] *Capital,* Eng. trans. p. 776. The German text says that force is an *oekonomische Potenz* (*Kapital,* 4th edition, p. 716) ; the French text says that force is an *agent économique.* Fourier calls geometric progressions *puissancielles* (*Nouveau Monde industriel et sociétaire,* p. 376). Marx evidently used the word *Potenz* in the sense of a multiplier ; cf. in *Capital,* p. 176, col. 1, the term *travail puissancié* for labour of a multiplied productivity. [The English translation has *economic power.* —*Trans. Note.*]

guaranteed, and perpetuated by the very mechanism of production." [1]

When we reach the last historical stage, the action of independent wills disappears, and the whole of society resembles an organised body, working automatically; observers can then establish an economic science which appears to them as exact as the sciences of physical nature. The error of many economists consisted in their ignorance of the fact that this system, which seemed natural or primitive to them,[2] is the result of a series of transformations which might not have taken place, and always remains a very unstable structure, for it could be destroyed by force, as it had been created by the intervention of force; moreover, contemporary economic literature is full of complaints respecting the intervention of the State, which has thereby upset *natural laws*.

Nowadays economists are little disposed to believe that these *natural laws* are in reality laws of Nature; they are well aware that the capitalist system was reached but slowly, but they consider that it was reached by a progress which should enchant the minds of all enlightened men. This progress, in fact, is demonstrated by three remarkable facts: it has become possible to set up a science of economics; laws can be stated in the simplest, surest, and most elegant formulas, since the law of contract dominates every country of advanced capitalism; [3] the caprices of the rulers of the State are no longer so apparent, and thus the path towards liberty is open. Any return

---

[1] *Capital*, tome i. p. 327, col. 1.

[2] *Natural*, in the Marxian sense, is that which resembles a physical movement as opposed to the idea of creation by an intelligent will; for the deists of the eighteenth century, *natural* was that which had been created by God, and which was both primitive and excellent; this is still, it seems, the view of G. de Molinari.

[3] In a very advanced capitalist régime questions of agricultural rights, women's dowries, the division of landed property go into the background; the first place is occupied by commercial associations, bills of exchange, sale of stocks and shares, etc.

to the past seems to them a crime against science, law, and human dignity.

Socialism looks upon this evolution as being a history of middle-class force, and it only sees differences of degree where the economists imagine that they are discovering difference of kind. Whether force manifests itself under the aspect of historical acts of coercion, or of fiscal oppression, or of conquest, or labour legislation, or whether it is wholly bound up with the economic system, it is always a middle-class force labouring with more or less skill to bring about the capitalist order of society.

Marx endeavoured to describe the details of this evolution very carefully ; he gave very little detail, however, about the organisation of the proletariat. This gap in his work has often been explained. He found in England an enormous mass of materials concerning the history of capitalism, which was fairly well arranged, and which had already been discussed by economists ; he was therefore able to investigate thoroughly the different peculiarities of middle-class evolution, but he was not very well furnished with matter on which he could argue about the organisation of the proletariat ; he was obliged, therefore, to remain content with an explanation, in very abstract formulas, of his ideas on the subject of the path which the proletariat must take, in order to arrive at the final revolutionary struggle. The consequence of this inadequacy of Marx's work was that Marxism has deviated from the path assigned to it by its real nature.

The people who pride themselves on being orthodox Marxians have made no attempt to add anything essential to what their master has written, and they have always imagined that, in order to argue about the proletariat, they must make use of what they had learned from the history of middle-class development. They have never suspected, th efore, that a distinction should be drawn between the *force* that aims at authority, endeavouring to bring about an automatic obedience, and the *violence* that would smash that authority. According to them, the proletariat must acquire force just as the middle class acquired it, use it as the latter used it, and end finally by establishing a Socialist State which will replace the middle-class State.

As the State formerly played a most important part in the revolutions which abolished the old economic systems, so it must again be the State which should abolish capitalism. The workers should therefore sacrifice every-thing to one end alone—that of putting into power men who promise them solemnly to ruin capitalism for the benefit of the people ; that is how a Parliamentary Socialist party is formed. Former militant Socialists provided with modest jobs, middle-class people, educated, frivolous, and eager to be in the public eye, and Stock Exchange speculators imagine that a golden age might spring up for them as the result of a cautious—a very cautious—revolution, which would not seriously disturb the traditional State. Quite naturally, these future masters of the world harbour the thought of reproducing the history of middle-class force, and they are organising themselves so that they may be able to draw the greatest possible profit from this revolution. Quite a number of such people might find a place in the new hierarchy, and what Paul Leroy Beaulieu calls the " Fourth Estate " would become really a *lower middle class*.[1]

The whole future of democracy might easily depend

---

[1] In an article in the *Radical* (January 2, 1906), Ferdinand Buisson shows that those classes of workers who are more favoured at the present time will continue to rise above the others ; the miners, the railway workers, employees in the State factories or municipal services who are well organised form a " working-class aristocracy," which succeeds all the more easily because it has continually to discuss all kinds of affairs with corporative bodies who " stand for the recognition of the rights of man, national supremacy, and the authority of universal suffrage." Beneath this nonsense is to be found merely the recognition of the relationship existing between politicians and obsequious followers.

on this *lower middle class*, which hopes to make use of the strength of the really proletarian organisations for its own great personal advantage.[1] The politicians believe that this class will always have peaceful tendencies, that it may be organised and disciplined, and that since the leaders of such sane syndicates understand equally with the politicians the action of the State, this class will form an excellent body of followers. They would like to make use of it to govern the proletariat; it is for this reason that Ferdinand Buisson and Jaurès are in favour of syndicates of the minor grades of civil servants, who, entering the *Bourses du Travail*, would inspire the proletariat with the idea of imitating their own feeble and peaceful attitude.

The political general strike concentrates the whole of this conception into one easily understood picture: it shows us how the State would lose nothing of its strength, how the transmission of power from one privileged class to another would take place, and how the mass of the producers would merely change masters. These new masters would very probably be less able than those of to-day; they would make more flowery speeches than the capitalists, but there is every evidence that they would be much harder and much more insolent than their predecessors.

The *new school* approaches the question from quite another point of view : it cannot accept the idea that the historical mission of the proletariat is to imitate the middle class ; it cannot conceive that a revolution as vast as that which would abolish capitalism could be attempted for a trifling and doubtful result, for a change of masters, for the satisfaction of theorists, politicians,

[1] " A portion of the nation throwing in its lot with the proletariat to demand its just rights," says Maxime Leroy, in a book devoted to the defence of the syndicates of civil servants (*Les Transformations de la puissance publique*, p. 216).

and speculators—all worshippers and exploiters of the State. It does not wish to restrict itself to the formulas of Marx ; although he gave no other theory than that of middle-class force, that, in its eyes, is no reason why it should confine itself to a scrupulous imitation of middle-class force.

In the course of his revolutionary career, Marx was not always happily inspired, and too often he followed inspirations which belong to the past ; he even allowed from time to time a quantity of old rubbish which he found in the Utopists to creep into his writings. The *new school* does not in the least feel itself bound to admire the illusions, the faults, and the errors of the man who did so much to work out revolutionary ideas ; it endeavours to separate what disfigures the work of Marx from what will immortalise his name ; its attitude is thus the reverse of that of official Socialists, who admire especially in Marx that which is not Marxian. We shall therefore attach no importance whatever to the numerous extracts which may be quoted against us to prove that Marx often understood history as the politicians do.

We know now the reason for his attitude : he did not know the distinction, which appears to us nowadays so obvious, between middle-class force and proletarian violence, because he did not move in circles which had acquired a satisfactory notion of the general strike.[1] We now possess sufficient material to enable us to understand the Syndicalist strike as thoroughly as we do the political strike ; we know what differentiates the proletarian movement from the older middle-class movement ; we find in the attitude of the revolutionaries towards the

[1] The inadequacy of, and the errors contained in Marx's work in respect to everything concerning the revolutionary organisation of the proletariat may be cited as memorable examples of that law which prevents us from *thinking* anything but that which has actual bases in life. Let us not confuse *thought* and *imagination.*

State a means of elucidating ideas which were still very confused in Marx's mind.

The method which has served us to mark the difference which exists between middle-class force and proletarian violence may also serve to solve many questions which crop up in the course of researches about the organisation of the proletariat. In comparing attempts to organise the Syndicalist strike, and attempts to organise the political strike, we may often judge what is good and what is bad, *i.e.* what is specifically socialistic and what has middle-class tendencies.

Popular education, for example, seems to be wholly carried on in a middle-class spirit ; history shows us that the whole effort of capitalism has been to bring about the submission of the masses to the conditions of the capitalist economic system, so that society might become an organism ; the whole revolutionary effort tends to create *free men*, but democratic rulers adopt as their mission the accomplishment of the *moral unity* of France. This moral unity is the automatic discipline of the producers, who would doubtless be happy to work for the glory of their intellectual leaders.

It may be said, too, that the greatest danger which threatens Syndicalism would be an attempt to imitate democracy ; it would be better for it to remain content for a time with weak and chaotic organisations rather than that it should fall beneath the sway of syndicates which would copy the political forms of the middle class.

The revolutionary Syndicalists have never yet made that mistake, because those who seek to lead them into an imitation of middle-class methods happen to be adversaries of the Syndicalist general strike, and have thus stood confessed as enemies.

CHAPTER VI

THE ETHICS OF VIOLENCE

I

THERE are so many legal precautions against violence, and our upbringing is directed towards so weakening our tendencies towards violence, that we are instinctively inclined to think that any act of violence is a manifestation of a return to barbarism. Peace has always been considered the greatest of blessings and the essential condition of all material progress, and it is for this reason that industrial societies have so often been contrasted favourably with military ones. This last point of view explains why, almost uninterruptedly since the eighteenth century, economists have been in favour of strong central authorities, and have troubled little about political liberties. Condorcet levels this reproach at the followers of Quesnay, and Napoleon III. had probably no greater admirer than Michel Chevalier.[1]

It may be questioned whether there is not a little stupidity in the admiration of our contemporaries for gentle methods. I see, in fact, that several authors, remarkable for their perspicacity and their interest in the ethical side of every question, do not seem to have the same fear of violence as our official professors.

P. Bureau was extremely surprised to find in Norway a rural population which had remained profoundly Christian. The peasants, nevertheless, carried a dagger at their belt ; when a quarrel ended in a stabbing affray, the police enquiry generally came to nothing for lack of witnesses ready to come forward and give evidence.

The author concludes thus : " In men, a soft and effeminate character is more to be feared than their feeling of independence, however exaggerated and brutal, and a stab given by a man who is virtuous in his morals, but violent, is a social evil less serious and more easily curable than the excessive profligacy of young men reputed to be more civilised." [2]

I borrow a second example from P. de Rousiers, who, like P. Bureau, is a fervent Catholic and interested especially in the moral side of all questions. He narrates how, towards 1860, the country of Denver, the great mining centre of the Rocky Mountains, was cleared of the bandits who infested it ; the American magistracy being impotent, courageous citizens undertook the work. " Lynch law was frequently put into operation ; a man accused of murder or of theft might be arrested, condemned and hanged in less than a quarter of an hour, if

[1] " One day Michel Chevalier came beaming into the editorial room of the *Journal des débats*. His first words were : ' I have achieved liberty ! ' Everybody was all agog ; he was asked to explain. He meant the liberty of the slaughter-houses " (Renan, *Feuilles détachées*, p. 149).

[2] P. Bureau, *Le Paysan des fjords de Norwège*, pp. 114 and 115.

an energetic Vigilance Committee could get hold of him. The American who happens to be honest has one excellent habit—he does not allow himself to be crushed on the pretext that he is virtuous. A law-abiding man is not necessarily a craven, as is often the case with us ; on the contrary, he is convinced that his interests ought to be considered before those of an habitual criminal or of a gambler. Moreover, he possesses the necessary energy to resist, and the kind of life which he leads makes him capable of resisting effectively, even of taking the initiative and the responsibility of a serious step when circumstances demand it. . . . Such a man, placed in a new country, full of natural resources, wishing to take advantage of the riches it contains and to acquire a superior situation in life by his labour, will not hesitate to suppress, in the name of the higher interests he represents, the bandits who compromise the future of this country. That is why, twenty-five years ago at Denver, so many corpses were dangling above the little wooden bridge thrown across Cherry Creek." [1]

This is a considered opinion of P. de Rousiers, for he returns elsewhere to this question. " I know," he says, " that lynch law is generally considered in France as a symptom of barbarism . . . ; but if honest virtuous people in Europe think thus, virtuous people in America think quite otherwise." [2] He highly approved of the Vigilance Committee of New Orleans which, in 1890, " to the great satisfaction of all virtuous people," hanged *maffiosi* acquitted by the jury.[3]

In Corsica, at the time when the *vendetta* was the regular means of supplying the deficiencies or correcting the action of a too halting justice, the people do not appear to have

---

[1] De Rousiers, *La Vie américaine : ranches, fermes et usines*, pp. 224-225.
[2] De Rousiers, *La Vie américaine, l'education et la société*, p. 218.
[3] De Rousiers, *loc. cit.* p. 221.

been less moral than to-day. Before the French conquest, Kabylie had no other means of punishment but private vengeance, yet the Kabyles were not a bad people.

It may be conceded to those in favour of mild methods that violence may hamper economic progress, and even, when it goes beyond a certain limit, that it is a danger to morality. This concession cannot be used as an argument against the doctrine set forth here, because I consider violence only from the point of view of its influence on social theories. It is, in fact, certain that a great development of brutality accompanied by much blood-letting is quite unnecessary in order to induce the workers to look upon economic conflicts as the reduced facsimiles of the great battle which will decide the future. If a capitalist class is energetic, it is constantly affirming its determination to defend itself ; its frank and consistently reactionary attitude contributes at least as greatly as proletarian violence towards keeping distinct that cleavage between the classes which is the basis of all Socialism.

We may make use here of the great historical example provided by the persecutions which Christians were obliged to suffer during the first centuries. Modern authors have been so struck by the language of the Fathers of the Church, and by the details given in the Acts of the Martyrs, that they have generally imagined the Christians as outlaws whose blood was continually being spilt. The cleavage between the pagan world and the Christian world was extraordinarily well marked ; without this cleavage the latter would never have acquired all its characteristic features ; but this cleavage was maintained by a combination of circumstances very different from that formerly imagined.

Nobody believes any longer that the Christians took refuge in subterranean quarries in order to escape the searches of the police ; the catacombs were dug out at great expense by communities with large resources at their disposal, under land belonging generally to powerful families which protected the new cult. Nobody has any doubt now that before the end of the first century Christianity had its followers among the Roman aristocracy ; " in the very ancient catacomb of Priscilla . . . has been found the family vault in which was buried from the first to the fourth century the Christian line of the Acilii." [1] It seems also that the old belief that the number of the martyrdoms was very great must be abandoned.

Renan still asserted that the literature of martyrdom should be taken seriously. " The details of the Acts of the Martyrs," he said, " may be false for the most part ; the dreadful picture which they unroll before us was nevertheless a reality. The true nature of this terrible struggle has often been misconceived, but its seriousness has not been exaggerated." [2] The researches of Harnack lead to quite another conclusion : the language of the Christian authors was entirely disproportionate to the actual importance of the persecutions ; there were very few martyrs before the middle of the third century. Tertullian is the writer who has most strongly indicated the horror which the new religion felt for its persecutors, and yet here is what Harnack says : " If, with the help of the works of Tertullian, we consider Carthage and Northern Africa we shall find that before the year 180 there was in those regions no case of martyrdom, and that from that year to the death of Tertullian (after 220), and adding Numidia and the Mauritanias, scarcely more than two dozen could be counted." [3] It must be remembered that at that time there was in Africa a rather large number of Montanists, who extolled the glory of martyrdom,

---

[1] P. Allard, *Dix leçons sur le martyre,* p. 171.
[2] Renan, *Église chrétienne,* p. 137.
[3] P. Allard, *op. cit.* p. 137.

and denied that any one had the right to fly from persecution.

P. Allard combats Harnack's proposition with arguments which seem to me somewhat weak.[1] He is unable to understand the enormous difference which probably exists between the reality of the persecutions and the conceptions which the persecuted formed of them. " The Christians," says the German professor, " were able to complain of being persecuted flocks, and yet such persecution was exceptional ; they were able to look upon themselves as models of heroism, and yet they were rarely put to the proof " ; and I call attention to the end of this sentence : " They were able to place themselves above the grandeurs of the world, and yet at the same time to make themselves more and more at home in it." [2]

There is something paradoxical at first sight in the situation of the Church, which had its followers in the upper classes, who were obliged to make many concessions to custom, and who yet could hold beliefs based on the idea of an absolute cleavage. The inscriptions on the catacomb of Priscilla prove " the continuance of the faith through a series of generations of the Acilii, among whom were to be found not only consuls and magistrates of the highest order, but also priests, priestesses, even children, members of illustrious idolatrous colleges, reserved by privilege for patricians and their sons." [3] If the Christian system of ideas had been rigorously based on actual facts, such a paradox would have been impossible.

The statistics of persecutions therefore play no great part in this question ; what was of much greater importance than the frequency of the torments were the remarkable occurrences which took place during the scenes of

---

[1] *Revue des questions historiques*, July 1905.

[2] P. Allard, *op. cit.* p. 142. Cf. what I have said in *Le Système historique de Renan*, pp. 312-315.

[3] P. Allard, *op. cit.* p. 206.

martyrdom. The Christian ideology was based on these rather rare but very heroic events ; there was no necessity for the martyrdoms to be numerous in order to prove, by the test of experience, the absolute truth of the new religion and the absolute error of the old, to establish thus that there were two incompatible ways, and to make it clear that the reign of evil would come to an end. " In spite of the small number of martyrs," says Harnack, " we may estimate at its true value the courage needed to become a Christian and to live as one. Above all else we ought to praise the conviction of the martyr whom a word or a gesture could save, and who preferred death to such freedom." [1] Contemporaries who saw in martyrdom a *judicial proof*, testifying to the honour of Christ,[2] drew from these facts quite other conclusions than those which a modern historian, whose mind runs in modern grooves, might draw from them ; no ideology was ever more remote from the facts than that of the early Christians.

The Roman administration dealt very severely with any one who showed a tendency to disturb the public peace, especially with any accused person who defied its majesty. In striking down from time to time a few Christians who had been denounced to it (for reasons which have generally remained hidden from us) it did not think that it was accomplishing an act which would ever interest posterity ; it seems that the general public itself hardly ever took any great notice of these punishments ; and this explains why the persecutions left scarcely any trace on pagan literature. The pagans had no reason to attach to martyrdom the extraordinary importance which the faithful and those who already sympathised with them attached to it.

This ideology would certainly not have been formed

---

[1] P. Allard, *op. cit.* p. 142.
[2] G. Sorel, *Le Système historique de Renan*, pp. 335-336.

in so paradoxical a manner had it not been for the firm belief that people had in the catastrophes described by the numerous apocalypses which were composed at the end of the first century and at the beginning of the second ; it was the conviction of all that the world was to be delivered up completely to the reign of evil, and that Christ would then come and give the final victory to His elect.   Any case of persecution borrowed from the mythology of the Antichrist something of its dread dramatic character ; instead of being valued on its actual importance as a misfortune which had befallen a few individuals, a lesson for the community, or a temporary check on propaganda, it became an incident of the war carried on by *Satan, prince of this world,* who was soon to reveal his Antichrist.   Thus the cleavage sprang at the same time from the persecutions and from the feverish expectation of a decisive battle.   When Christianity had developed sufficiently, the apocalyptic literature ceased to be cultivated to any extent ; although the root idea contained therein still continued to exercise its influence, the Acts of the Martyrs were drawn up in such a way that they might excite the same feelings that the apocalypses excited ; it may be said that they replaced these : [1] we sometimes find in the literature of the persecutions, set down as clearly as in the apocalypses, the horror which the faithful felt for the ministers of Satan who persecuted them.[2]

It is possible, therefore, to conceive Socialism as being perfectly revolutionary, although there may only be a few short conflicts, provided that these have strength enough to evoke the idea of the general strike : all the

[1] It is probable that the first Christian generation had no clear idea of the possibility of replacing the apocalypses imitated from Jewish literature by the Acts of the Martyrs ; this would explain why we possess no accounts prior to the year 155 (letter of Smyrniotes telling of the death of Saint Polycarpe), and why all memory of a certain number of very ancient Roman martyrs has been lost.

[2] *Marc Aurèle,* p. 500.

events of the conflict will then appear under a magnified
form, and the idea of catastrophe being maintained, the
cleavage will be perfect. Thus one objection often urged
against revolutionary Socialism may be set aside—there
is no danger of civilisation succumbing under the consequences of a development of brutality, since the idea
of the general strike may foster the notion of the class
war by means of incidents which would appear to middle-
class historians as of small importance.

When the governing classes, no longer daring to govern,
are ashamed of their privileged situation, are eager to
make advances to their enemies, and proclaim their horror
of all cleavage in society, it becomes much more difficult
to maintain in the minds of the proletariat this idea of
cleavage which without Socialism cannot fulfil its historical
rôle. So much the better, declare the *worthy progressives* ;
we may then hope that the future of the world will not
be left in the hands of brutes who do not even respect the
State, who laugh at the lofty ideas of the middle class,
and who have no more admiration for the professional
expounders of lofty thought than for priests. Let us
therefore do more and more every day for the disinherited,
say these gentlemen ; let us show ourselves more Christian,
more philanthropic, or more democratic (according to the
temperament of each) ; let us unite for the accomplishment of *social duty*. We shall thus get the better of these
dreadful Socialists, who think it possible to destroy the
prestige of the Intellectuals now that the Intellectuals
have destroyed that of the Church. As a matter of fact,
these cunning moral combinations have failed ; it is not
difficult to see why.

The specious reasoning of these gentlemen—the
pontiffs of " social duty "—supposes that violence cannot
increase, and may even diminish in proportion as the
Intellectuals unbend to the masses and make platitudes

and grimaces in honour of the union of the classes. Unfortunately for these great thinkers, things do not happen in this way ; violence does not diminish in the proportion that it should diminish according to the principles of advanced sociology. There are, in fact, Socialist scoundrels, who, profiting by middle-class cowardice, entice the masses into a movement which every day becomes less like that which ought to result from the sacrifices consented to by the middle class in order to obtain peace. If they dared, the sociologists would declare that the Socialists cheat and use unfair methods, so little do the facts come up to their expectations.

However, it was only to be expected that the Socialists would not allow themselves to be beaten without having used all the resources which the situation offered them. People who have devoted their life to a cause which they identify with the regeneration of the world, could not hesitate to make use of any weapon which might serve to develop to a greater degree the spirit of the class war, seeing that greater efforts were being made to suppress it. Existing social conditions favour the production of an infinite number of acts of violence, and there has been no hesitation in urging the workers not to refrain from brutality when this might do them service. Philan-thropic members of the middle class having given a kindly reception to members of the syndicates who were willing to come and discuss matters with them, in the hope that these workmen, proud of their aristocratic acquaintances, would give peaceful advice to their comrades, it is not to be wondered their fellow-workmen soon suspected them of treachery when they became upholders of " social reform." Finally, and this is the most remarkable fact in the whole business, anti-patriotism becomes an essential element of the Syndicalist programme.[1]

[1] As we consider everything from the historical point of view, it is of small importance to know what reasons were actually in the mind of

The introduction of anti-patriotism into the working-class movement is all the more remarkable because it came just when the Government was about to put its theories about the solidarity of the classes into practice. It was in vain that Léon Bourgeois approached the proletariat with particularly amiable airs and graces ; in vain that he assured the workers that capitalist society was one great family, and that the poor had a right to share in the general riches ; he maintained that the whole of contemporary legislation was directed towards the application of the principles of solidarity ; the proletariat replied to him by denying the social compact in the most brutal fashion—by denying the duty of patriotism. At the moment when it seemed that a means of suppressing the class war had been found, behold, it springs up again in a particularly displeasing form.[1]

Thus all the efforts of the *worthy progressives* only brought about results in flat contradiction with their aims ; it is enough to make one despair of sociology ! If they had any common sense, and if they really desired to protect society against an increase of brutality, they would not drive the Socialists into the necessity of adopting the tactics which are forced on them to-day ; they would remain quiet instead of devoting themselves to " social duty " ; they would bless the propagandists of the general strike, who, as a matter of fact, endeavour to *render the maintenance of Socialism compatible with the minimum of brutality.* But these *well-intentioned* people are not blessed with common sense ; and they have yet to suffer many blows, many humiliations, and many losses

the first apostles of anti-patriotism; reasons of this kind are almost never the right ones ; the essential thing is that for the revolutionary workers anti-patriotism appears an inseparable part of Socialism.

[1] This propaganda produced results which went far beyond the expectations of its promoters, and which would be inexplicable without the revolutionary idea.

of money, before they decide to allow Socialism to follow its own course.

II

We must now carry our investigations farther, and enquire what are the motives behind the great aversion felt by moralists for acts of violence ; a very brief summary of a few very curious changes which have taken place in the manners of the working classes is first of all indispensable.

A. I observe, in the first place, that nothing is more remarkable than the change which has taken place in the methods of bringing up children ; formerly it was believed that the rod was the most necessary instrument of the schoolmaster ; nowadays corporal punishments have disappeared from our public elementary schools. I believe that the competition which the latter had to maintain against the Church schools played a very great part in this progress ; the Brothers applied the old principles of clerical pedagogy with extreme severity ; and these, as is well known, involve an excessive amount of corporal punishment inflicted for the purpose of taming the demon who prompted so many of the child's bad habits.[1] The Government was intelligent enough to set up in opposition to this barbarous system a milder form of education which brought it a great deal of sympathy ; it is not at all improbable that the severity of clerical punishments is largely responsible for the present tumult of hatred against which the Church is struggling with such difficulty.   In 1901 I wrote : " If (the Church) were well advised, it would suppress entirely that part of its activities which is devoted to children ; it would do away

[1] Cf. Renan, *Histoire du peuple d'Israël*, tome iv. pp. 289 and 296 ; Y. Guyot, *La Morale*, pp. 212-215 ; Alphonse Daudet, *Numa Roumestan*, chap. iv.

with its schools and workshops ; it would thus do away with the principal sources of anti-clericalism : far from showing any desire to adopt this course, it seems to be its intention to develop these establishments still further, and thus it is laying up for itself still further opportunities for displays of popular hatred for the clergy." [1] What has happened since 1901 surpasses my forecast.

In factories and workshops customs of great brutality formerly existed, especially in those where it was necessary to employ men of superior strength, to whom was given the name of *"grosses culottes"* (big breeches) ; in the end these men managed to get entrusted with the task of engaging other men, because " any individual taken on by others was subjected to an infinite number of humiliations and insults " ; the man who wished to enter *their* workshop had to buy them drink, and on the following day to treat all his fellow-workers. " The notorious *When's it to be ? (Quand est-ce ?)* [2] would be started ; everybody gets tipsy. . . . *When's it to be ?* is the devourer of savings ; in a workshop where *When's it to be ?* is the custom, you must stand your turn or beware." Denis Poulot, from whom I borrow these details, observes that machinery did away with the prestige of the *grosses culottes*, who were scarcely more than a memory when he wrote in 1870.[3]

The manners of the *compagnonnages* [4] (a kind of trade

---

[1] G. Sorel, *Essai sur l'église et l'état*, p. 63.

[2] *Quand est-ce ?* This was the question addressed to the new-comer in a workshop, to remind him that according to custom he must pay for drinks all round—" Pay your footing."

[3] Denis Poulot, *Le Sublime*, pp. 150-153. I quote from the edition of 1887. This author says that the *grosses culottes* very much hampered progress in the forges.

[4] The *compagnonnages* were very ancient workmen's associations, whose principal purpose was to enable carpenters, joiners, locksmiths, farriers, and others, to make a circular tour round France, in order to learn their trades thoroughly. In the towns on this circuit there was an hotel kept by the *Mère des compagnons* ; the newly arrived

union) were for a long time remarkable for their brutality. Before 1840 there were constant brawls, often ending in bloodshed, between groups with different rites. Martin Saint Léon, in his book on the *compagnonnage*, gives extracts from really barbarous songs.[1] Initiation into the lodge was accompanied by the severest tests ; young men were treated as if they were pariahs in the " *Devoirs de Jacques et de Subise* " :[2] " *Compagnons* (carpenters) have been known," says Perdiguier, " to call themselves the Scourge of the Foxes (candidates for admission), the Terror of the Foxes. . . . In the provinces, a ' fox ' rarely works in the towns ; he is hunted back, as they say, into the brushwood." [3] There were many secessions when the tyranny of the companions came into opposition with the more liberal habits which prevailed in society. When the workers were no longer in need of protection, especially for the purpose of finding work, they were no longer so willing to submit to the demands which had formerly seemed to be of little consequence in comparison with the advantages of the *compagnonnage*. The struggle for work more than once brought candidates into opposition with companions who wished to reserve certain privileges.[4] We might find still other reasons to explain

workman was received there and the older men found him work. The *compagnonnages* are now in a state of decay.

[1] Martin Saint-Léon, *Le Compagnonnage*, pp. 115, 125, 270-273, 277-278.

[2] Each trade possessed often several rival associations of workmen, which often engaged each other in bloody combats. Each association was called a *Devoir*. What was intended by *de Jacques* and *de Subise* has long been forgotten. They are traditional words indicating the rules, and so by extension, the associations which follow these rules.

[3] Martin Saint-Léon, *op. cit.* p. 97. Cf. pp. 91-92, p. 107.

[4] In 1823, the companion joiners claimed La Rochelle as theirs, a town which they had for a long time neglected as being of too little importance ; they had previously only stopped at Nantes and Bordeaux (Martin Saint-Léon, *op. cit.* p. 103). *L'Union des travailleurs du tour de France* was formed in 1830 to 1832 as a rival organisation to the

the decline of an institution which, while rendering many important services, had contributed very much to maintaining the idea of brutality.

Everybody agrees that the disappearance of these old brutalities is an excellent thing. From this opinion it was so easy to pass to the idea that all violence is an evil, that this step was bound to have been taken ; and, in fact, the great mass of the people, who are not accustomed to thinking, have come to this conclusion, which is accepted nowadays as a dogma by the *bleating herd* of moralists. They have not asked themselves what there is in brutality which is reprehensible.

When we no longer remain content with current stupidity we discover that our ideas about the disappearance of violence depend much more on a very important transformation which has taken place in the criminal world than on ethical principles. I shall endeavour to prove this.

B. Middle-class scientists are very chary of touching on anything relating to the dangerous classes ;[1] that is one of the reasons why their observations on the history of morals always remain superficial ; it is not very difficult to see that it is a knowledge of these classes which alone enables us to penetrate the mysteries of the moral thought of peoples.

The dangerous classes of past times practised the simplest form of offence, that which was nearest to hand, that which is nowadays left to groups of young scoundrels without experience and without judgment. Offences of brutality seem to us nowadays something abnormal ; so

---

compagnonnage, following the refusals with which the latter had met a few rather modest demands for reforms presented by the candidates for election (pp. 108-116, 126, 131).

[1] On March 30, 1906, Mє ⸱3 said in the Senate : " We cannot write in a legal text that prostitution *exists* in France for both sexes."

much so, that when the brutality has been great we often
ask ourselves whether the culprit is in possession of all
his senses.　This transformation has evidently not come
about because criminals have become moral, but because
they have changed their method of procedure to suit
the new economic conditions, as we shall see farther on.
This change has had the greatest influence on popular
thought.

We all know that by using brutality, associations of
criminals manage to maintain excellent discipline among
themselves.　When we see a child ill-treated we instinctively suppose that its parents have criminal habits.　The
methods used by the old schoolmasters, which the ecclesiastical houses persist in preserving, are those of vagabonds
who steal children to make clever acrobats or interesting
beggars of them.　Everything which reminds us of the
habits of dangerous classes of former times is extremely
odious to us.

There is a tendency for the old ferocity to be replaced
by cunning, and many sociologists believe that this is a
real progress.　Some philosophers who are not in the habit
of following the opinions of the herd, do not see exactly
how this constitutes progress, from the point of view of
morals : " If we are revolted by the cruelty, by the
brutality of past times," says Hartmann, " it must not
be forgotten that uprightness, sincerity, a lively sentiment
of justice, pious respect before holiness of morals characterised the ancient peoples ; while nowadays we see
predominant lies, duplicity, treachery, the spirit of
chicane, the contempt for property, disdain for instinctive
probity and legitimate customs—the value of which is
not even understood.[1]　Robbery, deceit, and fraud

[1] Hartmann here bases his statements on the authority of the
English naturalist Wallace, who has greatly praised the simplicity of
life among the Malays ; there must surely be a considerable element of
exaggeration in this praise, although other travellers have made similar
observations about some of the tribes of Sumatra.　Hartmann wishes

increase in spite of legal repression more rapidly than brutal and violent crimes, like pillage, murder, and rape, etc., decrease. Egoism of the basest kind shamelessly breaks the sacred bonds of the family and friendship in every case in which these oppose its desires." [1]

At the present time money losses are generally looked upon as accidents to which we are constantly exposed and easily made good again, while bodily accidents are not so easily reparable. Fraud is therefore regarded as infinitely less serious than brutality ; criminals benefit from this change which has come about in legal sentences.

Our penal code was drawn up at a time when the citizen was pictured as a rural proprietor occupied solely with the administration of his property, as a good family man, saving to secure an honourable position for his children ; large fortunes made in business, in politics, or by speculation were rare and were looked on as real monstrosities ; the defence of the savings of the middle classes was one of the first concerns of the legislator. The previous judicial system had been still more severe in the punishment of fraud, for a royal declaration of August 5, 1725, punished a fraudulent bankrupt with death ; it would be difficult to imagine anything further removed from our customs. We are now inclined to consider that offences of this sort can, as a rule, only be committed as the result of the imprudence of the victims, and that it is only exceptionally that they deserve severe penalties ; we, on the contrary, content ourselves with light punishment.

In a rich community where business is on a very large scale, and in which everybody is wide awake in defence of his own interests, as in America, crimes of fraud never have the same consequences as in a community which is forced to practise rigid economy ; as a matter of fact,

---

to show that there is no progress towards happiness, and this pre-occupation leads him to exaggerate the happiness of the ancients.

[1] Hartmann, *Philosophy of the Unconscious*, French trans., pp. 464-465.

these crimes seldom cause a serious and lasting disturbance in the economic system ; it is for this reason that Americans put up with the excesses of their politicians and financiers with so little complaint.   P. de Rousiers compares the American to the captain of a ship who, during a dangerous voyage, has no time to look after his thieving cook. " When you point out to Americans that they are being robbed by their politicians, they usually reply, ' Of course we are quite aware of that !   But as long as business is good and politicians do not get in the way, it will not be very difficult for them to escape the punishment they deserve.' " [1]

In Europe also, since it has become easy to gain money, ideas, analogous to those current in America, have spread among us.   Great company promoters have been able to escape punishment because in their hour of success they were clever enough to make friends in all circles.   We have finally come to believe that it would be extremely unjust to condemn bankrupt merchants and lawyers who retire ruined after moderate catastrophes, while the princes of financial swindling continue to lead gay lives.   Gradually the new industrial system has created a new and extraordinary indulgence for all crimes of fraud in the great capitalist countries.[2]

In those countries where the old parsimonious and non-speculative family economy still prevails, the relative estimation of acts of fraud and acts of brutality has not followed the same evolution as in America, England, and France ; this is why Germany has preserved so many of the customs of former times,[3] and does not feel the same

[1] De Rousiers, *La Vie américaine : l'éducation et la société*, p. 217.

[2] Several small countries have adopted these ideas, thinking by such imitation to reach the greatness of the large countries.

[3] It must be noticed that in Germany there are so many Jews in the world of speculation that American ideas do not spread very easily. The majority look upon the speculator as a *foreigner who is robbing the nation.*

horror that we do for brutal punishments ; these never seem to them, as they do to us, only suitable to the most dangerous classes.

Many philosophers have protested against this mitigation of sentences ; after what we have related earlier about Hartmann, we shall expect to meet him among those who protest. " We are already," he says, " approaching the time when theft and lying condemned by law will be despised as vulgar errors, as gross clumsiness, by the clever cheats who know how to preserve the letter of the law while infringing the rights of other people. For my part, I would much rather live amongst the ancient Germans, at the risk of being killed on occasion, than be obliged, as I am in modern cities, to look on every man as a swindler or a rogue unless I have evident proofs of his honesty."[1] Hartmann takes no account of economic conditions ; he argues from an entirely personal point of view, and never looks at what goes on round him. Nobody to-day wants to run the risk of being slain by ancient Germans ; fraud or a theft are very easily reparable.

C. Finally, in order to get to the heart of contemporary thought on this matter, it is necessary to examine the way in which the public judges the relations existing between the State and the criminal associations. Such relations have always existed ; these associations, after having practised violence, have ended by employing craft alone, or at least their acts of violence have become somewhat exceptional.

Nowadays we should think it very strange if the magistrates were to put themselves at the head of armed bands, as they did in Rome during the last years of the Republic. In the course of the Zola trial, the Anti-Semites recruited bands of paid demonstrators, who were commissioned to manifest patriotic indignation ; the Govern-

---

[1] Hartmann, *loc. cit.*, p. 465.

ment of Méline protected these antics, which for some
months had considerable success and helped considerably
in hindering a fair revision of the sentence on Dreyfus.

I believe that I am not mistaken in saying that these
tactics of the partisans of the Church have been the
principal cause of all the measures directed against
Catholicism since 1901 ; the middle-class liberals would
never have accepted these measures if they had not still
been under the influence of the fear they had felt during
the Dreyfus affair.   The chief argument which Clemenceau
used to stir up his followers to fight against the Church
was that of fear ; he never ceased to denounce the danger
which the Republic ran in the continued existence of the
Romish faction ; the laws about the congregations, about
education and the administration of the churches were
made with the object of preventing the Catholic party
again taking up its former warlike attitude, which Anatol
France so often compared to that of the League ; [1] they
were *laws inspired by fear*.   Many Conservatives felt this
so strongly that they regarded with displeasure the
resistance recently opposed to the inventories of churches ;
they considered that the employment of bands of *pious
apaches* would make the middle classes still more hostile
to their cause.[2]   It was not a little surprising to see
Brunetière, who had been one of the admirers of the anti-
Dreyfus apaches, advise submission ; this was because
experience had enlightened him as to the consequences
of violence.

[1] [The League was a political organisation directed by the partisans
of the Duc de Guise against the Protestants ; it resisted Henri IV. for
a considerable time.—*Trans. Note.*]

[2] At a meeting of the Municipal Council of Paris on March 26, 1906,
the Prefect of Police said that the resistance was organised by a committee sitting at 86. rue de Richelieu, which hired *pious apaches* at
between three and four francs a day.   He asserted that fifty-two
Parisian curés had promised him either to facilitate the inventories or
to be content with a merely passive resistance.   He accused the Catholic
politicians of having forced the hands of the clergy.

Associations which work by craft provoke no such reactions in the public ; in the time of the " clerical republic," [1] the society of Saint Vincent de Paul was an excellent centre of surveillance over officials of every order and grade ; it is not surprising, then, that free-masonry has been able to render services to the Radical Government of exactly the same kind as those which Catholic philanthropy was able to render to former Governments. The history of recent spying scandals has shown very plainly what the point of view of the country actually was.

When the nationalists obtained possession of the documents containing information about officers of the army, which had been compiled by the dignitaries of the masonic lodges, they believed that their opponents were lost ; the panic which prevailed in the Radical camp for some time seemed to justify their hopes, but before long the democracy showed only derision for what they called the " petty virtue " of those who publicly denounced the methods of General André and his accomplices. In those difficult days Henry Bérenger showed that he understood admirably the ethical standards of his contemporaries ; he did not hesitate to approve of what he called the " legitimate supervision of the governing classes exercised by the organisations of the vanguard " ; he denounced the cowardice of the Government which had " allowed those who had undertaken the difficult task of opposing the military caste and the Roman Church, of examining and denouncing them, to be branded as informers " (*Action*, Oct. 31, 1904) ; he loaded with insults the few Dreyfusards who dared to show their indignation ; the attitude of Joseph Reinach appeared particularly scandalous to him ; in his opinion the latter should have felt himself extremely honoured by being tolerated in the " League of the Rights of Man," which had decided at last to lead " the good

[1] [*I.e.* in the time when MacMahon was President.—*Trans. Note.*]

fight for the defence of rights of the citizen, sacrificed too
long to those of one man " (*Action*, Dec. 12, 1904). Finally,
a law of amnesty was voted declaring that no one wanted
to hear anything more of these trifles.

There was some opposition in the provinces,[1] but was
it very serious ?   I am inclined to think not, when I read
the documents published by Peguy in the ninth number
of the sixth series of his *Cahiers de la quinzaine*.   Several
people, accustomed to speaking a verbose, sonorous, and
nonsensical language, doubtless found themselves a little
uncomfortable under the smiles of the leading grocers and
eminent chemists who constituted the élite of the learned
and musical societies before which they had been
accustomed to hold forth on Justice, Truth, and Light.
They found it necessary to adopt a stoical attitude.

Could anything be finer than this passage from a letter
of Professor Bougle, an eminent doctor of social science,
which I find on page 13 : " I am very happy to learn that
at last the League is going to speak. *Its silence astonishes
and frightens us.*"   He must be a man who is easily
astonished and frightened ! Francis de Pressensé also
suffered some anxiety of mind—he is a specialist in that
kind of thing—but his feelings were of a very distinguished
kind, as is only proper for an aristocratic Socialist ; he
was afraid that democracy was threatened with a new
guillotine sèche,[2] resembling that which had done so
much harm to virtuous democrats during the Panama
scandal.[3]   When he saw that the public quietly accepted

[1] The people in the provinces are not, as a matter of fact, so
accustomed as the Parisians are to indulgence towards non-violent
trickery and brigandage.

[2] [" Dry guillotine," popular expression meaning persecution.—*Trans.*]

[3] *Cahiers de la quinzaine* 9th of the VIth series, p. 9. F. de Pressensé
was at the time of the Panama affair Hébrard's principal clerk ; we
know that the latter was one of the principal beneficiaries from the
Panama booty, but that has not injured his position in the eyes of
the austere Huguenots ; the *Temps* continues to be the organ of moderate
democracy and of the ministers of the Gospel.

the complicity of the Government with a philanthropic association which had turned into a criminal association, he hurled his avenging thunders against the protestors. Among the most comical of these protestors I pick out a political pastor of St-Etienne called L. Comte. He wrote, in the extraordinary language employed by the members of the League of the Rights of Man : " I had hoped that the [Dreyfus] affair would have definitely cured us of the moral malaria from which we suffer, and that it would have cleansed the republican conscience of the clerical virus with which it was impregnated. It has done nothing. We are more clerical than ever." [1] Accordingly this austere man remained in the League ! Protestant and middle-class logic ! It is always possible, you see, that the League might one of these days be able to render some small service to the deserving ministers of the Gospel.

I have insisted rather lengthily on these grotesque incidents because they seem to me to characterise very aptly the moral ideas of the people who claim to lead us. Henceforth it must be taken for granted that politico-criminal associations which work by craft have a recognised place in any democracy that has attained its maturity. P. de Rousiers believes that America will one day cure itself of the evils which result from the guilty manœuvres of its politicians. Ostrogorski, after making a long and minute inquiry into " Democracy, and the organisation of political parties," believes that he has found remedies which will enable modern states to free themselves from exploitation by political parties. These are platonic vows ; no historical experience justifies the hope that a democracy can be made to work in a capitalist country, without the criminal abuses experienced everywhere nowadays. When Rousseau demanded that the democracy should not tolerate the existence in its midst of any private association, he reasoned from his knowledge of the republics

[1] *Cahiers de la quinzaine, loc. cit.* p. 13.

of the Middle Ages ; he knew that part of history better than his contemporaries did, and was struck with the enormous part played at that time by the politico-criminal associations ; he asserted the impossibility of reconciling a rational democracy with the existence of such forces, but we ought to learn from experience that there is no way of bringing about their disappearance.[1]

III

The preceding explanations enable us to understand the ideas about the proper function of the worker's syndicates formed by the enlightened democrats and the *worthy progressives.* Waldeck-Rousseau has often been congratulated on having carried the law on syndicates in 1884. In order to give an account of what was expected from this law we must recall the situation of France at that epoch. Severe financial embarrassments had compelled the Government to sign agreements with the railway companies which the Radicals denounced as acts of brigandage ; the colonial policy gave opportunities for extremely violent attacks and was thoroughly unpopular ;[2] the discontent which a few years later took the form of Boulangism was already very marked, and in the elections of 1885 very nearly gave a majority to the Conservatives.

Waldeck-Rousseau, without being a very profound seer, was yet sharp enough to understand the danger which might threaten the opportunist republic, and cynical enough to look for a means of defence in a politico-

----

[1] Rousseau, stating the question in an abstract way, appeared to condemn every kind of association, and our Governments for a long time used his authority to subject every association to authority.

[2] In his *Morale*, published in 1883, Y. Guyot violently attacks this policy. " In spite of the disastrous experiences [of two centuries], we are taking Tunisia, we are on the point of going to Egypt, we are setting out for Tonkin, we dream of the conquest of Central Africa " (p. 339).

criminal association capable of checkmating the Conservatives.

At the time of the Empire the Government had tried to manipulate the benefit societies in such a way as to control the employés and a section of the artisans. Later on, it believed it might be possible to find, in the workmen's associations, a weapon with which it might be capable of ruining the authority which the Liberal party had with the people, and terrorising the rich classes, who had obstinately opposed the Government since 1863. Waldeck-Rousseau was inspired by these examples and hoped to organise among the workmen a hierarchy under the direction of the police.[1]

In a circular of August 25, 1884, Waldeck-Rousseau explained to the prefects that they ought not to confine themselves to their too limited function of enforcing respect for the law ; they must stimulate the spirit of association and " smooth away the difficulties which were bound to arise from inexperience and lack of practice in this new liberty," their task would be so much the more useful and important if they succeeded in inspiring greater confidence in the workmen ; in diplomatic terms the Minister advised them to undertake the moral leadership of the Syndicalist movement.[2] " Although the Government is not obliged by the law of 1884 to take any part in the search for the solutions of the great economic and social problems, it cannot be indifferent to them, and I am convinced that it is its duty to participate and to put its services and zeal at the disposal of all the parties

---

[1] I have pointed this out in the *Ère nouvelle*, March 1894, p. 339.

[2] According to the Socialist deputy, Marius Devèze, the Prefect du Gard undertook this leadership of the Syndicalist movement under the minister Combes (*Études socialistes*, p. 323). I find in the *France du Sud-Ouest* (January 25, 1904) a notice announcing that the Prefect of La Manche, delegated by the Government, together with the under-prefect, the mayor, and the municipality, officially inaugurated the Bourse du Travail at Cherbourg.

concerned." It will be necessary to act with a great deal of prudence so as " not to excite mistrust," to show the workmen's associations how very much the Government interests itself in their development, and to advise them " when they make applications." The prefects must prepare themselves for " this rôle of counsellor and *energetic collaborator* by a thorough study of legislation, and of the similar organisations which exist in France and abroad."

In 1884 the Government did not in the least foresee that the syndicates might participate in a great revolutionary agitation, and the circular spoke with a certain irony of " the hypothetical peril of an anti-social federation of the whole of the workers." Nowadays one is very tempted to smile at the ingenuousness of the man who has so often been represented to us as the *prince of cunning* ; but to account for his illusions it is necessary to go back to the writings of the democrats of that period. In 1887, in the preface to the third edition of *Sublime*, Denis Poulot, an experienced manufacturer, former mayor of the 11th arrondissement and a follower of Gambetta, said that the syndicates would kill strikes ; he believed that the revolutionaries had no serious influence on the organised workmen, and he saw in the primary schools a sure means of bringing about the disappearance of Socialism ; like nearly all the opportunists of that time, he was much more preoccupied with *blacks* than with *reds*.[1] Yves Guyot himself does not seem to have had much more insight than Waldeck-Rousseau, because in his *Morale* (1883) he considered collectivism to be merely a word, he denounced the existing legislation which " aims at hindering the organisation of workmen for the sale of their labour at the highest possible price and for the discussion of their interests," and he expected that what the syndicates would lead to would be the

[1] Blacks and reds—clericals and Socialists.

" organisation of the sale of labour on a wholesale basis."
He makes violent attacks on the priests, and the Chagot
family is denounced because it forces the miners of
Monceau to go to Mass.[1] Everybody then counted on
the working men's organisations to destroy the power
of the clerical party.

If the Waldeck-Rousseau had had the slightest fore-
sight, he would have perceived the advantage that the
Conservatives have tried to draw from the law on syndicates, with a view to attempting the restoration of *social
peace* in the country districts under their own leadership.
For several years the peril which the Republic ran in the
formation of an agrarian party has been denounced ; [2] the
result has not answered to the hopes of the promoters of
agricultural syndicates, but it might have been serious.
Waldeck-Rousseau never suspected it for an instant ; he
does not seem, in his circular, to have suspected even the
material services which the new associations would render
to agriculture.[3] If he had had any idea of what might come
to pass, he would have taken precautions in the drawing
up of the law ; it is certain that neither the minister who
drew up the law, nor the " rapporteur " [4] understood the
importance of the word " agricultural " which was introduced by means of an amendment proposed by D'Oudet,
the senator for Doubs.[5]

Workmen's associations directed by democrats, using
cunning, threats, and sometimes even a certain amount

[1] Y. Guyot, *Morale*, pp. 293, 183-184, 122, 148 and 320.

[2] De Rocquigny, *Les Syndicats agricoles et leur œuvre*, pp. 42, 391-394.

[3] This is all the more remarkable since the syndicates are represented
in the circular as *capable of aiding French industry* in its struggle against
foreign competition.

[4] [See note p. 80.—*Trans.*]

[5] It was thought to be merely a question of permitting agricultural
labourers to form themselves into syndicates ; Tolain declared, in the
name of the Committee, that he had never thought of excluding them
from the benefits of the new law (De Rocquigny, *op. cit.* p. 10). As a
rule, the agricultural syndicates have served as commercial agencies for
farm bailiffs, landowners, etc.

of violence, could have been of the greatest service to the Government in the struggle against the Conservatives, then so threatening.   Those people who have recently transformed Waldeck-Rousseau into the father of his country will probably protest against such a disrespectful interpretation of his policy ; but this interpretation will not seem altogether improbable to the people who remember the cynicism with which he, who is now repre- sented as a *great Liberal*, governed ; one had the impression that France was about to enter on a régime which would recall the follies, the luxuries, and the brutality of the Cæsars.   Moreover, when unforeseen circumstances brought back Waldeck-Rousseau to power, he immediately resumed his former policy and tried to use the syndicates against his adversaries.

In 1899 it was no longer possible to attempt to put the workmen's associations under the direction of the prefects in the way indicated by the circular of 1884 ; but there were other methods which might be tried, and in including Millerand in his ministry, Waldeck-Rousseau thought he had carried out a master-stroke.   As Millerand had been able to make himself the leader of the Socialists, who had, until then, been divided into irreconcilable groups, might he not become the *broker* who would discreetly manipulate the syndicates by influencing their leaders ?   Every means of seduction was employed in order to bring the workmen to reason, and to inspire them with confidence in the higher officials of the " Government of Republican Defence."

One cannot help being reminded of the policy that Napoleon, in signing the Concordat, intended to follow ; he had recognised that it would not be possible for him, as for Henry VIII., to directly influence the Church. "Failing that method," said Taine, " he adopts another, which leads to the same end.   He does not want to change the opinions of his people, he respects spiritual things and wishes to *control them without interfering with them* and without becoming entangled himself in them ; he wants to make them square with his policy, but by the influence of temporal things." [1] In the same way, Millerand was commissioned to assure the workmen that their Socialist convictions would not be interfered with ; the Government only wanted to direct the action of the syndicates and to make them fit in with its own policy.

Napoleon had said, " You will see how I shall be able to utilise the priests." [2] Millerand was instructed to gratify in every way the vanity of the leaders of the syndicates,[3] while the mission of the prefects was to induce the employers to grant material advantages to the workers ; it was thought that this Napoleonic policy would give results as considerable as those obtained from the policy pursued in regard to the Church. Dumay, the Minister of Public Worship, had succeeded in creating a docile episcopacy formed of men whom the ardent Catholics contemptuously called the *"préfets violets."* [4] Might it not be possible, by putting a shrewd principal clerk in the office of the minister, to create *"préfets rouges."* All this was fairly well thought out and corresponded perfectly with the kind of talent possessed by Waldeck-Rousseau, who was all his life a great partisan of the Concordat and was fond of negotiating with Rome. It was not unpleasing to him to negotiate with the *reds* ; the very originality of the enterprise would have been enough to charm a mind like his, that delighted in subtlety.

[1] Taine, *Le Régime moderne*, vol. ii. p. 10.

[2] Taine, *loc. cit.* p. 11.

[3] This is what Mme. Georges Renard very sensibly points out in her report of a workmen's fête given by Millerand (L. de Seilhac, *Le Monde socialiste*, p. 308).

[4] [*Préfets violets* ; this expression was used ironically by several papers to designate bishops who were too submissive to the Government. Catholic bishops wear a violet robe.—*Trans. Note.*]

In a speech on December 1, 1905, Marcel Sembat, who had been in a particularly good position to know how things happened in the time of Millerand, related several anecdotes which very much astounded the Chamber. He told them how the Government, in order to make itself disagreeable to the nationalist municipal councillors of Paris, and to reduce their influence on the Bourse du Travail,[1] had asked the syndicates "to make applications to it that would justify" the reorganisation of that establishment. A certain amount of scandal was caused by the march past of the red flags before the official platform at the inauguration of the monument to Dalou in the Place de la Nation. We now know that this happened as the result of negotiations ; the prefect of police had hesitated, but Waldeck-Rousseau had authorised these revolutionary ensigns. The fact that the Government denied having any relations with the syndicates is of no importance — a lie more or less would not trouble a politician of Waldeck-Rousseau's calibre.

The exposure of these manœuvres shows us that the ministry depended on the syndicates to frighten the Conservatives. Ever since then it has been easy to understand the attitude they have adopted in the course of several strikes : on the one hand, Waldeck-Rousseau proclaimed with great fervour the necessity of giving

[1] Millerand did not keep on the former Director of the *Office du Travail*, who was doubtless not pliant enough for the new policy. It seems to me to be clearly established that at that time considerable attention was being given in this Government department to a kind of enquiry as to the state of feeling among the militants of the syndicates, evidently in order to ascertain in what way they might be advised. This was revealed by Ch. Guieysse in the *Pages libres* of December 10, 1904 ; the protestations of the department and those of Millerand do not appear to have been very serious (*Voix du peuple*, December 18, 25, 1904, January 1, 1905, June 25, August 27). [The *Office du Travail* is a ministerial office, which makes enquiries about labour and publishes statistics ; it was created principally in the hope that it would serve to put the Government into connection with the leaders of the syndicates.—*Trans.*]

the protection of public force to every single workman who wished to·work in spite of the strikers ; on the other hand, he has more than once shut his eyes to acts of violence. The reason of this is, that he found it necessary to annoy and frighten the progressists,[1] and because he meant to reserve to himself the right of forcible intervention at the moment when his political interests require the disappearance of all disorder. In the precarious state of his authority in the country he believed it possible to govern only by fear and by imposing himself as the supreme arbitrator in industrial disputes.[2]

Since 1884 Waldeck-Rousseau's plan had been to transform the syndicates into politico-criminal associations which could serve as auxiliaries to the democratic Government. The syndicates were to play a part analogous to that played by the lodges, the latter being useful in spying on the officials, and the former designed to threatening the interests of those employers who were not on the side of the administration ; the freemasons being rewarded by decorations and favours given to their friends, the workmen being authorised to extract extra wages from their employers. This policy was simple and cheap.

In order that this system may work properly, a certain moderation in the conduct of the workmen is necessary. Not only must violence be used with discretion, but the workmen's demands also must not exceed certain limits. The same principles must be applied in this case as in the case of the bribery of politicians. Everybody approves

[1] It may be questioned whether Waldeck-Rousseau did not go too far, and thus started the Government on a very different road from that which he wanted it to take ; I do not think that the law about associations would have been voted except under the influence of fear, but it is certain that its final wording was much more anti-clerical than its promoter would have wished.

[2] In a speech on June 21, 1907, Charles Benoist complains that the Dreyfus case had thrown discredit on " reasons of State," and had led the Government to appeal to the elements of disorder in the nation in order to create order.

of that as long as the politicians are reasonable in their demands. People who are in business know that there is quite a complete art of bribery ; certain intermediaries have acquired a special skill in estimating the amount of the presents that should be offered to high officials, or to deputies who can get bills passed. If financiers are almost always obliged to have recourse to the services of specialists, there is all the more reason why the workmen, who are quite unaccustomed to the customs of this world, must need intermediaries to fix the sum which they can exact from their employers without exceeding reasonable limits.[1]

We are thus led to consider arbitration in an entirely new light and to understand it in a really scientific manner, since, instead of allowing ourselves to be duped by abstractions, we shall explain it by means of the dominant ideas of middle-class society, who invented it, and who want to impose it on the workers. It would be evidently absurd to go into a pork butcher's shop, order him to sell us a ham at less than the marked price, and then ask him to submit the question to arbitration ; but it is not absurd to promise to a group of employers the advantages to be derived from the fixity of wages for several years, and to ask the *specialists* what present remuneration this guarantee is worth ; this remuneration may be considerable if business is expected to be good during that time. Instead of bribing some influential person, the employers raise their workmen's wages ; from their point of view there is no difference. As for the Government, it becomes the benefactor of the people, and hopes that it will do well in the elections ; to the politician, the electoral advantages which result from a successful conciliation are worth more than a very large bribe.

It is easy to understand now why all politicians have

---

[1] I suppose that no one is ignorant of the fact that no important undertaking is carried through without bribery.

so great an admiration for arbitration ; it is because an
enterprise conducted without bribery is inconceivable to
them.   Many of our politicians are lawyers, and clients
who confide their cases to them attach great weight to
their Parliamentary influence.   It is for this reason that
a former Minister of Justice is always sure of getting
remunerative law-suits even when he is not very talented,
because he has means of influencing the magistrates, with
whose failings he is very familiar, and whom he could
ruin if he wished.   The great political advocates are sought
out by financiers who have serious difficulties to overcome
in the law courts, who are accustomed to bribe on a large
scale and in consequence pay royally.   The world of
employers thus appears to our rulers as a world of
adventurers, gamblers, and parasites of the stock exchange ; they consider that this rich and criminal class
must expect to submit from time to time to the demands
of other social groups.   Their conception of the ideal
capitalist society would be a *compromise between con-
flicting appetites under the auspices of political lawyers.*[1]

The Catholics would not be sorry, now they are in

[1] I borrow from a celebrated novel by Léon Daudet a description of
the character of the barrister Méderbe. " The latter was a curious
character, tall, thin, of a well-set-up figure, surmounted by a head like
a dead fish, green impenetrable eyes, oiled and flattened hair, his whole
appearance being frozen and rigid. . . . He had chosen the profession
of a barrister as being one which would supply his own and his wife's
need of money. . . . He took part chiefly in financial cases, on account
of the large profit to be made out of them, and of the secrets he learned
from them ; he was employed in such cases on account of his semi-
political, semi-judicial relations, which always secured him victory in
any case he pleaded. He charged fabulous fees. *What he was paid
for was certain acquittal.* This man then had enormous power. . . .
He gave one the impression of a *bandit armed* for social life and sure of
impunity. . . ." (*Les Morticoles*, pp. 287-288). It is clear that many
of these traits are copied from those of the man the Socialists so often
called the Eiffel barrister, before they made him the demi-god of
Republican Defence. [In the Panama affair, Eiffel was prosecuted for
having illegally appropriated a large sum. Waldeck-Rousseau defended
him in the law courts.—*Trans.*]

opposition, to find support in the working classes. It is not only flattery that they address to the workers, in order to convince them that it would be greatly to their advantage to abandon the Socialists. They also would very much like to organise politico-criminal associations, just as Waldeck-Rousseau hoped to do twenty years ago ; but the results they have obtained up till now have been very moderate. Their aim is to save the Church, and they think that the well-disposed capitalists might sacrifice a part of their profits to give to the Christian syndicates the concessions necessary to assure the success of this religious policy. A well-informed Catholic, who interests himself in social questions, lately told me that in a few years the workers would be obliged to recognise that their prejudices against the Church had no foundation. I think that he deluded himself as much as Waldeck-Rousseau did when in 1884 he regarded the idea of a revolutionary federation of syndicates as ridiculous, but the material interest of the Church so blinds Catholics that they are capable of every kind of stupidity.

The Social Catholics [1] have a way of looking at economic questions that makes them resemble our vilest politicians very closely. In fact it is difficult for the clerical world to conceive that things can happen otherwise than by grace, favouritism, and bribery.

I have often heard a lawyer say that a priest can never be made to understand that certain actions which the Code never punished are nevertheless villainies ; and I have been told by a bishop's lawyer, that while a clientèle composed of convents is an excellent one, yet at the same time it is very dangerous, because convents frequently want fraudulent deeds drawn up. Many people seeing during the last fifteen years so many gorgeous monuments

[1] [The "catholiques soceaun" form a definite party. De Mutz has been for a long time the recognised leader of the party and still exercises considerable influence.—*Trans. Note.*]

erected by the religious congregations have wondered if a wave of madness was not passing over the Church. They are unaware that these building operations enable a crowd of pious rascals to live at the expense of the Church treasury. The imprudence of those congregations which persist in carrying on long and costly lawsuits against the public treasury has often been pointed out, for such tactics enable the Radicals to work up a lively agitation against the monks by denouncing the avarice of people who claim to have taken vows of poverty. But these law-suits make plenty of business for the army of pious rascality. I do not think I am exaggerating when I say that more than a third of the fortune of the Church has been wasted for the benefit of these vampires.

A widespread dishonesty therefore prevails in the Catholic world, which leads the devout to believe that economic conditions depend chiefly on the caprices of the people who hold the purse. Everybody who has profited by an unexpected gain—and all profit from capital is an unexpected gain to them [1]—ought to share the profit with those people who have a right to his affection or to his esteem : first of all the priests,[2] and then their parishioners. If he does not respect this obligation, he is a rascal, a freemason, or a Jew ; no violence is too great to be used against such an imp of Satan. When priests, then, are heard using revolutionary language, we need not take them literally and believe that these vehement orators have socialistic sentiments. It simply indicates that the capitalists have not been sufficiently generous.

Here again, then, there is a case for arbitration ; recourse

[1] I do not think that there exists a class less capable of understanding the economics of production than the priests.

[2] In Turkey when a high palace dignitary receives a bribe, the Sultan takes the money and then gives a certain proportion of it back to his employé ; what proportion is given back depends on the Sultan's disposition at the moment. The Sultan's ethical code in these matters is also that of our Catholic social reform group.

must be had to men with great experience of life in order
to ascertain exactly what sacrifices the rich must submit
to on behalf of the poor dependants of the Church.

IV

The study we have just made has not led us to think
that the theorists of " social peace " are on the way to an
ethic worthy of acknowledgment.   We now pass to a
counterproof and enquire whether proletarian violence
might not be capable of producing the effect in vain
expected from tactics of moderation.

First of all, it must be noticed that modern philosophers
seem to agree in demanding a kind of sublimity from the
ethics of the future, which will distinguish it from the
petty and insipid morality of the Catholics.   The chief
thing with which the theologians are reproached is that
they make too great use of the conception of probabilism ;
nothing seems more absurd (not to say more scandalous)
to contemporary philosophers than to count the opinions
which have been emitted for and against a maxim, in order
to find out whether we ought to shape our conduct by it
or not.

Professor Durkheim said recently, at the *Société
française de philosophie* (February 11, 1906), that it would
be impossible to suppress the religious element in ethics,
and that what characterised this element was its incom-
mensurability with other human values.   He recognised
that his sociological researches led him to conclusions
very near those of Kant ;   he asserted that utilitarian
morality had misunderstood the problem of duty and
obligation.   I do not want to discuss these here ;   I simply
cite them to show to what point the character of the
sublime impresses itself on authors who, by the nature of
their work, would seem the least inclined to accept it.

No writer has defined more forcibly than Proudhon

the principles of that morality which modern times have
in vain sought to realise. " To feel and to assert the
dignity of man," he says, " first in everything in connection with ourselves, then in the person of our neighbour,
and that without a shadow of egoism, without any consideration either of divine or communal sanction—therein
lies Right. To be ready to defend that dignity in every
circumstance with energy, and, if necessary, against oneself, that is Justice." [1] Clemenceau, who doubtless can
hardly be said to make a personal use of this morality,
expresses the same thought when he writes : " Without
the dignity of the human person, without independence,
liberty, and justice, life is but a bestial state not worth
the trouble of preserving " (*Aurore*, May 12, 1905).

One well-founded reproach has been brought against
Proudhon, as well as against many others of the great
moralists ; it has been said that his maxims were admirable, but that they were doomed to remain ineffective.
And, in fact, experience does prove, unfortunately, that
those precepts which the historians of ideas call the most
elevated precepts are, as a rule, entirely ineffective. This
was evident in the case of the Stoics, it was no less remarkable in Kantism, and it does not seem as if the practical
influence of Proudhon has been very noticeable. In order
that a man may suppress the tendencies against which
morality struggles, he must have in himself some source
of conviction which must dominate his whole consciousness,
and act before the calculations of reflection have time to
enter his mind.

It may even be said that all the fine arguments by
which authors hope to induce men to act morally are more
likely to lead them down the slope of probabilism ; as
soon as we consider an act to be accomplished, we are
led to ask ourselves if there is not some means of escaping

[1] Proudhon, *De la justice dans la révolution et dans l'église*, vol. i.
216.

the strict obligations of duty.   A. Comte supposed that human nature would change in the future and that the cerebral organs which produce altruism (?) would destroy those which produce egoism ; in saying this he very likely bore in mind the fact that moral decision is instantaneous, and, like instinct, comes from the depth of man's nature.

At times Proudhon is reduced, like Kant, to appeal to a kind of scholasticism for an explanation of the paradox of moral law.   " To feel himself in others, to the point of sacrificing every other interest to this sentiment, to demand for others the same respect as for himself, and to be angry with the unworthy creature who suffers others to be lacking in respect for him, as if the care of his dignity did not concern himself alone, such a faculty at first sight seems a strange one. . . . There is a tendency in every man to develop and force the acceptance of that which is essentially himself—which is, in fact, his own dignity. It results from this that the essential in man being identical and one for all humanity, each of us is aware of himself at the same time as individual and as species ; and that an insult is felt by a third party and by the offender himself as well as by the injured person, that in consequence the protest is common.   This precisely is what is meant by Justice." [1]

Religious ethics claim to possess this source of action which is wanting in lay ethics,[2] but here it is necessary to make a distinction if an error, into which so many authors have fallen, is to be avoided.   The great mass of Christians do not carry out the real Christian ethic, that which the philosopher considers as really peculiar to their religion ; worldly people who profess Catholicism are chiefly preoccupied with probabilism, mechanical

[1] Proudhon, *loc. cit*. pp. 216-217.

[2] Proudhon thinks that this was also lacking in pagan antiquity : " During several centuries, polytheistic societies had customs, but no ethics. In the absence of a morality solidly based on principles, the customs gradually disappeared " (*loc. cit.* p. 173).

rites and proceedings more or less related to magic and which are calculated to assure their present and future happiness in spite of their sins.[1]

Theoretical Christianity has never been a religion suited to worldly people ; the doctors of the spiritual life have always reasoned about those people who were able to escape from the conditions of ordinary life. " When the Council of Gangres, in 325," said Renan, " declared that the Gospel maxims about poverty, the renunciation of the family and virginity, were not intended for the ordinary Christian, the perfectionists made places apart where the evangelical life, too lofty for the common run of men, could be practised in all its rigour." He remarks, moreover, very justly, that the " monastery took the place of martyrdom so that the precepts of Jesus might be carried out somewhere," [2] but he does not push this comparison far enough ; the lives of the great hermits were a material struggle against the infernal powers which pursue them even to the desert,[3] and this struggle was to continue that which the martyrs had waged against their adversaries.

These facts show us the way to a right understanding of the nature of lofty moral convictions ; these never depend on reasoning or on any education of the individual will, but on a state of war in which men voluntarily participate and which finds expression in well-defined myths. In Catholic countries the monks carry on the struggle against the prince of evil who triumphs in this world, and would subdue them to his will ; in Protestant countries

[1] Heinrich Heine claims that the Catholicism of a wife is a very good thing for the husband, because the wife is never oppressed by the burden of her sins ; after confession she begins again " to chatter and laugh." Moreover, there is no danger of her relating her sin (*L'Allemagne*, 2nd edition, vol. ii. p. 322).

[2] Renan, *Marc-Aurèle*, p. 558.

[3] Catholic saints do not struggle against abstractions but often against apparitions which present themselves with all the signs of reality. Luther also had to fight the Devil, at whom he threw his inkpot.

small fanatical sects take the place of the monasteries.[1] These are the battle-fields which enable Christian morality to hold its own, with that character of sublimity which to-day still fascinates many minds and gives it sufficient lustre to beget in the community a few pale imitations.

When one considers a less accentuated state of the Christian ethic, one is struck by seeing to what extent it depends on strife. Le Play, who was an excellent Catholic, often contrasted (to the great scandal of his co-religionists) the solidity of the religious convictions he met with in countries of mixed religions, with the spirit of inactivity which prevails in the countries exclusively submitted to the influence of Rome. Among the Protestant peoples, the more vigorously the Established Church is assailed by dissident sects the greater the moral fervour developed. We thus see that conviction is founded on the competition of communions, each of which regards itself as the army of truth fighting the armies of evil. In such conditions it is possible to find sublimity ; but when religious warfare is much weakened, probabilism, mechanical rites having a certain resemblance to magic, take the first place.

We can point out quite similar phenomena in the history of modern Liberal ideas. For a long while our fathers regarded from an almost religious point of view the Declaration of the Rights of Man, which seems to us nowadays only a colourless collection of abstract and confused formulas, without any great practical bearing. This was due to the fact that formidable struggles had been undertaken on account of the institutions which originated in this document ; the clerical party asserted that it would demonstrate the fundamental error of Liberalism ; everywhere it organised fighting societies intended to enforce its authority on the people and on the Government ; it boasted that it would be able to destroy

[1] Renan, *loc. cit.* p. 627.

the defenders of the Revolution before long. At the time when Proudhon wrote his book on Justice, the conflict was far from being ended ; thus the whole book is written in a warlike tone astonishing to the reader of to-day : the author speaks as if he were a veteran in the wars of Liberty ; he would be revenged on the temporary conquerors who threaten the acquisitions of the Revolution ; he announces the dawn of the great revolt.

Proudhon hopes that the duel will be soon, that the forces will meet with their whole strength, and that there will be a Napoleonic battle, finally destroying the opponent. He often speaks in a language which would be appropriate to an epic. He did not perceive that when later on his belligerent ideas had disappeared, his abstract reasonings would seem weak. There is a ferment all through his soul which colours it and gives a hidden meaning to his thought, very far removed from the scholastic sense.

The savage fury with which the Church proceeded against Proudhon's book shows that the clerical camp had exactly the same conception of the nature and consequences of the conflict as he had.

As long as the " sublime " imposed itself in this way on the modern spirit, it seemed possible to create a lay and democratic ethic ; but in our time such an enterprise would seem almost comic. Everything is changed now that the clericals no longer seem formidable ; there are no longer any Liberal convictions, since the Liberals have ceased to be animated by their former warlike passions. Nowadays everything is in such confusion that the priests claim to be the best of democrats ; they have adopted the *Marseillaise* as their party hymn, and if a little persuasion is exerted they will have illuminations on the anniversary of August 10, 1792. Sublimity has vanished from the ethics of both parties, giving place to a morality of extraordinary meanness.

Kautsky is evidently right when he asserts that in our time the advancement of the workers has depended on their revolutionary spirit.   At the end of a study on social reform and revolution he says, " It is hopeless to try, by means of moral homilies, to inspire the English workman with a more exalted conception of life, a feeling of nobler effort.   The ethics of the proletariat spring from its revolutionary aspirations, these are what give it the greatest force and elevation.   It is the idea of revolution which has raised the proletariat from its degradation." [1]   It is clear that for Kautsky morality is always subordinate to the idea of sublimity.

The Socialist point of view is quite different from that of former democratic literature ;   our fathers believed that the nearer man approached Nature the better he was, and that a man of the people was a sort of savage ;   that consequently the lower we descend the more virtue we find.   The democrats have many times, in support of this idea, called attention to the fact that during revolutions the poorest people have often given the finest examples of heroism ;   they explain this by taking for granted that these obscure heroes were true children of Nature.   I explain it by saying that, these men being engaged in a war which was bound to end in their triumph or their enslavement, the sentiment of sublimity was bound to be engendered by the conditions of the struggle.   As a rule, during a revolution the higher classes show themselves in a particularly unfavourable light, for this reason, that, belonging to a defeated army, they experience the feelings of conquered people, suppliant, or about to capitulate.

When working - class circles are *reasonable*, as the

[1] Karl Kautsky, *La Révolution sociale*, French trans., pp. 123-124. I have pointed out elsewhere that the decay of the revolutionary idea in the minds of former militants who have become moderate seems to be accompanied by a moral decadence that I have compared to that which as a rule one finds in the case of a priest who has lost his faith (*Insegnamente sociali*, pp. 344-345).

professional sociologists wish them to be, when conflicts are confined to disputes about material interests, there is no more opportunity for heroism than when agricultural syndicates discuss the subject of the price of guano with manure merchants. It has never been thought that discussions about prices could possibly exercise any ethical influence on men ; the experience of sales of live stock would lead to the supposition that in such cases those interested are led to admire cunning rather than good faith ; the *ethical values* recognised by horse-dealers have never passed for very elevated. Among the important things accomplished by agricultural syndicates, De Rocquigny reports that in 1896, " the municipality of Marmande having wanted to impose on beasts brought to the fair a tax which the cattle-breeders *considered iniquitous* . . . the breeders struck, and stopped supplying the market of Marmande, with such effect that the municipality found itself forced to give in.[1] This was a very peaceful procedure which produced results profitable to the peasants ; but it is quite clear that nothing ethical was involved in such a dispute.

When politicians intervene there is, almost necessarily, a noticeable lowering of ethical standards, because they do nothing for nothing and only act on condition that the favoured association becomes one of their customers. We are very far here from the path of sublimity, we are on that which leads to the practices of the political-criminal societies.

In the opinion of many well-informed people, the transition from violence to cunning which shows itself in contemporary strikes in England cannot be too much admired. The great object of the Trades Unions is to obtain a recognition of the right to employ threats

[1] De Rocquigny, *op. cit.* pp. 379-380. I am curious to know how exactly a tax can be iniquitous. These *worthy progressives* speak a special language.

disguised in diplomatic formulas; they desire that their delegates should not be interfered with when going the round of the workshops charged with the mission of bringing those workmen who wish to work to understand that it would be to their interests to follow the *directions* of the Trades Unions; they consent to express their desires in a form which will be perfectly clear to the listener, but which could be represented in a court of justice as a solidarist[1] sermon. I protest I cannot see what is so admirable in these tactics, which are worthy of Escobar. In the past the Catholics have often employed similar methods of intimidation against the Liberals; I understand thus perfectly well why so many *worthy progressives* admire the Trades Unions, but the morality of the *worthy-progressives* does not seem to me very much to be admired.

It is true that for a long time in England violence has been void of all revolutionary character. Whether corporative advantages are pursued by means of blows or by craft, there is not much difference between the two methods; yet the pacific tactics of the Trades Unions indicate an hypocrisy which would be better left to the " *well intentioned progressives.*" In a country where the conception of the general strike exists, the blows exchanged between workmen and representatives of the middle classes have an entirely different import, their consequences are far reaching and they may beget heroism.

I am convinced that in order to understand part, at any rate, of the dislike that Bernstein's doctrines rouse in German social democracy we must bear in mind these conclusions about the nature of the sublime in ethics. The German has been brought up on sublimity to an

---

[1] [This is a reference to the "solidarista" doctrine, invented by Buisson; the interests of the classes are not opposed, and the more wealthy have their duties toward the poorer.—*Trans. Note.*]

extraordinary extent, first by the literature connected with the wars of independence,[1] then by the revival of the taste for the old national songs which followed these wars, then by a philosophy which pursues aims very far removed from sordid considerations. It must also be remembered that the victory of 1871 has considerably contributed toward giving Germans of every class a feeling of confidence in their strength that is not to be found to the same degree in this country at the present time ; compare, for instance, the German Catholic party with the chicken - hearted creatures who form the clientèle of the Church in France ! Our clergy only think of humiliating themselves before their adversaries and are quite happy, provided that there are plenty of evening parties during the winter ; they have no recollection of services which are rendered to them.[2]

The German Socialist party drew its strength particularly from the catastrophic idea everywhere spread by its propagandists, and which was taken very seriously as long as the Bismarckian persecutions maintained a warlike spirit in the groups. This spirit was so strong in the masses that they have not yet succeeded in understanding thoroughly that their leaders are anything but revolutionaries.

[1] Renan even wrote : " The war of 1813 to 1815 is the only one of our century that had anything epic and elevated about it . . . [it] corresponded to a movement of ideas and had a real intellectual significance. A man who had taken part in this great struggle told me that, awakened by the cannonade on the first night that he passed with the volunteer troops collected in Silesia, he felt that he was witnessing an immense divine service " (*Essais de morale et de critique*, p. 116). Compare Manzoni's ode entitled " Mars 1821," dedicated to " the illustrious memory of Théodore Koerner, poet and soldier of German independence and killed on the field of battle at Leipzig, a name dear to all those peoples who are struggling to defend or to reconquer their fatherland." Our own wars of Liberty were also epic, but they have not been so well written up as the war of 1813.

[2] Drumont has often denounced this state of mind of the fashionable religious world.

When Bernstein (who was too intelligent not to know what was the real spirit of his friends on the directing committee) announced that the grandiose hopes which had been raised must be given up, there was a moment of stupefaction ; very few people understood that Bernstein's declarations were courageous and honest actions, intended to make the language of Socialism accord more with the real facts. If hereafter it was necessary to be content with the policy of social reform, the parliamentary parties and the ministry would have to be negotiated with—that is, it would be necessary to behave exactly as the middle classes did. This appeared monstrous to men who had been brought up on a catastrophic theory of Socialism. Many times had the tricks of the middle class politicians been denounced, their astuteness contrasted with the candour and disinterestedness of the Socialists, and the large element of artificiality and expediency in their attitude of opposition pointed out. It could never have been imagined that the disciples of Marx might follow in the footsteps of the Liberals. With the new policy, heroic characters, sublimity, and convictions disappear ! The Germans thought that the world was turned upside down.

It is plain that Bernstein was absolutely right in not wanting to keep up a revolutionary semblance which was in contradiction with the real state of mind of the party ; he did not find in his own country the elements which existed in France and Italy ; he saw no other way then of keeping Socialism on a basis of reality than that of suppressing all that was deceptive in a revolutionary programme which the leaders no longer believed in. Kautsky, on the contrary, wanted to preserve the veil which hid from the workmen the real activity of the Socialist party ; in this way he achieved much success among the politicians, but more than any one else he has helped to intensify the Socialist crisis in Germany. The ideas of Socialism cannot be kept intact by diluting the phrases of Marx in verbose commentaries, but by continually adapting the spout of Marx to facts which are capable of assuming a revolutionary aspect. The general strike alone can produce this result at the present day.

One serious question must now be asked. " Why is it that in certain countries acts of violence grouping themselves round the idea of the general strike, produce a Socialist ideology capable of inspiring sublimity, and why in others do they seem not to have that power ? " Here national traditions play a great part ; the examination of this problem would perhaps help to throw a strong light on the genesis of ideas ; but we will not deal with it here.

CHAPTER VII

THE ETHICS OF THE PRODUCERS

I

FIFTY years ago Proudhon pointed out the necessity of giving the people a morality which would fit new needs. The first chapter of the preliminary discourses placed at the beginning of *Justice in the Revolution and in the Church* is entitled " The State of Morals in the Nineteenth Century. Invasion of moral scepticism ; society in danger. What is the remedy ? " There one reads these noteworthy sentences : " France has lost its morals. Not that, as a matter of fact, the men of our generation are worse than their fathers. . . . When I say that France has lost its morals I mean that it has ceased to

believe in the very principles of morality, a very different
thing. She has no longer moral intelligence or conscience,
she has almost lost the idea of morals itself ; as a result
of continual criticism we have come to this melancholy conclusion : that right and wrong, between which
we formerly thought we were able to distinguish dogmatic-
ally, are now vague and indeterminate conventional terms ;
that all these words, Right, Duty, Morality, Virtue, etc.,
of which the pulpit and the school talk so much, serve
to cover nothing but pure hypotheses, vain Utopias,
and unprovable prejudices ; that thus ordinary social
behaviour, which is apparently governed by some sort of
human respect or by convention, is in reality arbitrary." [1]

However, he did not think that contemporary society
was mortally wounded ; he believed that since the
Revolution, humanity had acquired an idea of Justice
which was sufficiently clear to enable it to triumph over
temporary lapses ; by this conception of the future he
separated himself completely from what was to become the
most fundamental idea of contemporary official Socialism,
which sneers at morality. "This juridical faith . . . this
science of right and duty, which we seek everywhere in
vain, that the Church has never possessed, and without
which it is impossible for us to live, I say that the Revolution created all its principles ; that these principles,
unknown to us, rule and uphold us, but while at the
bottom of our hearts affirming them, we shrink from
them through prejudice, and it is this infidelity to ourselves
that makes our moral poverty and servitude." [2] He

[1] Proudhon, *De la justice dans la révolution et dans l'eglise* vol. i.
p. 70.

[2] Proudhon, *loc. cit.* p. 74. By *juridical* faith Proudhon here
understands a triple faith, which dominates the family, contracts, and
political relations. The first is " the conception of the mutual dignity
(of husband and wife) which, raising them above the level of the senses,
renders them more sacred to the other even than dear, and makes their
fertile community a religion for them, sweeter than love itself "—the
second " raising the mind above egoistical appetites, is made happier

maintains the possibility of bringing light to our minds, of presenting what he calls " the exegesis of the Revolution " ; in order to do this, he examines history, showing how humanity has never ceased to strive towards Justice, how religion has been the cause of corruption, and how " the French Revolution by bringing about the predominance of the juridical principle (over the religious principle) opens a new epoch, an entirely contrary order of things, the different elements of which it is now our task to determine." [1]   Whatever may happen in the future to our worn-out race, he says at the end of this discourse, " posterity will recognise that the third age of humanity [2] has its start in the French Revolution ; that an understanding of this new law has been given to some of us in all its fulness ; that we have not been found quite wanting in the practice of it ; and that to perish in this sublime childbirth was, after all, not without grandeur.   At that hour the Revolution became clear, then it lived.   The rest of the nation (*i.e.* those who had not understood the Revolution) does not think at all.   *Will that part which lives and thinks be suppressed by that which does not ?* " [3]

I said in the preceding chapter that the whole doctrine of Proudhon was subordinated to revolutionary enthusiasm and that this enthusiasm has been extinct since the Church has ceased to be formidable ; thus there is nothing astonishing in the fact that the undertaking which Proudhon considered so easy (the creation of a morality absolutely free from all religious belief) seems very uncertain to many of our contemporaries.   I find a proof

by respect for the right of another than by its own fortune "—without the third " citizens submitting to the attraction of individualism could not form, whatever they did, anything other than a mere aggregate of incoherent and repulsive existences that the first wind will disperse like dust " (*loc. cit.* pp. 72-73).   In the strict sense of the word, juridical faith would be the second of these three.

[1] Proudhon, *loc. cit.* p. 93.

[2] The two first epochs are those of paganism and of Christianity.

[3] Proudhon, *loc. cit.* p. 104.

of this way of thinking in a speech by Combes delivered during a discussion of the budget of Public Worship, January 26, 1903 : " At the present moment we look upon the moral ideas taught by the Church as necessary ideas. For my part I find it difficult to accept the idea of a society composed of philósophers like M. Allard,[1] whose primary education would have sufficiently guaranteed them against the perils and trials of life." Combes is not the kind of man to have ideas of his own ; he reproduced an opinion current in his circle.

This declaration created a great commotion in the Chamber. All the deputies who prided themselves on their knowledge of philosophy took part in the debate ; as Combes had referred to the superficial and narrow instruction of our primary schools, F. Buisson felt that as the leading pedagogue of the third Republic, he ought to protest : " The education that we give to the child of the people," he said, " is not a half education, it is the very flower and fruit of civilisation gathered during the centuries, from among many peoples, in the religions and legal systems of all ages and of all mankind." An ethic of this abstract kind must be entirely devoid of efficacy. I remember having read, in a manual by Paul Bert, that the fundamental principles of morality are based on the teachings of Zoroaster, and the Constitution of the year III. These do not seem to me the kind of principles

[1] This deputy had made a very anticlerical speech from which I quote this curious idea that " the Jewish religion was the most clerical of all religions, possessing the most *sectarian* and narrowest type of clericalism." A little before this he said, "I myself *am not an anti-Semite*, and only make one reproach to the Jews, that of having poisoned Aryan thought, so elevated and broad, with Hebraic monotheism." He demanded the introduction of the history of religions into the curriculum of the primary schools in order to ruin the authority of the Church. According to him the Socialist party saw in " the intellectual emancipation of the masses the necessary preface to the progress and social evolution of societies." Is it not rather the contrary which is true ? Does not this speech prove that there is an anti-Semitism in free-thinking circles quite as narrow and badly informed as that of the clericals ?

which would be powerful enough to influence a man's conduct.

It might be imagined that the University had arranged its present programme in the hope of imposing moral conduct on its pupils by means of the repetition of precepts ; moral courses are multiplied to such an extent that one might ask oneself if (with a slight difference) the well-known verse of Boileau might not be applied :

Aimez-vous la *muscade* ?   On en a mis partout.[1]

I do not think that there are many people who share the naïve confidence of F. Buisson and the members of the University in this ethic.   Exactly like Combes, G. de Molinari believes that it is necessary to have recourse to religion, which promises men a reward in the other world, and which is thus, " the surety of justice. . . . It is religion which in the infancy of humanity, raised the edifice of morality ; it is religion which supports and which alone can support it.   Such are the functions which religion has filled and which it continues to fill and which, unpleasant as it may be to the apostles of independent morality, constitute its usefulness." [2]   " We must look for help to a more powerful and more active instrument than the interests of society, to effect those reforms demonstrated by political economy to be necessary, and this instrument can only be found in the religious senti-ment associated with the sentiment of justice." [3]

G. de Molinari expresses himself in intentionally vague terms ; he seems to regard religion as do many modern Catholics (of the Brunetière type) ; that is, as a means of social Government, which must be suited to the needs of the different classes ; people of the higher classes have always considered that they had less need of moral discipline than their subordinates, and it is by making this

[1] So do like musk ?   It has been put everywhere.
[2] G. de Molinari, *Science et religion*, p. 94.
[3] G. de Molinari, *op. cit.* p. 198.

fine discovery the basis of their theology that the Jesuits have had so much success in contemporary middle classes. Our author distinguishes four motive forces capable of assuring the accomplishment of duty—" the power of society invested in the Governmental organism, the power of public opinion, the power of the individual conscience, and the power of religion " ; and he considers that this spiritual mechanism perceptibly lags behind the material mechanism.[1]   The two first motive forces may have some influence on capitalists, but none in the workshop ; for the workers the last two motive forces are alone effective, and they will become every day more important on account of " the growth of responsibility in those who are charged with the direction and surveillance of the working of machinery." [2]   But according to Molinari we could not conceive the power of the individual conscience without that of religion.[3]

I believe, then, that G. de Molinari would be inclined to approve of the employers who protect religious institutions ; he would only, however, like it done with a little more circumspection than Chagot used at Monceaules Mines.[4]

The Socialists for a long time have been greatly prejudiced against morality, on account of these Catholic institutions that the large employers established for their workpeople.   It seemed to them that, in our capitalist society, morality was only a means of assuring the docility of workmen, who are kept in the fear created by superstition.   The literature which the middle class have admired for so long describes conduct so outrageous, so scandalous even, that it is difficult to credit the rich

[1] G. de Molinari, op. cit. p. 61.
[2] G. de Molinari, op. cit. p. 54.
[3] G. de Molinari, op. cit. pp. 87 and 93.
[4] I have already mentioned that in 1883 Y. Guyot violently denounced the conduct of Chagot, who placed his workmen under the direction of the priests, and forced them to go to Mass (Morale, p. 183).

classes with sincerity when they speak of inculcating morality in the people.

The Marxists had a particular reason for showing themselves suspicious in all that concerned ethics ; the propagators of social reforms, the Utopists and the democrats, had so abused the idea of Justice that it was only reasonable to consider all discussions on such a subject as an exercise in rhetoric, or as sophistry intended to mislead those who were interested in the working-class movement. This is why, several years ago, Rosa Luxemburg called the idea of Justice " this old post horse, on which all the regenerators of the world, deprived of surer means of locomotion, have ridden; this ungainly Rosinante, mounted on which so many Quixotes of history have gone in search of the great reform of the world, bringing back from these journeys nothing but black eyes." [1] From these sarcasms about a fantastic Justice springing from the imagination of Utopists, they often used to pass, too easily, to coarse facetiousness about the most ordinary morality ; a rather sordid selection could easily be made of paradoxes supported by the official Marxists on this subject. Lafargue distinguishes himself particularly from this point of view.[2]

The principal reason which prevented the Socialists from studying ethical problems as they deserved was the democratic superstition which has dominated them for so long and which has led them to believe that above everything else the aim of their actions must be the acquisition of seats in political assemblies.

[1] *Mouvement socialiste*, June 15, 1889, p. 649.

[2] See, for example, the *Socialiste* of June 30, 1901. " As in a communist society the *morals which clogs the brains of the civilised* will have vanished like a *frightful nightmare*, perhaps to be replaced by another ethic, *which will incite women to flutter about like butterflies*, to use Ch. Fourier's expression, instead of submitting to being the property of a male. . . . In savage tribes and among barbarous communists women are much more honoured when they distribute their favours to a great number of lovers."

From the moment one has anything to do with elections, it is necessary to submit to certain general conditions which impose themselves unavoidably on all parties in every country and at all times. If one is convinced that the future of the world depends on the electoral programme, on compromises between influential men and on the sale of privileges, it is not possible to pay much attention to the moral constraints which prevent a man going in the direction of his most obvious interests. Experience shows that in all countries where democracy can develop its nature freely, the most scandalous corruption is displayed without any one thinking it even necessary to conceal his rascality. Tammany Hall of New York has always been cited as the most perfect type of democratic life, and in the majority of our large towns politicians are found who ask for nothing better than to follow the paths of their confrères in America. So long as a man is faithful to his party he only commits peccadilloes, but if he is unwise enough to abandon it, he is immediately discovered to have the most shameful vices. It would not be difficult to show, by means of well-known examples, that our Parliamentary Socialists practise this singular morality with a certain amount of cynicism.

There is a great resemblance between the electoral democracy and the Stock Exchange ; in one case as in the other it is necessary to work upon the simplicity of the masses, to buy the co-operation of the most important papers, and to assist chance by an infinity of trickery. There is not a great deal of difference between a financier who puts big sounding concerns on the market which come to grief in a few years, and the politician who promises an infinity of reforms to the citizens which he does not know how to bring about,[1] and which resolve

[1] On June 21, 1907, Clemenceau, replying to Millerand, told him that in introducing the bill to establish old age pensions, without concerning himself with where the money was to come from, he had not

themselves simply into an accumulation of Parliamentary papers. Neither one nor the other know anything about production, and yet they manage to obtain control over it, to misdirect and exploit it shamelessly ; they are dazzled by the marvels of modern industry, and it is their private opinion that the world is so rich that they can rob it on a large scale without causing any great outcry among the producers ; the great art of the financier and the politician is to be able to bleed the taxpayer without bringing him to the point of revolt. Democrats and business men have quite a special science for the purpose of making the deliberative assemblies approve of their swindling ; the Parliaments are as packed as shareholders' meetings. It is probable that they both understand each other as perfectly as they do because of profound psychological affinities resulting from these methods of operation ; democracy is the paradise of which unscrupulous financiers dream.

The disheartening spectacle presented to the world by these financial and political parasites [1] explains the success which anarchist writers have had for so long ; these latter founded their hopes of the regeneration of the world on the intellectual progress of individuals ; they never ceased urging the workmen to educate themselves, to realise more fully their dignity as men, and to show their devotion to their comrades. This attitude

---

acted as " a statesman nor even as a responsible person." Millerand's reply is quite characteristic of the pride of the political parvenu : " Don't talk about things that you know nothing about." Of what then does he himself speak ?

[1] I am pleased here to be able to support myself in the incontestable authority of Gérault-Richard who in the *Petite République* on March 19, 1903, denounced the " intriguers, people who wish to get on at all costs, starvelings and ladies' men (who) are only after the spoils " and who at that time were trying to bring about the fall of the Combes ministry. From the following number we see that he is speaking of Waldeck-Rousseau's friends, who, like him, were opposed to the destruction of the congregations.

was imposed on them by their principles : in fact, how was the formation of a society of free men conceivable if it was not taken for granted that individuals had not already acquired the capacity of guiding themselves ? Politicians assert that this is a very naïve idea, and that the world will enjoy all the happiness it can desire on the day when messengers of the new Gospel are able to profit from the advantages that power procures ; nothing will be impossible for a State which turns the editors of *Humanité* into princes. If in that time it is considered useful to have free men, they will be manufactured by a few good laws ; but it is doubtful if the friends and shareholders of Jaurès will find that necessary ; it will be sufficient for them if they have servants and taxpayers.

The *new school* is rapidly differentiating itself from official Socialism in recognising the necessity of the improvement of morals.[1] It is thus customary for the dignitaries of Parliamentary Socialism to accuse it of anarchical tendencies ; for my part, I should not object to acknowledge myself as an anarchist in this respect, since Parliamentary Socialism professes a contempt for morality equalled only by that which the vilest representatives of the stockbroking middle class have for it.

The new school also has sometimes been reproached with returning to the dreams of the Utopists. This criticism shows how much our adversaries misunderstand the works of the old Socialists as well as the present situation. The aim of the early Socialists was to build up ethical ideas capable of influencing the feelings of the upper classes, in such a way as to make them sympathise with those who in pity are called " the disinherited classes," and of inducing them to make some sacrifice in favour of their unfortunate brethren. The writers of

[1] This is what Benedetto Croce pointed out in the *Critica* of July 17, 1907, pp. 317-319. This writer is well known in Italy as a remarkably acute critic and philosopher.

that time picture the manufactory of the future in a very different light from that which it may have in a society of proletarians carrying on industry in a technically progressive and inventive way ; they suppose that it might resemble drawing-rooms in which ladies meet to do embroidery ; in this way they gave a middle-class setting to the mechanism of production. Finally, they credited the proletariat with feelings closely resembling those which eighteenth- and nineteenth-century explorers attributed to savages—goodness, simplicity, and an anxiety to imitate a superior race of men. With such hypotheses it was an easy matter to conceive an organisation of peace and happiness ; it was only necessary to make the rich better and the poorer class more enlightened. These two operations seemed easily realisable, and then the fusion of the drawing-room and the factory, which has turned the heads of so many Utopists, would be brought about.[1] The " new school " never conceives things on an idyllic, Christian, and middle-class model ; it knows that the process of production requires entirely different qualities from those met with in the upper classes ; it is only on account of the moral qualities, which are necessary to improve production, that it deals so much with ethical questions.

The new school, then, resembles the economists much more than the Utopists ; like G. de Molinari, it considers that the moral progress of the proletariat is as necessary as material improvement in machinery, if modern industry is to be lifted to the increasingly higher levels that technical science allows it to attain ; but it descends farther than this author does into the depths of this problem, and does not content itself with vague recommendations about religious duty.[2] In its insatiable

[1] In the New-Harmony colony founded by R. Owen the work done was little and bad, but amusements were abundant ; in 1826 the Duke of Saxe-Weimar was dazzled by the music and the balls (Dolléans, *Robert Owen*, pp. 247-268).

[2] G. de Molinari appears to believe that a natural religion like that

desire for reality, it tries to arrive at the real roots of this process of moral perfection and desires to know how to *create to-day the ethic of the producers of the future.*

II

At the beginning of any research on modern ethics this question must be asked, Under what conditions is regeneration possible ? The Marxists are absolutely right in laughing at the Utopists and in maintaining that morality is never created by mild preaching, by the ingenious constructions of theorists, or by fine gestures. Proudhon, having neglected this problem, suffered from many illusions about the persistence of the forces which gave life to his own ethics ; experience was soon to prove that his undertaking was to remain fruitless. And if the contemporary world does not contain the roots of a new ethic what will happen to it ? The sighs of a whimpering middle class will not save it, if it has for ever lost its morality.

Very shortly before his death Renan was much engrossed with the ethical future of the world : " Moral values decline, that is a certainty, sacrifice has almost disappeared ; one can see the day coming when everything will be syndicalised,[1] when organised selfishness will take the place of love and devotion. There will be strange upheavals. The two things which alone until now have resisted the decay of reverence, the army [2] and the Church, will soon be swept away in the universal torrent."[3] Renan showed a remarkable insight in writing this at the very

of J. J. Rousseau or Robespierre would suffice. We know to-day that such means have no moral efficacy.

[1] Renan is complaining that the corporative associations dominate society too much. It is clear that he had none of the veneration for the corporative spirit that so many contemporary idealists display.

[2] He did not foresee that his son-in-law would agitate violently against the army in the Dreyfus affair.

[3] Renan, *Feuilles détachées*, p. 14.

moment when so many futile intellects were announcing the renascence of idealism and foreseeing progressive tendencies in a Church that was at length reconciled with the modern world. But all his life Renan had been too favoured by fortune not to be optimistic ; he believed, therefore, that the evil of the future would consist simply in the necessity of passing through a bad period, and he added : " No matter, the resources of humanity are infinite. The eternal designs will be fulfilled, the springs of life ever forcing their way to the surface will never be dried up."

He had finished, several months before, the fifth volume of his *History of the People of Israel*, and this volume, having been printed from the unaltered manuscript, contains a more imperfect expression of his ideas on this subject ; (it is known that he corrected his proofs very carefully). We find in this the most gloomy presentiments; the author even questions whether humanity will ever attain its real end. " If this globe should happen not to fulfil its purpose, there will be others to carry on to its final end the programme of all life—Light, Reason, and Truth." [1] The times to come frightened him. " The immediate future is dark. The triumph of Light is not assured." He dreaded Socialism, and there is no doubt that by Socialism he meant the humanitarian idiocy which he saw emerging in the stupid middle-class world ; it was, in this way, that he came to think that Catholicism might perhaps be the accomplice of Socialism. [2]

On the same page he speaks of the divisions which may exist in a society, and this is of considerable importance. " Judea and the Greco-Roman world were like two universes revolving one beside the other under opposing influences. . . . The history of humanity by no means synchronises in its various parts. Tremble ! At this

---

[1] Renan, *Histoire du peuple d'Israël*, vol. v. p. 421.
[2] Renan, *loc. cit.* p. 420.

moment perhaps the religion of the future is being
created . . . and we have no part in it. I envy wise
Kimri who saw beneath the earth. It is there that everything is prepared, it is there that we must look." There
is in these words nothing that the theorists of the class-
war could not approve of ; in them I find the commentary
to what Renan said a little later on the subject of " the
springs of life ever forcing their way to the surface " ;
regeneration is being brought about by a class which works
subterraneously, and which is separating itself from the
modern world as Judaism did from the ancient world.

Whatever the official sociologists may think, the lower
classes are by no means condemned to live on the crumbs
which the upper classes let fall ; we are glad to see Renan
protest against this imbecile doctrine. Syndicalism claims
to create a real proletarian ideology, and whatever the
middle-class professors say of it, historical experience, as
proclaimed by the mouth of Renan, tells us that this is
quite possible, and that out of it may come the salvation
of the world. The syndicalist movement is really being
developed underground ; the men who devote themselves
to it do not make much noise in the world ; what a
difference between them and the former leaders of democracy, whose sole aim was the conquest of power !

These men were intoxicated by the hope that the
chances of life might some day make them *republican
princes*. While waiting for the wheel of fortune to turn
to their advantage in this way, they obtained the moral
and material advantages that celebrity procures for all
virtuosi, in a society which is accustomed to paying well
those who amuse it. The chief motive force behind many
of them was their immeasurable pride, and they fancied
that, as their name was bound to shine with singular
brilliancy in the annals of humanity, they might buy that
future glory by a few sacrifices.

None of these motives for action exist for the Syndicalists

of to-day ; the proletariat has none of the servile instincts of democracy ; it no longer aspires to walk on all fours before a former comrade who has become a chief magistrate, or to swoon for joy before the toilettes of ministers' wives.[1] The men who devote themselves to the revolutionary cause know that they must always remain poor. They carry on their work of organisation without attracting attention, and the meanest hack who scribbles for *L'Humanité* is much better known than the militants of the *Confédération du Travail* ;[2] for the great majority of the French public, Griffuelhes will never have the notoriety of Rouanet ;[3] and in the absence of the material advantages, which they could hardly expect, they have not even the satisfaction that celebrity can give. Putting their whole trust in the movements of the masses, they have no

[1] The essence of democracy is concentrated in the *mot* attributed to Mme. Flocon. " It is we who are the princesses.". The democracy is happy when it sees a ridiculous creature like Félix Faure, whom Joseph Reinach compared to the *bourgeois gentilhomme*, treated with princely honours (*Histoire de l'affaire Dreyfus*, vol. iv. p. 552).

[2] Parliamentary Socialism is very keen on good manners, as we can assure ourselves by consulting Gérault-Richard's numerous articles. I quote at random several specimens. On June 1, 1903, he declared in the *Petite République* that Queen Nathalie of Servia should have been called to order " for having listened to the preaching of P. Coubé at Aubervilles, and he demands that she be admonished by the police commissary of her district." On September 26 he is roused to indignation by the coarseness and the ignorance of good manners exhibited by Admiral Maréchal. The socialist code has its mysteries ; the wives of socialists are sometimes called ladies and sometimes *citizenesses* ; in the society of the future there will evidently be disputes about the order of precedence as there were at Versailles. On July 30, 1903, Cassagnac makes great fun in the *Autorité* of his having been taken to task by Gérault-Richard, who had given him lessons in good manners.

[3] Griffuelhes, who had been a shoemaker, was at one time secretary of the *Confédération du Travail* ; he was remarkably intelligent ; cf. a pamphlet by him entitled *Voyage révolutionnaire*.

[Rouanet was Malon's principal disciple ; he was for some time a deputy, very much opposed to the Marxists, naturally a great adversary of the *Confédération du Travail*, a type of socialist politician who occupies a considerable place in journalism and in Parliament, but who does not count at all intellectually.—*Trans.*]

expectation of a Napoleonic glory, and they leave the superstition of great men to the middle classes.

It is well that it is so, because the proletariat will be able to develop itself much more surely if it organises itself in obscurity ; Socialist politicians shun occupations which do not provide celebrity (and which are consequently not profitable) ; they are, then, not at all disposed to trouble themselves with the work of the syndicates, the object of which is to remain proletarian ; they make a show on the Parliamentary stage, but that, as a rule, does not amount to much. The men who do participate in the real working-class movement are an example of what have always been looked upon as the greatest virtues ; they cannot, in fact, acquire any of those things which the middle classes regard as especially desirable. If, then, as Renan asserts,[1] history rewards the resigned abnegation of men who strive uncomplainingly, and who accomplish, without profit, a great historical work, we have a new reason for believing in the advent of Socialism, since it represents the highest moral ideal ever conceived by man. This time it is not a new religion which is shaping itself underground, without the help of the middle-class thinkers, it is *the birth of a virtue*, a virtue which the middle-class Intellectuals are incapable of understanding, a virtue which has the power to save civilisation, as Renan hoped it would be saved—but by the total elimination of the class to which Renan belonged.

Let us now consider closely the reasons which made Renan dread a decadence of the middle-class ; [2] he was

---

[1] Renan, *op. cit.* vol. iv. p. 267.

[2] Renan pointed out one symptom of decadence, on which he did not insist enough and which does not seem to have particularly impressed his readers ; he was irritated by the restlessness, the claims to originality, and the naïve rivalry of the young metaphysicians: " But, my dear fellows, it is useless to give oneself so much headache, merely to change from one error to another " (*Feuilles détachées*, p. 10). A restlessness of this kind (which puts on nowadays a sociological, socialist, or humanitarian air) is a sure sign of anæmia.

struck by the decay of religious ideas : " An immense moral, and *perhaps intellectual*, degeneracy will follow the disappearance of religion from the world. We, at the present day, can dispense with religion, because others have it for us. Those who do not believe are carried along by the more or less believing majority ; but on the day when the majority lose this impulse, the men of spirit themselves will go feebly to the attack." It is the absence of the sentiment of sublimity which Renan dreaded ; like all old people in their days of sadness, he thinks of his childhood, and adds, " Man is of value in proportion to the religious sentiment which he preserves from his first education and which colours his whole life." He himself had lived all his life under the influence of the sentiment of sublimity inculcated in him by his mother ; we know, in fact, that Madame Renan was a woman of lofty character. But the source of sublimity is dried up : " Religious people live on a shadow. We live on the shadow of a shadow. On what will those who come after us live ? " [1]

Renan, as was his wont, tried to mitigate the gloom of the outlook which his perspicacity presented to him ; he is like many other French writers who, wishing to please a frivolous public, never dare to go to the bottom of the problems that life presents ; [2] he does not wish to frighten his amiable lady admirers, so he adds, therefore, that it is not necessary to have a religion burdened with dogmas, such a religion, for example, as Christianity ; the religious sentiment should suffice. Since Renan, there has been no lack of chatter about this vague religious sentiment which " should suffice " to replace the positive

[1] Renan, *Feuilles détachées*, pp. 17-18.

[2] Brunetière addressed this reproach to French literature : " If you wish to know why Racine or Molière, for example, never attained the depth we find in a Shakespeare or a Goethe . . . *cherchez la femme*, and you will find that the defect is due to the influence of the salons, and of women " (*Évolution des genres*, 3rd edition, p. 128).

religions which are coming to grief. F. Buisson informs us that " no religious doctrines will survive, but only religious emotions, which, far from contradicting either science, art, or morality, will steep them in a feeling of profound harmony with the life of the Universe." [1] This, unless I am unable to see beyond my nose, is the merest balderdash.

" On what will those who come after us live ? " This is the great problem posed by Renan and which the middle classes will never be able to solve. If any doubt is possible on this point, the stupidities uttered by the official moralists would show that the decadence is henceforth fatal. Speculations on the harmony of the Universe (even when the Universe is personified) are not the kind of thing which will give men that courage which Renan compared to that of the soldier in the moment of attack. Sublimity is dead in the middle classes, and they are doomed to possess no ethic in the future.[2] The winding-up of the Dreyfus affair, which the Dreyfusards, to the great indignation of Colonel Picquart,[3] knew how to put to such good account, has shown that middle-class sublimity is a Stock Exchange asset. All the intellectual and moral defects of a class tainted with folly showed themselves in that affair.

[1] *Questions de morale* (lectures given by several professors) in the *Bibliothèque des sciences sociales*, p. 328.

[2] I must call attention to the extraordinary prudence shown by Ribot in his *Psychologie des sentiments* in dealing with the evolution of morality ; it might have been expected that, on the analogy of the other sentiments, he would have come to the conclusion that there was an evolution towards a purely intellectual state and to the disappearance of its efficacy ; but has not dared to draw this conclusion for morality as he did for religion.

[3] I refer to an article published in the *Gazette de Lausanne*, April 2, 1906, from which the *Libre Parole* gave a fairly long extract (cf. Joseph Reinach, *op. cit.* vol. vi. p. 36). Several months after I had written these lines Picquart was himself the object of exceptionally favourable treatment ; he had been conquered by the fatalities of Parisian life. which have ruined stronger men than he.

III

Before examining what qualities the modern industrial system requires of free producers, we must analyse the component parts of morality. The philosophers always have a certain amount of difficulty in seeing clearly into these ethical problems, because they feel the impossibility of harmonising the ideas which are current at a given time in a class, and yet imagine it to be their duty to reduce everything to a unity. To conceal from themselves the fundamental heterogeneity of all this civilised morality, they have recourse to a great number of subterfuges, sometimes relegating to the rank of exceptions, importations, or survivals, everything which embarrasses them— sometimes drowning reality in an ocean of vague phrases and, most often, employing both methods the better to obscure the problem. My view, on the contrary, is that the *best way of understanding any group of ideas in the history of thought is to bring all the contradictions into sharp relief.* I shall adopt this method and take for a starting-point the celebrated opposition which Nietzsche has established between two groups of moral values, an opposition about which much has been written, but which has never been properly studied.

A. We know with what force Nietzsche praised the values constructed by the *masters*, by a superior class of warriors who, in their expeditions, enjoying to the full freedom from all social constraint, return to the simplicity of mind of a wild beast, become once more triumphant monsters who continually bring to mind " the superb blond beast, prowling in search of prey and bloodshed," in whom " a basis of hidden bestiality needs from time to time a purgative." To understand this thesis properly, we must not attach too much importance to formulas which have at times been intentionally exaggerated, but should examine the historical facts ; the author tells **us** that he has in mind " the aristocracy of Rome, Arabia, Germany, and Japan, the *Homeric heroes*, the Scandinavian vikings."

It is chiefly the Homeric heroes that we must bear in mind in order to understand what Nietzsche wished to make clear to his contemporaries. We must remember that he had been professor of Greek at the University of Bâle, and that his reputation began with a book devoted to the glorification of the Hellenic genius (*The Origin of Tragedy*). He notices that, even at the period of their highest culture, the Greeks still preserved a memory of their former character of masters. " Our daring," said Pericles, " has traced a path over earth and sea, raising everywhere imperishable monuments both of good and evil." It was of the heroes of Greek legend and history that he was thinking when he speaks of " that audacity of noble races, that mad, absurd, and spontaneous audacity, their indifference and contempt for all security of the body, for life, for comfort." Does not " the terrible gaiety and the profound joy which the heroes tasted in destruction, in all the pleasures of victory and of cruelty," apply particularly to Achilles ? [1]

It was certainly to the type of classic Greek that Nietzsche alluded when he wrote " the moral judgments of the warrior aristocracy are founded on a powerful bodily constitution, a flourishing health without forgetfulness of what was necessary to the maintenance of that overflowing vigour—war, adventure, hunting, dancing, games, and physical exercises, in short, everything implied by a robust, free, and joyful activity." [2]

That very ancient type, the Achaean type celebrated by Homer, is not simply a memory ; it has several times reappeared in the world. " During the Renaissance there was a superb reawakening of the classic ideal of the

[1] Nietzsche, *Généalogie de la moral*, trad. franç., pp. 57-59.
[2] Nietzsche, *op. cit.* p. 43.

aristocratic valuation of all things ; and after the Revolution " the most prodigious and unexpected event came to pass, the antique ideal stood in person with unwonted splendour before the eyes and consciousness of humanity. . . . (Then) appeared Napoleon, isolated and belated example though he was." [1]

I believe that if the professor of philology had not been continually cropping up in Nietzsche he would have perceived that the *master* type still exists under our own eyes, and that it is this type which, at the present time, has created the extraordinary greatness of the United States. He would have been struck by the singular analogies which exist between the Yankee, ready for any kind of enterprise, and the ancient Greek sailor, sometimes a pirate, sometimes a colonist or merchant ; above all, he would have established a parallel between the ancient heroes and the man who sets out on the conquest of the Far West.[2] P. de Rousiers has described the *master* type admirably. " To become and to remain an American, one must look upon life as *a struggle and not as a pleasure*, and seek in it, victorious effort, energetic and efficacious action, rather than pleasure, leisure embellished by the cultivation of the arts, the refinements proper to other societies. Everywhere—we have seen that what makes the American succeed, what constitutes his type—is character, personal energy, energy in action, creative energy." [3] The profound contempt which the Greek had for the Barbarian is matched by that of the Yankee for the foreign worker who makes no effort to become truly American. " Many of these people would be better if we took them in hand,"

---

[1] Nietzsche, *op. cit.* pp. 78-80.

[2] P. de Rousiers observes that everywhere in America approximately the same social environment is found, and the same type of men at the head of big businesses ; but " it is in the West that the qualities and defects of this extraordinary people manifest themselves with the greatest energy ; . . . *it is there that the key to the whole social system is to be found* " (*La Vie américaine : ranches, fermes, et usines*, pp. 8-9 ; cf. p. 261).

[3] De Rousiers, *La Vie américaine : l'éducation et la société*, p. 325.

an old colonel of the War of Secession said to a French traveller, but we are a proud race ; a shopkeeper of Pottsville spoke of the Pennsylvania miners as " the senseless populace." [1] J. Bourdeau has drawn attention to the strange likeness which exists between the ideas of A. Carnegie and Roosevelt, and those of Nietzsche, the first deploring the waste of money involved in maintaining incapables, the second urging the Americans to becoming conquerors, a race of prey.[2]

I am not among those who consider Homer's Achaean type, the indomitable hero confident in his strength and putting himself above rules, as necessarily disappearing in the future. If it has often been believed that the type was bound to disappear, that was because the Homeric values were imagined to be irreconcilable with the other values which spring from an entirely different principle ; Nietzsche committed this error, which all those who believe in the necessity of unity in thought are bound to make. It is quite evident that liberty would be seriously compromised if men came to regard the Homeric values (which are approximate the same as the Cornelian values) as suitable only to barbaric peoples. Many moral evils would for ever remain unremedied if some hero of revolt did not force the people to become aware of their own state of mind on the subject. And art, which is after all of some value, would lose the finest jewel in its crown.

The philosophers are little disposed to admit the right of art to support the cult of the " will to power " ; it seems to them that they ought to give lessons to artists, instead

---

[1] De Rousiers, *La Vie américaine : ranches, fermes, et usines*, pp. 303-305.

[2] J. Bourdeau, *Les Maîtres de la pensée contemporaine*, p. 145. The author informs us on the other hand that " Jaurès greatly astonished the people of Geneva by revealing to them that the hero of Nietzsche, the *superman*, was nothing else but the proletariat " (p. 139). I have not been able to get any information about this lecture of Jaurès ; let us hope that he will some day publish it, for our amusement.

of receiving lessons from them ; they think that only those
sentiments which have received the stamp of the Universities have the right to manifest themselves in poetry.
Like industry, art has never adapted itself to the demands
of theorists ; it always upsets their plans of social harmony,
and humanity has found the freedom of art far too satisfactory ever to think of allowing it to be controlled by the
creators of dull systems of sociology.   The Marxists are
accustomed to seeing the ideologists look at things the
wrong way round, and so, in contrast to their enemies,
they should look upon art as a reality which begets ideas
and not as an application of ideas.

B. To the values created by the *master* type, Nietzsche
opposed the system constructed by sacerdotal castes—
the ascetic ideal against which he has piled up so much
invective.   The history of these values is much more
obscure and complicated than that of the preceding ones.
Nietzsche tries to connect the origin of asceticism with
psychological reasons which I will not examine here.   He
certainly makes a mistake in attributing a preponderat-
ing part to the Jews.   It is not at all evident that antique
Judaism had an ascetic character ; doubtless, like the
other Semitic religions, it attached importance to pilgrim-
ages, fasts, and prayers recited in ragged clothes.   The
Hebrew poets sang the hope of revenge which existed in the
heart of the persecuted, but, until the second century of
our era, the Jews looked to be revenged by arms : [1] on the
other hand, family life, with them, was too strong for the
monkish ideal ever to become important.

Imbued with Christianity as our civilisation may be,
it is none the less evident that, even in the Middle Ages,
it submitted to influences foreign to the Church, with
the result that the old ascetic values were gradually
transformed.   The values to which the contemporary

[1] It is always necessary to remember that the resigned Jew of the
Middle Ages was more like the Christians than his ancestors.

world clings most closely, and which it considers the true *ethical values*, are not realised in convents, but in the family ; respect for the human person, sexual fidelity and devotion to the weak, constitute the elements of morality of which all high - minded men are proud ; morality, even, is very often made to consist of these alone.

When we examine in a critical spirit the numerous writings which treat, to-day, of marriage, we see that the reformers who are in earnest propose to improve family relations in such a way as to assure the better realisation of these ethical values ; thus, they demand that the scandals of conjugal life shall not be exposed in the law courts, that unions shall not be maintained when fidelity no longer exists, and that the authority of the head of the family shall not be diverted from its moral purpose to become mere exploitation, etc.

On the other hand, it is curious to observe to what extent the modern Church misunderstands the values that classico-Christian civilisation has produced. It sees in marriage, above all, a contract directed by financial and worldly interests ; it is unwilling to allow of the union being dissolved when the household is a hell, and takes no account of the duty of devotion.[1] The priests are wonderfully skilful in procuring rich dowries for impoverished nobles, so much so, indeed, that the Church has been accused of considering marriage as a mating of noblemen living as " bullies " with middle-class women reduced to the rôle of the women who support such men. When it is heavily recompensed, the Church finds unexpected reasons for divorce, and finds means of annulling inconvenient unions for ridiculous motives. Proudhon asks ironically : " Is it possible for a responsible man of a serious turn of mind and a true Christian to care for the love of his wife ? . . . If the husband seeking divorce, or the wife seeking separation, alleges the refusal of the

[1] Epistle to the Ephesians, v. 25-31.

conjugal right, then, *of course*, there is a legitimate reason
for a rupture, for the service for which the marriage is
granted has not been carried out." [1]

Our civilisation having come to consider nearly all
morality as consisting of values derived from those
observed in the normally constituted family, two serious
consequences have been produced : (1) it has been asked
if, instead of considering the family as an application of
moral theories, it would not be more exact to say that it
is the base of these theories ; (2) it seems that the Church,
having become incompetent on matters connected with
sexual union, must also be incompetent as regards morality.
These are precisely the conclusions to which Proudhon
came. " Sexual duality was created by Nature to be the
instrument of Justice. . . . To produce Justice is the
higher aim of the bisexual division ; generation, and what
follows from it, only figure here as accessory." [2] " Marriage,
both in principle and in purpose, being the *instrument of
human right*, and the living negation of the divine right,
is thus in formal contradiction with theology and the
Church." [3]

Love, by the enthusiasm it begets, can produce that
sublimity without which there would be no effective
morality. At the end of his book on Justice, Proudhon
has written pages, which will never be surpassed, on the
rôle of women.

C. Finally we have to examine the values which escape

[1] Proudhon is alluding sarcastically to the frequently very comic
nullifications of marriage, pronounced by the Roman courts, for
physiological reasons. Proudhon, *op. cit.* vol. vi. p. 39. We know that
the theologians do not like curious people to consult ecclesiastical
writings about *conjugal duty* and the legitimate method of fulfilling it.

[2] Proudhon, *loc. cit.* p. 212.

[3] Proudhon, *Œuvres*, vol. xx. p. 169. This is extracted from the
memoir he wrote in his own defence, after he had been condemned to
three years in prison for his book on Justice. It is worth while noting
that Proudhon was accused of attacking marriage ! This affair is one
of the shameful acts which dishonoured the Church in the reign of
Napoleon III.

Nietzsche's classification and which treat of *civil relations*. Originally magic was much mixed up in the evaluation of these values ; among the Jews, until recent times, one finds a mixture of hygienic principles, rules about sexual relationships, precepts about honesty, benevolence and national solidarity, the whole wrapped up in magical superstitions ; this mixture, which seems strange to the philosopher, had the happiest influence on their morality so long as they maintained their traditional mode of living, and one notices among them even now a particular exactitude in the carrying out of contracts.

The ideas held by modern ethical writers are drawn mainly from those of Greece in its time of decadence ; Aristotle, living in a period of transition, combined ancient values with values that, as time went on, were to prevail ; war and production had ceased to occupy the attention of the most distinguished men of the towns, who sought, on the contrary, to secure an easy existence for themselves ; the most important thing was the establishment of friendly relations between the better educated men of the community, and the fundamental maxim was that of the golden mean. The new morality was to be acquired principally by means of the habits which the young Greek would pick up in mixing with cultivated people. It may be said that here we are on the level of an ethic adapted to consumers ; it is not astonishing then that Catholic theologians still find Aristotle's ethics an excellent one, for they themselves take the consumer's point of view.

In the civilisation of antiquity, the ethics of producers could hardly be any other than that of slave-owners, and it did not seem worth developing at length, at the time when philosophy made an inventory of Greek customs. Aristotle said that no far-reaching science was needed to employ slaves : " For the master *need only know how to order what the slaves must know how to execute*. So, as soon as a man can save himself this trouble, he leaves it in the charge of a steward, so as to be himself free for a political or philosophical life." [1] A little farther on he wrote : " It is manifest, then, that the master ought to be the source of excellence in the slave ; but not merely because he possesses the art which trains him in his duties." [2] This clearly expresses the point of view of the urban consumer, who finds it very tiresome to be obliged to pay any attention whatever to the conditions of production. [3]

As to the slave, he needs very limited virtues. " He only needs enough to prevent him neglecting his work through intemperance or idleness." He should be treated with " more indulgence even than children," although certain people consider that slaves are deprived of reason and are only fit to receive orders. [4]

It is quite easy to see that during a considerable period the moderns also did not think that there was anything more to be said about workers than Aristotle had said ; they must be given orders, corrected with gentleness, like children, and treated as passive instruments who do not need to think. Revolutionary Syndicalism would be impossible if the world of the workers were under the

[1] Aristotle, *Politics*, book i. chap. vii. 4-5.

[2] Aristotle, *op. cit.* book i. chap. v. 13, 14.

[3] Xenophon, who represents in everything a conception of Greek life very much earlier than the time in which he lived, discusses the proper method of training an overseer for a farm (*Economics*, pp. 12-14). Marx remarks that Xenophon speaks of the division of labour in the workshop, and that appears to him to show a *middle-class instinct* (*Capital*, vol. i. p. 159, col. 1) ; I myself think that it *characterises* an observer who understood the importance of production, an importance of which Plato had no comprehension. In the *Memorabilia* (book ii. p. 7) Socrates advises a citizen who had to look after a large family, to set up a workshop with the family ; J. Flach supposes that this was something new (*Leçon du 19ᵉ avril 1907*) : it seems to me to be rather a return to more ancient customs. The historians of philosophy appear to me to have been very hostile to Xenophon because he is too much of an *old Greek*. Plato suits them much better since he is more of an *aristocrat*, and consequently more detached from production.

[4] Aristotle, *op. cit.* book i. chap. v. 9 and 11.

influence of such a *morality of the weak*. State Socialism, on the contrary, could accommodate itself to this morality perfectly well, since the latter is based on the idea of a society divided into a class of producers and a class of thinkers applying results of scientific investigation to the work of production. The only difference which would exist between this sham Socialism and Capitalism would consist in the employment of more ingenious methods of procuring discipline in the workshop.

At the present moment, officials of the *Bloc* are working to create a kind of ethical discipline which will replace the hazy religion which G. de Molinari thinks necessary to the successful working of capitalism. It is perfectly clear, in fact, that religion is daily losing its efficacy with the people ; something else must be found, if the intellectuals are to be provided with the means of living on the margin of production.

IV

The problem that we shall now try to solve is the most difficult of all those which a Socialist writer can touch upon. We are about to ask how it is possible to conceive the transformation of the men of to-day into the free producers of to-morrow working in manufactories where there are no masters. The question must be stated accurately ; we must state it, not for a world which has already arrived at Socialism, but solely for our own time and for the preparation of the transition from one world to the other ; if we do not limit the question in this way, we shall find ourselves straying into Utopias.

Kautsky has given a great deal of attention to the question of the conditions immediately following a social revolution ; the solution he proposes seems to me quite as feeble as that of G. de Molinari. If the syndicates of to-day are strong enough to induce the workmen of to-day to abandon their workshops and to submit to great sacrifices, during the strikes kept up against the capitalists, he thinks that they will then doubtless be strong enough to bring the workmen back to the workshops, and to obtain good and regular work from them, when once they see that this work is necessary for the general good.[1] Kautsky, however, does not seem to feel much confidence in the value of his own solution.

Evidently no comparison can be made between the kind of discipline which forces a general stoppage of work on the men and that which will induce them to handle machinery with greater skill. The error springs from the fact that Kautsky is more of a theorist than he is a disciple of Marx ; he loves reasoning about abstractions and believes that he has brought a question nearer to solution when he manages to produce a phrase with a scientific appearance ; the underlying reality interests him less than its academic presentment. Many others have committed the same error, led astray by the different meanings of the word *discipline*, which may be applied both to regular conduct founded on the deepest feelings of the soul or to a merely external restraint.

The history of ancient corporations furnishes us with no really useful information on this subject ; they do not seem to have had any effect whatever in promoting any kind of improvement, or invention in technical matters ; it would seem rather that they served to protect routine. If we examine English Trade Unionism closely, we find that it also is strongly imbued with this industrial routine springing from the corporative spirit.

Nor can the examples of democracy throw any light on the question. Work conducted democratically would be regulated by resolutions, inspected by police, and subject to the sanction of tribunals dealing out rewards or imprisonment. The discipline would be an exterior

[1] Karl Kautsky, *La Révolution sociale*, French translation, p. 153.

compulsion closely analogous to that which now exists in
the capitalist workshops; but it would probably be still
more arbitrary because the committee would always have
their eye on the next elections.[1] When one thinks of
the peculiarities found in judgments in penal cases one
feels convinced that repression would be exercised in a
very unsatisfactory way. It seems to be generally agreed
that light offences cannot be satisfactorily dealt with in
law courts, when hampered by the rules of a strict legal
system; the establishment of administrative councils to
decide on the future of children has often been suggested;
in Belgium mendicity is subject to an administrative
arbitration which may be compared to the " police des
mœurs "; it is well known that this police, in spite of
innumerable complaints, continues to be almost supreme
in France. It is very noticeable that administrative intervention in the case of important crimes is continually
increasing. Since the power of mitigating or even of suppressing penalties is being more and more handed over
to the heads of penal establishments, doctors and
sociologists speak in favour of this system, which tends
to give the police as important a function as they had
under the *ancien régime*. Experience shows that the
discipline of the capitalist workshops is greatly superior
to that maintained by the police, so that one does not
see how it would be possible to improve capitalist discipline by means of the methods which democracy would
have at its disposal.[2]

I think that there is one good point, however, in

[1] The managers of manufactories would constantly be busying themselves with how to ensure the success of the government party at the
next election. They would be very indulgent to workmen who were
influential speakers, and very hard on men suspected of lack of
electoral zeal.

[2] We might ask if the ideal of the relatively honest and enlightened
democrats is not at the present moment the discipline of the capitalist
workshop. The increase of the power given to the mayors and State
governors in America seems to me to be a sign of this tendency.

Kautsky's hypothesis ; he seems to have been aware that the motive force of the revolutionary movement must also be the motive force of the ethic of the producers ; that is a view quite in conformity with Marxist principles, but the idea must be applied in quite a different way from that in which he applied it.   It must not be thought that the action of the syndicates on work is direct, as he supposes ; this influence of the syndicates on labour should result from complex and sometimes distant causes, acting on the general character of the workers rather than from a quasi-military organisation.   This is what I try to show by analysing some of the qualities of the best workmen.

A satisfactory result can be arrived at, by starting from the curious analogies which exist between the most remarkable qualities of the soldiers who took part in the wars of Liberty, the qualities which engendered the propaganda in favour of the general strike, and those that will be required of a free worker in a highly progressive state of society.   I believe that these analogies constitute a new (and perhaps decisive) proof, in favour of revolutionary syndicalism.

In the wars of Liberty each soldier considered himself as an *individual* having something of importance to do in the battle, instead of looking upon himself as simply one part of the military mechanism committed to the supreme direction of a leader.   In the literature of those times one is struck by the frequency with which the *free men* of the republican armies are contrasted with the *automatons* of the royal armies ; this was no mere figure of rhetoric employed by the French writers ; I have convinced myself as a result of a thorough first-hand study of one of the wars of that time, that these terms corresponded perfectly to the actual feelings of the soldiers.

Battles under these conditions could, then, no longer be likened to games of chess in which each man is comparable to a pawn ; they became collections of heroic

exploits accomplished by individuals under the influence
of an extraordinary enthusiasm. Revolutionary literature is not entirely false, when it reports so many grandiloquent phrases said to have been uttered by the combatants;
doubtless none of these phrases were spoken by the people
to whom they are attributed, their form is due to men
of letters used to the composition of classical declamation ;
but the basis is real in this sense, that we have, thanks
to these lies of revolutionary rhetoric, a perfectly exact
representation of the aspect under which the combatants
looked on war, a true expression of the sentiments aroused
by it, and the *actual accent of the truly Homeric conflicts*
which took place at that time. I am certain that none
of the actors in these dramas ever protested against the
words attributed to them ; this was no doubt because
each found beneath these fantastic phrases, a true expression of his own deepest feelings.[1]

Until the moment when Napoleon appeared the war had
none of the scientific character which the later theoretists
of strategy have sometimes thought it incumbent on
them to attribute to it. Misled by the analogies they
discovered between the triumphs of the revolutionary
armies and those of the Napoleonic armies, historians
imagined that generals anterior to Napoleon had made
great plans of campaign ; such plans never existed, or at
any rate had very little influence on the course of operations. The best officers of that time were fully aware
that their talent consisted in furnishing their troops with
the suitable opportunities of exhibiting their ardour ; and
victory was assured each time that the soldiers could
give free scope to all their enthusiasm, unfettered by bad
commissariat, or by the stupidity of representatives of the
people who looked upon themselves as strategists. On

---

[1] This history has also been burdened by a great number of adventures, which have been fabricated by imitating real ones, and which are
very like those which later on *The Three Musketeers* rendered popular.

the battle-field the leaders gave an example of daring courage and were merely the first combatants, like true Homeric kings ; it is this which explains the enormous prestige with the young troops, immediately gained by só many of the non-commissioned officers of the *ancien régime*, who were borne to the highest rank by the unanimous acclamations of the soldiers at the outset of the war.

If we wished to find, in these first armies, what it was that took the place of the later idea of discipline, we might say that the soldier was convinced that the slightest failure of the most insignificant private might compromise the success of the whole and the life of all his comrades, and that the soldier acted accordingly. This presupposes that no account is taken of the relative values of the different factors that go to make up a victory, so that all things are considered from a *qualitative and individualistic* point of view. One is, in fact, extremely struck by the individualistic characters which are met with in these armies, and by the fact that nothing is to be found in them which at all resembles the obedience spoken of by our contemporary authors. There is some truth then in the statement that the incredible French victories were due to intelligent bayonets.

The same spirit is found in the working-class groups who are eager for the general strike ; these groups, in fact, picture the Revolution as an immense uprising which yet may be called individualistic ; each working with the greatest possible zeal, each acting on his own account, and not troubling himself much to subordinate his conduct to a great and scientifically combined plan. This character of the proletarian general strike has often been pointed out, and it has the effect of frightening the greedy politicians, who understand perfectly well that a Revolution conducted in this way would do away with all their chances of seizing the Government.

Jaurès, whom nobody would dream of classing with any but the most circumspect of men, has clearly recognised the danger which threatens him ; he accuses the upholders of the general strike of considering only one aspect of social life and thus going against the Revolution.[1] This rigmarole should be translated thus : the revolutionary Syndicalists desire to exalt the individuality of the life of the producer ; they thus run counter to the interests of the politicians who want to direct the Revolution in such a way as to transmit power to a new minority ; they thus undermine the foundations of the State. We entirely agree with all this ; it is precisely this characteristic which so terrifies the Parliamentary Socialists, the financiers, and the ideologists, which gives such extraordinary moral value to the notion of the general strike.

The upholders of the general strike are accused of anarchical tendencies ; and as a matter of fact, it has been observed during the last few years that anarchists have entered the syndicates in great numbers, and have done a great deal to develop tendencies favourable to the general strike.

This movement becomes understandable when we bear the preceding explanations in mind ; because the general strike, just like the wars of Liberty, is a most striking manifestation of *individualistic force in the revolted masses*. It seems to me, moreover, that the official Socialists would do well not to insist too much on this point ; they would thus avoid some reflections which are not altogether to their advantage. We might, in fact, be led to ask if our official Socialists, with their passion for discipline, and their infinite confidence in the genius of their leaders, are not the authentic inheritors of the traditions of the royal armies, while the anarchists and the upholders of the general strike represent at the present time the spirit of the revolutionary warriors who, against

[1] Jaurès, *Études socialistes*, pp. 117-118.

all the rules of the art of war, so thoroughly thrashed the fine armies of the coalition. I can understand why the Socialists approved, controlled, and duly patented by the administrators of *Humanité*, have not much sympathy for the heroes of Fleurus,[1] who were very badly dressed, and would have cut a sorry figure in the drawing-rooms of the great financiers ; but everybody does not adapt his convictions to suit the tastes of M. Jaurès's shareholders.

V

I want now to point out some analogies which show how revolutionary syndicalism is the greatest educative force that contemporary society has at its disposal for the preparation of the system of production, which the workmen will adopt, in a society organised in accordance with the new conceptions.

A. The free producer in a progressive and inventive workshop must never evaluate his own efforts by any external standing ; he ought to consider the models given him as inferior, and desire to surpass everything that has been done before. Constant improvement in quality and quantity will be thus assured to production ; the idea of continual progress will be realised in a workshop of this kind.

Early socialists had had an intuition of this law, when they demanded that each should produce according to his faculties ; but they did not know how to explain this principle, which in their Utopias seemed made for a convent or for a family rather than for modern industrial life. Sometimes, however, they pictured their workers as possessed by an enthusiasm similar to that which we find in the lives of certain great artists ; this last point

---

[1] [The battle of Fleurus, won in 1794 by General Jourdain, was one of the first decisive triumphs of the revolutionary army. The *Chant du Départ* was written by J. M. Chénier shortly before this battle.—*Trans.*]

of view is by no means negligible, although the early
Socialists hardly understood the value of the comparison.

Whenever we consider questions relative to industrial
progress, we are led to consider art as an *anticipation* of the
highest and technically most perfect forms of production,
although the artist, with his caprices, often seems to be at
the antipodes of the modern worker.[1] This analogy is
justified by the fact that the artist dislikes reproducing
accepted types; the inexhaustibly inventive turn of
his mind distinguishes him from the ordinary artisan,
who is mainly successful in the unending reproduction
of models which are not his own. The inventor is an
artist who wears himself out in pursuing the realisation
of ends which practical people generally declare absurd ;
and who, if he has made any important discovery is often
supposed to be mad ; practical people thus resemble
artisans. One could cite in every industry important
improvements which originated in small changes made
by workmen endowed with the artist's taste for innovation.

This state of mind is, moreover, exactly that which was
found in the first armies which carried on the wars of
Liberty and that possessed by the propagandists of the
general strike. This passionate individualism is entirely
wanting in the working classes who have been educated
by politicians ; all they are fit for is to change their
masters. These *bad shepherds* [2] sincerely hope that it

[1] When we speak of the educative value of art, we often forget that
the habits of life of the modern artist, founded on an imitation of those
of a jovial aristocracy, are in no way necessary, and are derived from
a tradition which has been fatal to many fine talents.   Lafargue appears
to believe that the Parisian jeweller might find it necessary to dress
elegantly, to eat oysters, and run after women in order to be able to
keep up the artistic quality of his work (*i.e.* in order to keep his mind
active ; the artistic quality of his work, destroyed by the wear of daily
life in the workshop, will be reconstituted by the gay life he leads outside)
(*Journal des économistes*, September 1884, p. 386).   He gives no reasons
to support this paradox; we might moreover point out that the mentality
of Marx's son-in-law is always obsessed by aristocratic *prejudices*.

[2] [This is an allusion to a play by Octave Mirbeau with that title.—
Trans.]

will be so ; and the Stock Exchange people would not provide them with money, were they not convinced that Parliamentary Socialism is quite compatible with financial robbery.

B. Modern industry is characterised by an ever-growing care for exactitude ; as tools get more scientific it is expected that the product shall have fewer hidden faults, and that in use its quality shall be as good as its appearance.

If Germany has not yet taken the place in the economic world which the mineral riches of its soil, the energy of its manufacturers and the science of its technicians ought to give it, it is because its manufacturers for a long time thought it clever to flood the markets with trash ; although the quality of German manufactures has much improved during the last few years, it is not yet held in any very great esteem.

Here again it is possible to draw a comparison between industry in a high state of perfection and art. There have been periods in which the public appreciated above all the technical tricks by which the artist created an illusion of reality ; but these tricks have never been accepted in the great schools, and they are universally condemned by the authors who are accepted as authorities in matters of art.[1]

This honesty which now seems to us to-day as necessary in industry as in art, was hardly suspected by the Utopists ; [2] Fourier, at the beginning of the new era, believed that fraud in the quality of merchandise was characteristic

[1] See the chapter in Ruskin's *Seven Lamps of Architecture* entitled " Lamp of Truth."

[2] It must not be forgotten that there are two ways of discussing art ; Nietzsche attacks Kant for having " like all the philosophers meditated on art and the beautiful as a *spectator* instead of looking at the esthetic problem from the point of view of the artist, the *creator* " (*op. cit.* p. 178). In the time of the Utopists, esthetics was merely the babbling of amateurs, who were delighted with the cleverness with which the artist had been able to deceive the public.

of the relations between civilised people ; he turned his back on progress and showed himself incapable of understanding the world which was being formed about him ; like nearly all professional prophets this sham seer confused the future with the past. Marx, on the contrary, said that " deception in merchandise in the capitalist system of production is unjust," because it no longer corresponds with the modern system of business.[1]

The soldier of the wars of Liberty attached an almost superstitious importance to the carrying out of the smallest order. As a result of this he felt no pity for the generals or officers whom he saw guillotined after a defeat on the charge of dereliction of duty ; he did not look at these events as the historians of to-day do ; he had no means of knowing whether the condemned had really committed treason or not ; in his eyes failure could only be explained by some grave error on the part of his leaders. The high sense of responsibility felt by the soldier about his own duties, and the extreme thoroughness with which he carried out the most insignificant order, made him approve of rigorous measures taken against men who in his eyes had brought about the defeat of the army and caused it to lose the fruit of so much heroism.

It is not difficult to see that the same spirit is met with in strikes ; the beaten workmen are convinced that their failure is due to the base conduct of a few comrades who have not done all that might have been expected of them ; numerous accusations of treason are brought forward ; for the beaten masses, treason alone can explain the defeat of heroic troops ; the sentiment, felt by all, of the thoroughness that must be brought to the accomplishment of their duties, will therefore be accompanied by many acts of violence. I do not think that the authors who have written on the events which follow strikes, have sufficiently reflected on this analogy between strikes and the wars of

[1] Marx, *Capital*, French translation, vol. iii., first part, p. 375.

Liberty, and, consequently, between these acts of violence
and the executions of generals accused of treason.[1]

C. There would never have been great acts of heroism
in war, if each soldier, while acting like a hero, yet at the
same time claimed to receive a reward proportionate to
his deserts. When a column is sent to an assault, the
men at the head know they are sent to their death, and
that the glory of victory will be for those who passing
over their dead bodies enter the enemy's position. However, they do not reflect on this injustice, but march
forward.

The value of any army where the need of rewards
makes itself actively felt, may be said to be on the decline.
Officers who had served in the campaigns of the Revolution
and of the Empire, but who had served under the direct
orders of Napoleon only in the last years of their career,
were amazed to see the fuss made about feats of arms
which in the time of their youth would have passed un-
noticed : " I have been overwhelmed with praise," said
General Duhesne, " for things which would not have been
noticed in the army of Sambre-et-Meuse." [2] This theatri-
cality was carried by Murat to a grotesque degree, and
historians have not taken enough notice of the responsibility of Napoleon for this degeneracy of the true warlike
spirit. The extraordinary enthusiasm which had been
the cause of so many prodigies of valour on the part of
the men of 1794 was unknown to him ; he believed that
it was his function to measure all capacities, and to give

[1] P. Bureau has devoted a chapter of his book on the *Contrat de
Travail* to an explanation of the reasons which justify boycotting of
workmen who do not join their comrades in strikes ; he thinks that
these people merit their fate because they are notoriously inferior both
in courage and as workmen. This seems to me very inadequate as
an account of the reasons which, in the eyes of the working classes
themselves, explain these acts of violence. The author takes up a
much too intellectualist point of view.

[2] Lafaille, *Mémoires sur les campagnes de Catalogne de 1808 à 1814,*
p. 336.

to each a reward exactly proportionate to what he had accomplished ; this was the Saint-Simonian principle already coming into practice, and every officer was encouraged to bring himself forward. Charlatanism[1] exhausted the moral forces of the nation whilst its material forces were still very considerable. Napoleon formed very few distinguished general officers and carried on the war principally with those left him by the Revolution ; this impotence is the most absolute condemnation of the system.[2]

The scarcity of the information which we possess about the great Gothic artists has often been pointed out. Among the stone-carvers who sculptured the statues in the cathedrals there were men of great talent who seem always to have remained anonymous ; nevertheless they produced masterpieces. Viollet-le-Duc was surprised that the archives of Notre Dame had preserved for us no detailed information about the building of this gigantic monument and that, as a rule, the documents of the Middle Ages say very little about the architects ; he adds that " genius can develop itself in obscurity, and that it is its very nature to seek silence and obscurity."[3] We

[1] The charlatanism of the followers of Saint Simon was as disgusting as that of Murat ; moreover, the history of this school is unintelligible if we do not compare it with its Napoleonic models.

[2] General Donop strongly insists on the incapacity of Napoleon's lieutenants who passively obeyed instructions that they never tried to understand, and the fulfilment of which was minutely overlooked by their master (*op. cit.* pp. 22-29 and 32-34). Napoleon's armies were valued in proportion to the exactitude with which they carried out the orders of their master ; initiative being little valued, it was possible to estimate the conduct of the generals like the ability of a good pupil who has learnt his lessons well ; the Emperor gave pecuniary rewards to his lieutenants, proportionate to the measure of merit he recognised in them.

[3] Viollet-le-Duc, *Dictionnaire raisonné de l'architecture française*, vol. iv. pp. 42-43. This does not contradict what we read in the article " Architect." From that we learn that the builders often inscribed their names in the cathedrals (vol. i. pp. 109-111) ; from that it has been concluded that these works were not anonymous (Bréhier, *Les*

might even go farther and question whether their contemporaries suspected that these artists of genius had
raised edifices of unperishable glory ; it seems very
probable to me that the cathedrals were only admired
by the artists.

This striving towards perfection which manifests itself,
in spite of the absence of any personal, immediate, and
proportional reward, constitutes the *secret virtue* which
assures the continued progress of the world.   What would
become of modern industry if inventors could only be
found for those things which would procure them an
almost certain remuneration ?   The calling of an inventor is
much the most miserable of all, and yet there is no lack of
inventors.   How often in workshops have little modifica-
tions introduced by ingenious artisans into their work,
become by accumulation fundamental improvements,
without the innovators ever getting any permanent or
appreciable benefit from their ingenuity !   And has not
even simple piece-work brought about a gradual but
uninterrupted progress in the processes of production, a
progress which, after having temporarily improved the
position of a few workers and especially that of their
employers, has proved finally of benefit chiefly to the
consumer ?

Renan asked what was it that moved the heroes of
great wars.   " The soldier of Napoleon was well aware
that he would always be a poor man, but he felt that the
epic in which he was taking part would be eternal, that he
would live in the glory of France."   The Greeks had fought
for glory ; the Russians and the Turks seek death because
they expect a chimerical paradise.   "A soldier is not made
by promises of temporal rewards.   He must have immor-

Églises gothiques, p. 17), but what meaning had these inscriptions for
the people of the town ?   They could only be of interest to artists who
came later on to work in the same edifice and who were familiar with
the traditions of the *schools*.

tality. In default of paradise, there is glory, which is itself a kind of immortality." [1]

Economic progress goes far beyond the individual life, and profits future generations more than those who create it ; but does it give glory ? Is there an economic epic capable of stimulating the enthusiasm of the workers. The inspiration of immortality which Renan considered so powerful is obviously without efficacy here, because artists have never produced masterpieces under the influence of the idea that their work would procure them a place in paradise (as Turks seek death that they may enjoy the happiness promised by Mahomet). The workmen are not entirely wrong when they look on religion as a middle-class luxury, since, as a matter of fact, the emotions it calls up are not those which inspire workmen with the desire to perfect machinery, or which create methods of accelerating labour.

The question must be stated otherwise than Renan put it ; do there exist among the workmen forces capable of producing enthusiasm equivalent to those of which Renan speaks, forces which could combine with the ethics of good work, so that in our days, which seem to many people to presage the darkest future, this ethic may acquire all the authority necessary to lead society along the path of economic progress.

We must be careful that the keen sentiment which we have of the necessity of such a morality, and our ardent desire to see it realised does not induce us to mistake phantoms for forces capable of moving the world. The abundant " idyllic " literature of the professors of rhetoric is evidently mere chatter. Equally vain are the attempts made by so many scholars to find institutions in the past, an imitation of which might serve as a means of

---

[1] Renan, *Histoire du peuple d'Israël*, vol. iv. p. 191. Renan seems to me to have *identified* too readily glory and immortality : he has fallen a victim to a figure of speech.

disciplining their contemporaries ; imitation has never produced much good and often bred much sorrow ; how absurd the idea is then of borrowing from some dead and gone social structure, a suitable means of controlling a system of production, whose principal characteristic is that every day it must become more and more opposed to all preceding economic systems.   Is there then nothing to hope for ?

Morality is not doomed to perish because the motive forces behind it will change ; it is not destined to become a mere collection of precepts as long as it can still vivify itself by an alliance with an enthusiasm capable of conquering all the obstacles, prejudices, and the need of immediate enjoyment, which oppose its progress.   But it is certain that this sovereign force will not be found along the paths which contemporary philosophers, the experts of social science, and the inventors of *far-reaching reforms* would make us go.   There is only one force which can produce to-day that enthusiasm without whose co-operation no morality is possible, and that is the force resulting from the propaganda in favour of a general strike.   The preceding explanations have shown that the idea of the general strike (constantly rejuvenated by the feelings roused by proletarian violence) produces an entirely epic state of mind, and at the same time bends all the energies of the mind to that condition necessary to the realisation of a workshop carried on by free men, eagerly seeking the betterment of the industry ; we have thus recognised that there are great resemblances between the sentiments aroused by the idea of the general strike and those which are necessary to bring about a continued progress in methods of production.   We have then the right to maintain that the modern world possesses that prime mover which is necessary to the creation of the ethics of the producers.

I stop here, because it seems to me that I have accomplished the task which I imposed upon myself ; I have, in fact, established that proletarian violence has an entirely different significance from that attributed to it by superficial scholars and by politicians. In the total ruin of institutions and of morals there remains something which is powerful, new, and intact, and it is that which constitutes, properly speaking, the soul of the revolutionary proletariat. Nor will this be swept away in the general decadence of moral values, if the workers have enough energy to bar the road to the middle-class corrupters, answering their advances with the plainest brutality.

I believe that I have brought an important contribution to discussions on Socialism ; these discussions must henceforth deal exclusively with the conditions which allow the development of specifically proletarian forces, that is to say, *with violence enlightened by the idea of the general strike*. All the old abstract dissertations on the Socialist *régime* of the future become useless ; we pass to the domain of real history, to the interpretation of facts— to the ethical evaluations of the revolutionary movement.

The bond which I pointed out in the beginning of this inquiry between Socialism and proletarian violence appears to us now in all its strength. It is to violence that Socialism owes those high ethical values by means of which it brings *salvation* to the modern world.

APPENDIX

APOLOGY FOR VIOLENCE

MEN who make revolutionary speeches to the people are bound to set before themselves a high standard of sincerity, because the workers understand their words in their exact and literal sense, and never indulge in any symbolic interpretation. When in 1905 I ventured to write in some detail on proletarian violence I understood perfectly the grave responsibility I assumed in trying to show the historic bearing of actions which our Parliamentary Socialists try to dissimulate, with so much skill. To-day I do not hesitate to assert that Socialism could not continue to exist without an apology for violence.

It is in strikes that the proletariat asserts its existence. I cannot agree with the view which sees in strikes merely something analogous to the temporary rupture of commercial relations which is brought about when a grocer and the wholesale dealer from whom he buys his dried plums cannot agree about the price. The strike is a phenomenon of war. It is thus a serious misrepresentation to say that violence is an accident doomed to disappear from the strikes of the future.

The social revolution is an extension of that war. in which each great strike is an episode ; this is the reason why Syndicalists speak of that revolution in the language of strikes ; for them Socialism is reduced to the conception, the expectation of, and the preparation for the general strike, which, like he Napoleonic battle, is to completely annihilate a condemned *régime*.

Such a conception allows none of those subtle exegeses in which Jaurès excels. It is a question here of an overthrow in the course of which both employers and the State would be set aside by the organised producers. Our

Intellectuals, who hope to obtain the highest places from democracy, would be sent back to their literature; the Parliamentary Socialists, who find in the organisations created by the middle classes means of exercising a certain amount of power, would become useless.

The analogy which exists between strikes accompanied by violence and war is prolific of consequences. No one doubts (except d'Estournelles de Constant) that it was war that provided the republics of antiquity with the ideas which form the ornament of our modern culture. The social war, for which the proletariat ceaselessly prepares itself in the syndicates, may engender the elements of a new civilisation suited to a people of producers. I continually call the attention of my young friends to the problems presented by Socialism considered from the point of view of a civilisation of producers; I assert that to-day a philosophy is being elaborated according to this plan, whose possibility even was hardly suspected a few years ago; this philosophy is closely bound up with the apology for violence.

I have never had that admiration for *creative hatred* which Jaurès has devoted to it; I do not feel the same indulgence towards the guillotiners as he does; I have a horror of any measure which strikes the vanquished under a judicial disguise. War, carried on in broad daylight, without hypocritical attenuation, for the purpose of ruining an irreconcilable enemy, excludes all the abominations which dishonoured the middle-class revolution of the eighteenth century. The apology for violence in this case is particularly easy.

It would serve no purpose to explain to the poor that they ought not to feel sentiments of jealousy and vengeance against their masters; these feelings are too powerful to be suppressed by exhortations; it is on the widespread prevalence of these feelings that democracy chiefly founds its strength. Social war, by making an appeal to the honour which develops so naturally in all organised armies, can eliminate those evil feelings against which morality would remain powerless. If this were the only reason we had for attributing a high civilising value to revolutionary Syndicalism, this reason alone would, it seems to me, be decisive in favour of the apologists for violence.

The conception of the general strike, engendered by the practice of violent strikes, admits the conception of an irrevocable overthrow. There is something terrifying in this which will appear more and more terrifying as violence takes a greater place in the mind of the proletariat. But, in undertaking a serious, formidable, and sublime work, Socialists raise themselves above our frivolous society and make themselves worthy of pointing out new roads to the world.

Parliamentary Socialists may be compared to the officials whom Napoleon made into a nobility and who laboured to strengthen the State bequeathed by the Ancien Régime. Revolutionary Syndicalism corresponds well enough to the Napoleonic armies whose soldiers accomplished such heroic acts, knowing all the time that they would remain poor. What remains of the Empire ? Nothing but the epic of the Grande Armée. What will remain of the present Socialist movement will be the epic of the strikes.

Matin, May 18, 1908.

THE END